Losing Mom

Losing Mom

A Memoir of Life, Loss, and Letting Go

What grief taught me about finding grace in goodbye

Peggy Ottman

979-8-9938492-0-1 Paperback
979-8-9938492-1-8 Ebook

Prologue

I thought I was going to lose my mom so many times, I almost started to believe I never would. For six years, Mom's aging body threw her one health crisis after another, yet she pulled through again and again. My sisters and I laughed that maybe the tenacious bundle of energy that was our mother would be the first person in the world to ever *not* die.

The first time I thought I was losing her was when we were gathered for my husband John's birthday dinner around his mother's dining room table. Everyone was chatting away, enjoying their soup course, when I heard Bill, our oldest son, say, "Grandmom, are you all right?" Unable to see Mom through the lavish centerpiece and candelabra, I stood up to find her staring into her soup bowl talking to herself, the words recognizable but making no sense. Hurrying over to her side, I knelt down to try and get her attention, but she was somewhere else, and wouldn't, or couldn't, look at me. I tried to stay calm—as a former EMT I'm usually good in a crisis—but it was hard. It was my *mom,* and I was pretty sure she was having a stroke.

It was terrifying to see her so confused, so vulnerable. In her eighty-three years, Mom had rarely been sick and, except for childbirth, had never been in the hospital as far as I could remember. Watching the paramedics load her into the ambulance then back out of the driveway with red lights flashing ominously, I found myself, for the first time ever, staring into a future without her in it. It seemed impossible.

But after a couple of months of recuperation along with heart medication to control her newly diagnosed atrial fibrillation, Mom was practically as good as new. Life returned to normal, albeit a new normal, where my once invulnerable mother was suddenly a little less so.

Growing up, Mom had been a real go-getter—always game for any challenge that came her way, and if something needed doing, she just did it.

Too much litter on the streets? Mom got Dad to make her a litter stick out of an old broom handle and nail, decorated it with bright floral contact paper, and walked around town picking up every rusty soda can, discarded cigarette butt, and stray newspaper she could find.

Didn't like a decision from the town council? Out came her blue, electric Smith Corona typewriter from its shelf in the kitchen cabinet, and she would dash off a letter to the editor of the local paper, then attend every council meeting she could to make them change their minds.

Wanted to see Obama elected? Okay, no matter she was eighty years old and living in a town that had always voted Republican. Mom helped open an Obama campaign headquarters smack in the middle of Louisiana Avenue, the town's main street, going in every day to make phone call after phone call to her fellow residents, and succeeded in getting that small town to vote Democratic for the first time in its history.

Stubborn, tenacious, and strong-willed, my mother simply did not put things off. Ever. It was hard to see some of that never-say-never spirit get tamped down after her stroke—to see vulnerability pierce through the stable wall of self-confidence that was Kay Ball.

A year or so later, she took a fall down her front stairs, fracturing her back and landing her in the hospital for several weeks, where she developed congestive heart failure from all the fluids they had to keep pumping into her tiny, ninety-five-pound body. My sisters and I—Sal, the eldest, from Maine; Lib, the youngest, from California;

and me, the middle, from Connecticut—all flew to Perrysburg, the small Ohio town where we grew up, to try and rally our mother's flagging spirits. She was as down as I'd ever seen her, and for the second time in my life, I was scared I might be losing her.

But it seemed the combined presence of her three daughters was the key to rebooting Mom's depleted energy and, again, she found a way to bounce back. After six weeks in a rehab facility, and three months in a full, hard-shell plastic back brace, Mom returned to her normal routine, continuing to live in her big house alone as if nothing had ever happened.

I guess it made sense that Mom drew such strength from me and my sisters. When our dad died twenty-five years before from complications removing a blood clot, he left the four of us stranded together, teetering on the edge of the enormous hole his sudden absence had created, trying to keep each other, especially Mom, from falling in. The grief we shared propelled us toward each other, and we found more and more ways to be together—weekends in New York to see a show or a new art exhibit, spring vacations for 'just the girls' to Mom's and Dad's favorite island in the Bahamas, birthday trips to Sedona and Florida, summers at our family's camp in Maine, and of course, our many visits back to Perrysburg—all helped to create the strong bond between us we may never have known if Dad hadn't died when he did.

Mom's friends dubbed us the K-Team, Kay being Mom's first name, during that extended hospital stay after her fall. We named Sal the CIO—as a consultant in the healthcare industry she was well-equipped to gather all the necessary information Mom's medical situations required and was the welcome intermediary between us and the doctors. Libby, with her background in economics and health insurance, was anointed CFO, managing all of Mom's bills while she was in the hospital and the deluge of Medicare paperwork that followed. My strengths were a little less specific, but I was, I admit, pretty good at managing Mom. I'm not sure why—maybe from my years as an EMT and hospice volunteer—but I was often able to get her to do things she didn't want to do, a not infrequent situation with our ofttimes stubborn mother, so I was christened COO. Mom, of course, was the CEO—it being her life and all—and always had the final say in any decision.

It was a little silly—we may or may not have had a couple of cocktails when we came up with our titles—but having our roles defined in such a way allowed us to care for our aging mother without constantly stepping on each other's toes which, even under the best of circumstances, the three of us were wont to do. And because caring for our sick mother was, without a doubt, the absolute *worst* of circumstances, having some clear boundaries proved very helpful in the years to come, when Mom's health continued to throw us one curveball after another.

Thankfully, not all of Mom's health issues required the three of us to drop everything and fly to Ohio, but still, every time something happened—pancreatitis, weird seizures, the flu—I was sure it was, if not the immediate end, the beginning of the end. I was in a state of constant high alert—every time the phone rang with an unfamiliar Ohio number, I braced myself for bad news.

Even when, at age eighty-seven, Mom decided to move out of her big house to a smaller apartment in Sunrise Crest, an independent living facility in the next town over, I worried I was going to lose her. My grandmother, Mom's mom, barely lasted three months when she made a similar move after my grandfather died, fading away so fast it was as if she'd left her spirit behind in the home she and Granddad had built together. What if that happened to Mom? Not only was she leaving the house she and Dad had shared for so many years, but she'd be leaving Perrysburg, too—the town she had lived in for more than six decades. And even though she wasn't going far, just a ten-minute drive across the river, it felt far. Mom and Perrysburg were so intertwined in my mind, it was hard to imagine one without the other.

After a couple of months, though, she seemed to be doing okay and I started to worry less. In fact, it was a bit of a relief to have her somewhere safe, where help was a pull cord away. Mom didn't love living in Sunrise Crest—organized activities and forced camaraderie with people she didn't know were not her cup of tea—but she loved her apartment, and seemed, if not happy, content.

But then she fell again, tripping over a chair in her new living room, and though she didn't appear to have hurt herself too badly, she was sent to the hospital to get checked out, just in case. That decision turned out to be a good one, as she was diagnosed with advanced-stage lung disease, requiring full-time oxygen the rest of her life. The news was as surprising as it was devastating—how had something so far along been missed until then? Sal flew out first to get some answers and try to boost Mom's spirits, but after a couple of days hadn't made any headway, especially with the latter.

"I don't know, you guys," she said to Lib and me on one of our many phone calls, "there's something in her eyes I haven't seen before. Like she's given up. I think maybe you should come."

Lib and I didn't question her for a second, trusting that she wouldn't ask if the situation didn't warrant it. Even John, despite our basement having just flooded and Christmas being less than three weeks away, agreed I should go, and the next morning I was on the first flight to Ohio.

As soon as I walked into the hospital room, I could see what Sal meant. Mom forced out a little smile when she saw me, but it didn't reach her eyes. It didn't even come close. There was a dullness in them, from weariness or discouragement I wasn't sure, but the normal spark I was accustomed to seeing was missing. It was disconcerting and scary.

Lib arrived a little later, and the three of us hovered around Mom like so many nervous chicks—straightening things up, refilling the water pitcher, tempting her with ice cream and other treats. But she remained listless, uninterested in food, or newspapers, or even her daughters. We'd huddle outside her room, worried and frustrated, not used to this mother who didn't seem to want to even try.

"It must be exhausting for her to think about having to wear oxygen all the time," I speculated after another failed attempt to get her to eat something. "I wonder if we found some ways to make the oxygen part less daunting, she'd feel less overwhelmed?"

So, we tried. We talked to the oxygen supplier and learned there was tubing long enough to reach from one end of her apartment to the other so she could move about freely. We found a portable concentrator not much bigger than a purse that she could use for getting around outside, and even travel to our camp in Maine with. We reminded her about the time her friend Joanne visited there, and Mom had been able to rent an oxygen concentrator for her despite being in the middle of nowhere.

"We know it's hard, Mom," we kept telling her, "but maybe it won't be as bad as you think. We'll figure it out, we'll get you to Maine, you'll see! But you have to try, right?"

And much to our relief, she did. I'm not sure if it was allaying her fears about the oxygen, or dangling the promise of Maine in front of her like a carrot, but when we walked into her room the next morning, we saw glimpses of our real mother again. Her eyes were brighter. She smiled a little. She tried to eat something. And though it took a long time—two months in Sunrise Crest's skilled nursing with daily occupational and physical therapy sessions—Mom somehow found the strength to bounce back, *again*. Not only was she able to regain her independence in her own apartment, but was able to travel to Maine the following summer, oxygen and all.

She slowed down quite a bit in the months that followed, giving up many of the things she'd always enjoyed—bridge with friends, dinner at the club, the symphony. We didn't worry too much—between the arrival of colder weather and her oxygen constraints, it made sense to us she'd want to spend more time in her apartment. We did, however, decide to start taking turns visiting her every couple of months—not only to give us peace of mind that she was doing okay, but to give her something to look forward to as well.

And so it's been as we've planned for her eighty-ninth birthday coming up in early March, the four of us anticipating a fun few days together in Ohio to celebrate the occasion. Sal, Lib, and I haven't been there at the same time since Mom moved to Sunrise Crest, and we're excited to take her to all her favorite places—the museum to see a new exhibit, the country club for lunch with friends, a quiet birthday dinner in her apartment, just the four of us. It will be like old times.

But then a couple of weeks before we're scheduled to go, my phone rings early one morning and, just like that, nothing the four of us do together is ever the same again.

Day One

"Hello?" I answer cautiously, scared to hear whose voice is on the other end calling at such an hour. Bill? Elizabeth? Jack? Though our three children are all grown and starting lives of their own, I still worry about them out in the world without me.

"Peg, it's Sal." Her voice is low and urgent, and I push myself up a little straighter. "Mom fell and hit her head pretty bad. She's on her way to the ER."

"What? Oh my god!" Clutching the phone to my ear, I glance over at John, mouthing '*Mom*' in answer to his worried look. He offers me a sympathetic grimace and drops his head back on the pillow, relieved I'm sure that it isn't one of the kids, or his own aging mother. Not that he doesn't care about Mom, but needless to say it isn't the first early morning call we've gotten about her.

"Is anyone with her?" I ask, climbing out of bed.

"No. The night security man who answered her emergency button told me there was so much blood he didn't know what else to do but call 911. Said her bedroom looked like a scene from a horror movie. The ambulance just left."

Making my way down the stairs to the kitchen in the early morning shadows, I try not to picture Mom bleeding and alone in her apartment, struggling to get to the pull cord in her bedroom to call for help. *At least there was a cord to pull,* I remind myself, grateful she is where she is.

"I can go," Sal offers. "There's a flight I can get on this afternoon."

"No, no—that's okay. I can go. We don't have anything planned this weekend."

Living in Connecticut near all the New York airports, it's a lot easier, and usually much cheaper, for me to get to Ohio faster than either of my sisters. Sal lives way up in Maine, two hours from the nearest airport, while Lib is all the way out in California. Plus, they both have jobs, making it even harder to just jump on a plane. And Libby, on top of that, has Henry, her special needs son, which adds a whole other level of complication for her.

Sal hesitates, and I try to decipher her pause. Does she really want to go, I wonder, or is she just checking the box so she can say she offered? Sometimes it's hard to know with my older sister.

"Are you sure?" Sal finally asks. "I feel like it's my turn. You were just there."

She's right—I *had* just been there when I took Mom home after she'd spent a few weeks with us over Christmas. But the truth is, I like going. I like being the daughter running to her mother's rescue at the drop of a hat. Taking care of Mom gives me a sense of purpose. It makes me feel important.

"It's really okay," I assure her. "You're better talking to the ER anyway—you should keep doing that until we know what's going on."

I'm not sure why, but for some reason as I rush to pack and get myself to the airport, I'm not that worried about losing Mom. I mean, I'm worried she's fallen and cut her head, and I'm worried she's in the hospital in the height of flu season, but I'm not worried she's going to die. At least not yet.

A few hours later, though, I'm not so sure. Walking into the cramped hospital room where Mom had been moved for 'observation', she is hardly recognizable, and I'm grateful she's asleep so I have a moment to compose myself. Her head is swathed in gauze from chin to crown, making her look like some kind of tiny Russian babushka. Her bony, age-spotted shoulder peeks out from the hospital gown, and her crooked, arthritic hands are clutching the sheet to her chest. The nasal cannula is slightly askew under her nose, the tubing snaking out from the gauze wrapped under her chin. There's a dark pink tinge to her normally snow-white hair, and I feel a flash of anger that no one has bothered to clean her up.

The lights on the monitor beside the bed blink and beep in the dimly lit room, and I watch the numbers for a minute, trying to discern if Mom's heart is managing things alright. Everything seems normal, at least as far as I can tell, so I lean down to give her a kiss, and her eyes pop open, lighting up when she sees me.

"You came," she murmurs, reaching out her hand toward me. Grasping it, I give it a quick squeeze.

"Of course I came, Mom!"

"But what about John?"

"John's fine. He wanted me to come."

The nurse bustles into the room just then, a big-chested, heavyset woman who barely glances my way when I smile to introduce myself. *Uh oh*, I think, hoping my mother hasn't done something to alienate Betty, the nurse's name according to her uniform. Mom often takes out her frustration at being in the hospital on the same people who are trying to help her, snapping at the poor unsuspecting doctors and nurses like it's their fault she is where she is. We try to tell her she has to be nicer, that it's in her best interest that they *like* her, but she rarely listens.

Now, trying to stay out of Betty's way, I watch as she clamps an oximeter on one of Mom's fingers, sighing with impatience when she doesn't get a good reading. Pulling it off, she leans her heavy bosom over the bed to put it on Mom's other hand.

"Her fingers can be tricky because of the arthritis," I offer, wanting to be helpful so maybe she'll like me. "Sometimes her toe works better."

"I suppose that's what we'll have to do," Betty mutters, "if I can even find that kind of device." She shuffles out of the room, and Mom closes her eyes. I pull a chair up close to the bed and take her hand, holding it lightly as I watch the numbers on the monitor. It's comforting, almost mesmerizing, to see them blinking up, then down, keeping track of her heart.

Betty steps back in and, pulling the covers from Mom's feet, tapes the new oxygen reader to her big toe. Moments later, Mom's eyes flash open and she groans, pulling her hand from mine to reach down toward her legs.

"Mom! What's wrong?" Confused, I jump out of my chair to help her as she tries to sit up. I have no idea what's happening—did Betty inadvertently hurt Mom's foot when she taped on the new device? But when I look over to her for help, she's disappeared, having somehow slipped out of the room without my noticing.

"It's my legs. They keep cramping. Oh, oh..." Mom moans, arching her back. Unsure what else to do, I start rubbing them, her calf muscles so tight under my hand I fear they might burst right through the skin. But then as fast as the pain began, it stops, and Mom lays back on the pillow, closing her eyes in relief. "I'm sorry," she whispers. "I don't know what it is. I'm okay now."

"Maybe it's just from being in bed so long," I tell her, glancing toward the door as Betty reappears, wheeling a computer in front of her.

"So Mom just had the strangest pain..." I start to say, my voice trailing off as Betty frowns, plucking the oximeter off Mom's toe and moving it up to her earlobe. Her earlobe? I've never seen that before and I begin to worry that maybe the reason it's so hard to get a measurement is because Mom's oxygen level is, in fact, too low to measure.

I adjust her nasal cannula, checking to make sure there aren't any kinks in the tubing, forgetting the mysterious leg pain, at least for the moment.

The earlobe placement seems to do the trick and, satisfied, Betty peels the device off Mom's ear and plops it in her pocket. Turning to the computer, she taps heavily on the keyboard before wheeling it back out of the room without a glance our way.

"My goodness, she's a cranky nurse," I murmur to Mom, but she's already dozed off again, exhausted, I'm sure, from this whole draining ordeal. Digging my phone out of my bag, I send a quick update to Sal and Lib, then settle in to wait for the evening shift change. We've learned over the years that it's important to meet Mom's new nurses face-to-face whenever we can, so they'll know that this tiny, frail, sometimes stubborn, white-haired little old lady is, in fact, quite loved.

∾

Sitting in Mom's Sunrise Crest bedroom later that evening—after being shooed out of the hospital by the much friendlier night nurse who'd assured me she would call if there were any changes—I try to picture the scene that had taken place earlier that morning. Guessing Mom must have tripped on something getting up to use the bathroom, I glance down at the floor. There, wrapped around the vanity leg next to the bed, is a tangle of oxygen tubing from the nearby concentrator, and I sigh in dismay. How many times had I warned her to be careful when that stupid tubing would pool around her unsteady feet?

"Mom," I'd say, jumping up to help her get it unwrapped from between her legs, "you really have to pay attention! You're going to trip on this!"

But Mom, who loathes that she has to have the oxygen in the first place, would just get cross, sighing in frustration as she'd wait for me to untangle her. "I hate it!" she'd complain, like a petulant child. "I don't know why I have to wear it all the time."

"I know it's hard," I'd murmur, looping the extra length of tubing in a tidy coil behind her. "But you have to do what you have to do, right?"

Crazy how, without me noticing, our roles had somehow reversed. I liked it better the other way. I missed the mom who used to take care of *me*.

Bending over now to straighten out the twisted tubing, I see a tuft of white hair caught in one of the brass handles on the vanity drawer. *Oh my god.* Staring in horror at this stark, physical evidence of how hard Mom hit her head when she fell, I want to weep. She must have been so scared, especially when she realized how badly she was bleeding.

Earlier that evening, waiting for the Sunrise Crest security guard to come let me into the apartment, I'd been nervous about walking through the door and having to deal with Mom's blood splattered all over the place. Even though I knew Sal had called the front desk to ask that housekeeping stop by to clean things up, what if they hadn't been able to? Feeling anxious about what I was walking into, and a little annoyed at how long I'd been waiting, I was relieved when the security guard finally appeared, his keys jangling from his belt as he lumbered down the carpeted hall toward me.

"Sorry for the delay," he said, fitting a key into the lock and pushing the door open. "Busy night here for some reason."

"That's okay." I grabbed the handle of my roller bag and squeezed past him into the small entryway, twisting my hip to hold open the door so he could let go. "Thanks for coming."

"Your mom doing okay?" he asked as the door was swinging shut. "I was the one who answered her call button this morning."

I paused, caught off guard that this large, slightly balding man with a sagging tummy was the hero who had helped my mom.

"You were?" I exclaimed, catching the door before it closed in his face. "I mean, oh my gosh, thank you!"

"Yeah, it was a good gash she got on her head. Lots of blood. But she's a strong one, your mom. Put a pillow on it to stop the bleeding until I got here." He shook his head, as if still not quite believing it. "Took the ambulance a little while, so I sat with her until it came."

My throat tightened, trying to keep back the sudden tears springing up behind my eyes. "I'm so grateful you were there," I managed to say. "Twelve staples in her head, but she's doing alright. I think she'll be home tomorrow."

"Well, that's good news." He backed into the hallway, giving a little wave as he turned to leave. "You have a good night now, okay?"

I let the door close slowly behind him, listening to the sound of his keys fade away as the latch clicked softly into place.

Rolling my suitcase into the nearby guest room, I then made my way into the darkened living room, turning on lights as I went along. Everything seemed to be as it should—the kitchen counter was tidy, the furniture in the living room all in place, except one chair that the paramedics must have moved to get the gurney by. Pulling it back to where it belonged, I smiled when I saw Mom's emergency alert necklace still dangling from the arm where she'd hung it after she fell the last time. Somehow it made more sense to her to have the pendant there, in the place where she'd fallen, than around her neck. *Oh, Mom.*

The doorway to her bedroom was in deep shadows, and I walked toward it with trepidation, preparing myself for the worst-case scenario. Fumbling for the wall switch, I turned on the light and scanned the room, letting out a deep sigh of relief when I saw everything in order. The bed was neatly made, the carpet vacuumed, clean towels hanging in the adjacent bathroom. Not a trace of blood to be seen. I sent a quick, silent thank you to Sal for having the forethought to call and have it cleaned up before I got there.

I headed back out to the kitchen and poured myself a glass of wine, trying to decide if I had the energy to make myself something to eat. I was so tired. Plopping myself down on a stool, I noticed a folded piece of paper in the middle of the counter. It was a note from the housekeeper who had been there to clean:

"*Sorry I had to throw away a towel and a pillow,*" she wrote in a slanted, uncertain script. "*They were too soaked in blood and not worth saving.*" She'd signed her name, *Doris*, and then, I guess as an afterthought, had added, "*P.S. I hope Mrs. Ball is okay.*"

My head dropped to my hands on the counter, and I made myself take a few deep breaths. *Mom is okay*, I reminded myself. *She just cut her head. There was a lot of blood, but she's fine. She's* fine.

Now, sitting on Mom's bed, staring at the place she'd fallen, I try to imagine what happened next. There's a pull cord near the bed, but it's on the opposite side from where she'd tripped, so I doubt she went that way. There's another one in the bathroom, where I think she was trying to get to in the first place, so maybe she just kept going? But how did she get there? Could she stand up? Did she have to crawl? A picture flashes through my mind of Mom dragging herself across the floor—blood dripping down her face from the open gash on her head, oxygen tubing trailing behind her—and I give my head a quick shake to dispel it. Maybe she didn't go to the bathroom. Maybe when she saw how badly she was bleeding she got back on the bed and pulled the cord, using the pillow to try and stop it while she waited for help to come.

But no matter how it happened, if I know my mom, she was probably less worried about herself as she sat there waiting than she was about all the trouble this would cause for her daughters. Which makes me sad. I don't want her to worry about us. After all the times she dropped everything to come to our rescue—the birth of a grandchild, an unexpected surgery, babysitting so we young parents could recharge—helping her these last few years hasn't been a burden at all. She's our mom. We'd do anything for her.

Day Two

The next morning, under strict instructions from my sisters to get Mom out of the hospital as quickly as possible to avoid the risk of infection, I watch as she makes her way slowly, but determinedly, down the fluorescent-lit corridor under the watchful eye of the physical therapist. According to the head nurse, Mom had an uneventful night, so as long as she can prove she's capable of walking without help, she'll be discharged later in the afternoon.

I know I should be happy, but I'm not. I'm nervous. Mom looks so frail to me, her body seeming to have diminished overnight, swallowed up by the oversized hospital gown hanging down past her knees and the beige non-skid socks bunched loosely around her ankles. The bandaging on her head has loosened as well, her blood-matted hair sticking out from under it, making her look a little bit crazy.

She turns to walk back, flashing me a small smile that seems to say, "See, Peg? I'm doing just fine. Stop worrying!" I'm glad to see a flicker of her feisty spirit, and I try to shrug off the niggling unease in the back of my mind as I follow her back into the room.

It's Saturday, so the discharge process takes longer than usual, and we're left to ourselves while we wait for the paperwork to come through. Mom dozes in and out, nibbling at her lunch when it arrives but not eating much. She complains once or twice about leg pain, but it passes quickly and I don't pay much attention. Again.

It's mid-afternoon when an aide comes breezing into the room, a perky young woman who steps toward the bed with purpose, pulling the privacy curtain closed with a quick tug, the swoosh of its hooks on the metal track startling Mom awake.

"Time to get you dressed," she says in a loud, sing-songy voice. Cringing, I glance at Mom to see if I'm going to have to intercede—she hates being talked to like a child, and she especially hates being talked to like a child who can't hear.

But to my surprise, Mom isn't at all annoyed, sitting up docilely on the edge of the bed as the aide removes her hospital gown and starts getting her into the clothes I'd brought from her apartment. I stand back, watching as Mom tries to help pull up her underwear and elastic waist pants, but the aide is all-business, and Mom finally gives up, her efforts only slowing down the whole process.

"I don't think this is going to go over her bandaging," the aide says, holding up the turtleneck I'd automatically thrown in the bag, a mainstay of Mom's winter wardrobe.

"Oh, right. Of course not," I say, moving forward to grab it from her hand. Picking up the blue cashmere hoodie I'd also brought, I turn to Mom. "You're okay just wearing this until we get home, aren't you?"

"I don't care what I wear as long as I'm getting out of here," Mom replies, holding out her arms like a child so I can help her into the well-worn sweater. Leaning in to zip it up, I smell a slight metallic odor which I don't immediately recognize. *What is that?* I wonder, looking Mom up and down, trying to figure out where it's coming from. It takes a moment before I realize it's from the blood still caked in her hair and, not for the first time, I find myself angry that no one has bothered to clean my mother up.

But I guess I'm not angry enough because I don't do anything about it, which makes me angry at myself. I wish I wasn't so scared to make a scene. I wish I was more like Sal and Lib, who confront conflict head on, rather than shy away from it the way I always do. I often wonder why I'm so different from my sisters—we were brought up under the same roof, after all—but like our parents, the two of them tend to embrace conflict, while I avoid it at all costs.

Growing up, Mom and Dad *loved* to argue, especially during dinner. Most weeknights the five of us would gather around the table in our dining room—Libby and Sal together on one side with me across from them, and Mom and Dad at each end, anchoring us all in place. They'd ask us about our days, and tell each other about their own, and it was usually fine—except when it wasn't.

I remember one night in particular—I was maybe ten or eleven and, bored with my parents' conversation, sat picking at my food. A sudden shift in Mom's tone cut its way into my thoughts and I glanced up, dismayed to see her mouth set in a grim line. She was staring defiantly at my father, whose mouth was set in a similar line, his blue eyes piercing as he glowered back at her.

Across from me, my sisters' faces faded away behind the flickering candles, leaving me feeling even more stranded on my side of the table. My eyes drifted down to the white paper napkin crumpled in my lap, and I gripped it harder.

"You're wrong, Kay!" my father barked.

"I don't care what you think, Bill!" Mom hurled back.

Neither of them willing to concede, the argument intensified and, unable to bear it, I ran from the table, racing up the nearby stairs to my room.

Burrowing into the safety of my bed, face down on the pillow, I put my hands over my ears, tears spilling out the corners of my tightly clenched eyes, trying to shut out the voices echoing up the stairs into my room. My parents' fury was churning around me, and I couldn't get away from it. "*Stop, stop. Please stop*," a voice in my head kept whispering.

Then suddenly it did. As quickly as the argument had begun, it was over, my parents' angry voices replaced by the sound of dishes being cleared, the television being turned on. I tiptoed to the top of the stairs and listened closely, just to make sure, heaving a big sigh of relief when I realized everything was back to normal.

I'm not sure why I was so scared by my parents' argument that night because my sisters weren't. In fact, they teased me for days afterward about being such a crybaby. And maybe for good reason. It's not as though there was any sort of physical threat—Mom and Dad were never violent, except with their words. So maybe I *was* being a crybaby. Maybe I'm *still* one.

I'm certain if either Sal or Lib were here in this hospital room, they would be telling the aide that no one was going anywhere until every speck of blood was washed out of Mom's hair. And though I *want* to say something, and know I *should* say something, I don't. I stay quiet, reasoning with myself as I bundle Mom into her coat, that it would be too much for her to change gears at this point anyway—she's all dressed and ready to go. I'll figure out how to clean her up once we're home.

Bending down, I drape Mom's wool scarf over her head and tie it under her chin like a kerchief, trying to cover as much of her blood-tinged hair as I can.

"Oh, Peg," she chuckles as I stuff the fringed ends inside her coat, "I don't care how I look!"

Smiling, I plant a quick kiss on her forehead before standing back up. "I know, Mom, but trust me, I'm not doing it for you! I don't want you to scare anyone!"

It's a slow process getting her into a wheelchair, then down the elevator and into the car, and I worry the entire drive back to Sunrise Crest how I'll ever manage on the other end without the aide there to help me. Pulling up in front of the entrance, I pause for a moment to think through my strategy.

"Okay, Mom, here's the plan," I tell her in my most matter-of-fact voice. "You're going to stay right here while I go in and see if there's a wheelchair we can borrow. If

there's not, then I'm going to have to run up to the apartment and get your walker, so it may take me a few minutes.
Are you okay here alone?"

Mom nods and tries to smile, but I can see she's wearing out, her thin lips pursed tight. I turn up the heat—it's
a raw, blustery February afternoon—and, leaving the car
running, jump out and jog into the lobby, stopping at the
front desk to ask about a wheelchair.

"Oh no," the receptionist tells me, shaking her head.
"We don't keep those *here*. They might have one you can
borrow over at the health center if you want to try there."

But the Sunrise Crest health center is all the way on
the other side of the building, too far for me to go with
Mom sitting alone in the car, so mumbling a half-heart-
ed thank you, I head toward the elevator. I've discovered
over the past year that there are very strict lines between
Sunrise Crest's three levels of care and, in the independent
living level especially, it's frowned upon to cross them. So
even though I suppose I could ask for help, I don't bother.
Mom wouldn't want the attention anyway.

Lost in thought, I'm walking past the big glass window of the computer center and glance in from habit to see
if anyone's there. It's empty, as usual, but as I'm about to
pass by, something in the corner catches my eye. I pause,

not quite believing what I'm seeing, but there, folded up and tucked away on the other side of the window, is a wheelchair.

For a moment I'm scared to move, worried that even the slightest motion might disturb whatever vibrational frequency I've stepped into where this wheelchair some-how exists. It's like it popped out of my head and landed right in front of me.

Giddy with relief, I hurry in to get it, rolling it back out past the surprised receptionist, silently thanking whatever force in the universe made me glance through that window.

"Look what I found!" I exclaim to Mom as I open the car door, my excitement quickly fading when I see she's grown even paler in the short time I was gone. Another prickle of worry pokes at me, but again, I ignore it.

"Okay, let's get you out of here." Leaning over to un-latch the seat belt, I help her turn so she's facing the door and then, with one hand on her shoulder so she doesn't fall out, pull the wheelchair toward me with my other, try-ing to get it as close to the car as I can.

"Think you can pull yourself into it?" I ask.

Mom nods and reaches forward, but it's clear right away she doesn't have the strength.

"That's okay, don't worry, we can do this." Talking more to myself than to her, I grab her under the arms, lifting her out of the car and plunking her down into the chair. The oxygen tubing has wrapped itself around one of her ankles, scrunching up her pant leg and exposing her dry, vein-riddled calf. Bending down to try and unwind it over her sneaker, I pull the tubing tighter, tugging Mom forward with a jerk.

"Oh my god, Mom! I'm so sorry!"

"I'm the one who's sorry," she says, her voice feeble and hard to hear. "I'm no help at all."

"Don't be silly, you're doing great," I reassure her, forcing myself to slow down and take a deep breath. But it's hard not to rush—it's freezing outside, the cold wind snapping my hair in my eyes and face—and Mom is so pale, her lips taking on the worrisome bluish tint that means she's not getting enough oxygen.

Leaning in to turn off the engine, I push the car door shut with my hip as I turn to roll her—dwarfed like a child in the enormous wheelchair—up the walkway and through the sliding glass doors into the warm lobby as fast as I can.

∿

"Mom?" I whisper, poking my head in the bedroom door to check on her a couple of hours later. She'd fallen asleep as soon as I'd gotten her settled into her recliner, so the rest of the afternoon had passed quietly, with me on the phone trying to find someone to come help give her a shower. It wasn't easy—no one wanted to work on a Saturday—but finally a kind-hearted aide took pity on me and agreed to come by later that evening.

Now, having just run out to the pharmacy to pick up Mom's antibiotic prescription, I'm relieved to see that she's still asleep. Leaving the door ajar, I'm about to turn away when something in the angle of her head and the pallor of her skin gives me pause. A prickle of fear tingles through me—did she look this bad earlier? Mom's head has slipped off the pillow and her mouth is slightly agape, her lips as colorless as the pallid skin around them. The dark staples across her scalp stand out stark against the pink tufts of hair going every which way. She looks dead, I think, and for a moment I feel a certain detachment, as though it's not actually *me* having this thought about my mother.

But the next moment it *is* me, and it *is* my mother, and I'm paralyzed, scared to go check her, but equally scared not to. Tiptoeing over to her side, my heart thudding hard against my chest, I reach my hand toward her neck to feel for a pulse.

Oh, thank god. I can just make out a faint flutter under my fingertips, and I sink down to the floor next to the recliner in relief. My own heart is beating like crazy, and I lay my head in my hands, taking a few slow, deep breaths to try and calm it down. I'm still scared, though. Mom may be breathing but she looks *really* bad, making me worried there's more wrong with her than just the cut on her head. Not sure what to do, I pull my phone from my pocket and take a quick picture to send to Sal and Lib. I'm just pushing the send button when Mom wakes up, writhing in pain.

"Mom!" I cry, leaping up from the floor. "What is it? What's wrong?"

"Oh, my legs!" She's leaning forward, her eyes wide but unseeing, like an animal caught in a trap. I rub one leg then the other, thinking the pain will subside as quickly as it did in the hospital, but when it doesn't, when it seems to be getting even worse, I jump up and run to the bathroom, rifling through her medicine cabinet for some kind of pain reliever. I can only find Tylenol, which I'm not sure will do anything, but I grab it anyway, rushing out to the kitchen for a glass of water, then back to her side.

I can't get her to swallow the pills, though. She's moaning and clutching at her legs, her pain so intense I can almost feel it myself. I'm desperate to make it stop, but I can't seem to think what to do. Somehow, even though my brain is screaming orders at me, CALL HER DOCTOR! CALL 911! it's rejecting them as fast as I think them. I can't call her doctor, it's the weekend. And I can't call 911 and send her back to the hospital, not after what we just went through to get home. Can I?

Panicking, knowing I have to do something, I grab the phone and call Sal. She answers on the first ring and, at the sound of her voice, I start to cry.

"Peg, Peg, what is it? What's wrong?"

"I don't know! Mom's in so much pain!" I choke out through my tears. "But I can't bear to take her back to the hospital!"

"Peg, I don't think you have a choice. That picture you just sent—something's not right. Call 911. I'm making my reservation now. I'll be there tomorrow."

Relieved to have someone tell me what to do, I take a shaky breath and hang up to make the call. I can't believe this is happening. I can't believe I'm taking Mom back to the hospital less than three hours after I'd gotten her home.

"I'm so sorry, Mom. I'm so sorry," I murmur over and over, rubbing her legs, trying to keep her calm, trying to keep *myself* calm, as we wait in the fading afternoon light for help to come.

∾

It seems to take forever, but the paramedics finally arrive, two enormous men—one tall and heavyset, the other just tall—their masculine presence overwhelming in Mom's small apartment. Leading them into the bedroom, I move to the other side of the recliner to get out of their way.

"What seems to be the problem?" the heavier set one asks, opening up a large black case to reveal a portable heart monitor. Pulling out cords, he starts attaching them to Mom, who has stopped thrashing but is still moaning softly. I try to describe her leg pain, but he doesn't seem to be listening, or even that concerned, focused as he is on the numbers flashing on the monitor.

"Vitals are fine," he says, plucking the cords back off Mom one at a time. "Heart rate is good, respirations are a little high but nothing to be worried about." He starts to pack his things up.

"Wait! You're leaving?" Bewildered, I look from him to the other guy, but neither of them looks back.

"Her heart's doing fine," the big one repeats, "and to be honest, there's just not much we can do for her here. Do you want an ambulance?"

I look at him in confusion, not sure what he means. "Didn't you come in an ambulance?" I ask, surprised by his question. Where I live in Connecticut there is always an ambulance at the scene with the paramedics, otherwise how would they get anyone to the hospital?

"No, it's a separate service," he explains. "I can call for one, but it will take a while to get here. It would be faster if you took her yourself."

I stare at him, speechless. Is he kidding? I can't possibly get Mom to the hospital myself—I was barely able to get her home on my own when she *wasn't* in this much pain. And though waiting for an ambulance that's not even on its way feels equally impossible, I don't know what other choice I have.

"Well, there's no way I can take her," I snap, upset that he can't see how sick Mom is. "So I guess you better call for one."

Shrugging his shoulders, he pulls out his phone to make the call. Mom is still moaning, but the pain seems to be lessening, at least a little. Perching myself on the edge of the small rocker next to the bed, I sit and stare out the window, ignoring the two paramedics like a peevish child. But after a few uncomfortable minutes, the heavy, awkward silence in the room is as loud in my head as if I'm in the middle of a heated argument, and I can't bear it.

"Look," I blurt out, "I'm sorry to be so upset. I just can't understand why it takes so long to get an ambulance. It makes no sense!"

"Hey, no apology needed", the big paramedic replies. "Believe me, I understand. The system was changed a few months ago and this is what we're dealing with now. It's frustrating for everyone."

His candor surprises me, and for the next half hour, as we wait for the ambulance, he explains the new EMS system, and I find myself feeling bad I'd been so quick to judge. Rather than being the source of the problem, it seems this poor guy is just a cog in a wheel, doing his job the best he can to keep the wheel turning, despite the fact that it's broken.

A knock on the door interrupts us, and two more enormous EMT's arrive, wheeling a gurney between them. Mom's bedroom isn't big enough for all of us, so the first two paramedics, after giving a quick report on Mom's vitals, retreat to the living room to get out of the way. I hover in a corner, watching as the other two lift Mom out of the recliner and onto the stretcher, covering her tiny body with a crisp sheet before tightening the wide black straps firmly around her chest and legs, then laying a blanket on top.

"Okay, Mom," I whisper in her ear, leaning down to kiss her forehead as they get ready to roll her out. "You're in good hands. I'll be right behind you." I can hardly bear how small she looks surrounded by all these large men, but they're being so kind and gentle I'm able to step back and let them take her.

Gathering up my things for what I anticipate will be a long night, I follow them out a few minutes later, back to the hospital.

Still Day Two

By the time I get to the ER, Mom is already in an examining room and the EMT's are at the main desk filling out their paperwork. When they see me, one of them comes over and asks if Mom is ever confused.

"How do you mean?" I ask nervously.

"Well, she was talking to us on the ride over, but she wasn't making any sense." He clears his throat, glancing over at his partner. "We're just not sure if that's something new, or something that is normal for her."

"No, no, it's not normal," I tell him, shaking my head. "But it has happened before, when she had a stroke a few years ago."

Terrified it's happening again, I rush into the examining room, momentarily reassured to find Mom awake and alert, though relieved to see me. She reaches out her hand to grasp mine and I take it, giving it a gentle squeeze.

"Hey Mom," I smile. "You doing okay?"

"For maybe it dance off that place?" She looks at me expectantly, and my heart sinks. Oh no.

A nurse comes in and I explain Mom's history as best I can. "This is exactly what happened before," I tell her, "she's talking but it makes no sense."

The nurse doesn't waste any time, and within minutes, Mom is whisked away for a CT scan, leaving me alone to wait in the examining room. Grateful to have a moment to check in with Sal and Lib, I'm just pulling out my phone when another nurse hurries in. Clipboard in hand, she starts firing questions at me, trying to get me to pinpoint exactly when Mom's symptoms had begun. I'm reminded of that night six years before when a different nurse, in a different emergency room, was firing the same questions at me, with the same intense urgency. It's intimidating and scary because now I'm remembering that if Mom *is* having a stroke there's an extremely narrow window to give her medication to stop it. I'm also remembering that if that window is missed—perhaps because an overwrought daughter can't say for sure when her mother's symptoms began because the past few hours are a giant blur in her head and she can't remember a thing—then the medication could do more harm than good.

I try to answer the nurse's questions as accurately as I can, but I find myself second guessing everything I tell her, worried I might be hurting Mom more than helping her. Am I *sure* I didn't see any signs of confusion getting her home from the hospital? Had we *really* been home three hours before she woke up, or was it maybe closer to four? Was she *definitely* not mixing up her words while we waited for the ambulance, or *was* she and I assumed it was because of her pain?

The nurse, pen poised over her clipboard, pauses before writing down each of my answers, as if sensing my uncertainty. I wish there was someone I could call, someone who would say, "Yes, Peggy. That's exactly how it happened," so I could relax and stop worrying. But there's not. There's just me, and it's unnerving.

Because as much as I want to be my mother's best advocate, I'm finding it hard to navigate the murky fog of details clouding my head. So much has happened in the past twenty-four hours, and somehow, we've ended up right back where we started. How did that happen? Did I make a wrong decision somewhere along the line?

Relieved when the nurse finally seems satisfied and clicks her pen closed, I watch her disappear out the door as an aide wheels Mom back in. Pulling up a stool next to her,

I lean down, resting my arms on the side of the gurney so we're head-to-head. Mom turns her face to look at me, her blue eyes cloudy with confusion.

"We're going to get this figured out, Mom," I promise, trying to sound reassuring. We sit quietly for a few minutes when suddenly her eyes widen, filling with panic as the oxygen mask fogs up, and she starts to make a low, primal grunting sound I've never heard before. What is happening? Thinking she may be having a heart attack, I cry out for help, scared to leave her side, but when no one comes, I race to the door, looking both ways down the corridor. Where is everyone? An attendant appears around a corner and I call out, waving my hand to get his attention. He hurries toward me and into the room.

"I don't know what's wrong!" I cry, the guttural sound coming out of my sick mother making me frantic with worry. I rub her shoulder to try and calm her. "She was fine and then her mask fogged up!"

Without a word, the attendant checks Mom's mask, then leans down and disconnects the tubing from the portable tank under the gurney, reconnecting it to the oxygen unit on the wall. Immediately the mask clears and Mom stops grunting, relaxing back onto the pillow under her head. *Oh my god!* Mom wasn't having a heart attack! She was suffocating! The aide who brought her back from the CT scan forgot to switch the oxygen back to the wall unit, and the portable tank had run out.

The attendant adjusts the flow meter then checks Mom one more time before turning to leave, still without a word. His silence infuriates me, minimizing the seriousness of what just happened. Should I make a scene? Demand the aide's name so I can report her? What if she did this again, but to someone whose daughter wasn't sitting right next to them when the oxygen ran out?

I look down at Mom. Her eyes are closed and she's breathing easier, her gaunt chest rising and falling steadily under the thin hospital gown. The room feels chilly, so I pull the blanket up from where it's bunched around her waist, tucking it in over her shoulders. She's so old, so un-in charge of herself. What would happen to her if I wasn't here?

I'm reminded of the time when I was an EMT and we responded to a late night call from the local nursing home for an elderly woman who was having trouble breathing. As was often the case at that particular facility, the nursing staff disappeared once we arrived, leaving the poor woman alone and scared, surrounded as she was by paramedics and EMT's she'd never seen before. She was sweet, though, and trusting, and on the short drive to the hospital I learned that she didn't have any family in the immediate area. Her daughter lived about four hours away and would come the next day if she was still in the hospital.

Things got a little hectic once we rolled her into the emergency room, but I managed to poke my head into the cubicle to check on her before we left. The nurse was in the process of getting her out of her nightgown, but seeming without care that the woman's bare chest was exposed, not only to the chill of the sterile air, but to anybody that might be walking by. The nurse glanced up when I stepped to the side of the bed and tried, as discreetly as I could, to pull the sheet up over the poor woman's pale, sagging breasts.

"Do you know her?" the nurse asked, unfolding a hospital gown with a quick shake, then slipping it over one of the woman's arms, then the other, exposing her chest yet again.

"No—we just brought her in from Wilton. Her family can't get here until tomorrow so I just wanted to check on her before we go."

I smiled down at the woman, pulling the sheet up over her chest more firmly now that the nurse was done with her. "Are you warm enough?" I asked, "Do you want a blanket?"

"I'm fine, dear." She smiled bravely, slipping her hand out from under the sheet to take mine, giving it a feeble squeeze. "Thank you. You've been very kind."

It was hard to leave her there, so old and alone, at the mercy of the overworked nurses and doctors in the busy emergency room. And not for the first time, as I settled myself in the ambulance for the ride back to Wilton, I wondered if there was such a thing as a volunteer hand holder—someone the nursing home could call when one of their elderly patients had to go to the hospital and didn't have any family around. If there wasn't, maybe there could be, and I put it on my list of things to look into. Of course, not long after that I ended up with my own elderly person's hand to hold in the hospital, so I'd never followed up on the idea.

Watching Mom now, more grateful than ever that I'm here with her, I decide to let things be. She seems okay, no worse for the wear, and for the second time that day I find I'm just too tired to call out the nursing staff on their incompetence. It might backfire and make things worse, I reason with myself. We need these people to like us.

The emergency room doctor taps on the door and, seeing that Mom is resting, gestures for me to join him in the hall. A short, round gentleman with kind eyes and a gentle smile, he introduces himself and then gives me a quick update on Mom's condition.

"The good news is we can rule out stroke," he begins, looking down at the chart he's holding. "But she's lost a great deal of blood from the cut on her head, and combined with the fact that she can't maintain adequate oxygen levels without a full mask, we're going to admit her overnight."

He pauses, glancing through the door at Mom, then back at me. "I have to ask—did *this* hospital send your mother home looking like that?"

I nod, not trusting myself to speak. Finally, someone is paying attention.

"I am beyond sorry about this," he says, his dismay so genuine I want to hug him. "We are going to get her cleaned up right now."

And true to his word, a few minutes later a tall, smiling young nurse walks into the room, her dark hair pulled back in a tidy bun at the nape of her neck, her skin so smooth it's almost translucent under the harsh fluo-rescent light. In one hand she's carrying a pink, plastic basin filled with water, and in the other a small bottle of shampoo and a comb. She sets it all on top of the rolling tray table, then, lifting Mom's head, spreads a towel over the pillow underneath before settling herself on a stool next to her.

"This could take a while," she warns, her fingers gently probing the area around the staples where the matted blood is the thickest. "But there's no rush. We'll get it out."

It's a tedious job, but she's patient and meticulous, rinsing one small section of hair at a time and then combing through it over and over until not a trace of pink remains. She doesn't rush. She doesn't complain. She chats about this and that, apologizing softly when she has to tug harder to get through one of the bigger clumps of dried blood, although I'm not sure Mom even notices. The nurse's gentle ministrations seem to have lulled her to sleep, or if not sleep, at least something close to it.

It *is* peaceful watching her work, and by the time she's done, I feel soothed, like a warm salve's been poured over me, calming my anxious nerves. And when Mom opens her eyes, she seems calmer, too, less confused. Her beautiful white hair is clean and combed neatly to the side, and despite the dark line of staples traversing her head, she looks more like her old self. She's clearly not out of the woods, but for the first time since I'd arrived twenty-four hours before, I feel hopeful that she's going to be okay.

Day Three

"Yes, yes, I have a telephone." Mom's voice pulls me out of a deep sleep, and I sit up with a start, momentarily disoriented until I remember where I am. Leaning forward in the recliner that I'd pulled up next to her hospital bed late the night before, I squint through the dim, early morning light to see her more clearly, my eyes so scratchy from lack of sleep I can barely open them.

Mom is staring at something intently, her cloudy blue eyes wide and alert above the oxygen mask covering the rest of her face. Confused, I look around the shadow-filled room, but it's empty.

"Do you want to come in and see it?" she asks, cocking her head to one side. Her words are muffled under the mask, her voice raspy and dry, but oddly clear. "Well, everyone has one I think, but you're welcome to use mine."

Holding my breath, I listen to this exchange with a mixture of fear and awe. As a hospice volunteer, I know that people close to death can often 'see' loved ones who have already passed and will talk to them as though they are right there in the room. I had never witnessed it before—though I'd always hoped to—and wonder if that's what's happening now. Is Mom talking to someone on the other side? Is she getting ready to die? I feel eerily calm that the thing I've been dreading for so long may be happening right in front of me.

Although if Mom *is* talking to someone on the other side, what a strange conversation to be having! And it doesn't seem like she recognizes whoever it is, which makes no sense either. Wouldn't it be someone she knows, like Dad, or her parents?

"Oh, well, I suppose that's alright," Mom murmurs, interrupting my thoughts. She closes her eyes and relaxes back against the pillow. "Maybe tomorrow it will work better."

I watch her for signs of distress, but she seems to be okay, and way more restful than she's been the past few hours. It had been a long and grueling night, her oxygen level dipping perilously low just after she was moved up from the emergency room into her new room. The leg pain continued to come and go in rolling waves, reminding me of labor contractions, building to unbearable peaks where Mom would be moaning and writhing to get away from them, then slowly subsiding, giving her a few blessed moments of relief. The nurse and aide had buzzed around her, fiddling with the IV, readjusting her mask, checking the tubing, all the while conferring with each other in low, serious voices. I was relieved when the nurse finally pulled out her phone.

"Your Mom's oxygen is just too low and we don't know why," she explained, stepping past me out into the hall. "I'm going to see if we can get a specialist up here to do a blood gas test."

It's funny how differently I'd pictured that night in my head. I'd assumed once we'd gotten Mom settled, I'd stick around until she fell asleep, then head back to her apartment for a long overdue shower and glass of wine, the way I always would whenever she'd been in the hospital in the past. There may have been one or two times when I thought *maybe* I should stay, but Mom would have none of it, stubbornly insisting she was in good hands and would sleep better knowing I was someplace more comfortable. I never argued—the lure of a warm bed easily persuading me that she was right, I'd be a much better advocate for her with a good night's sleep under my belt.

But standing there in the corner of Mom's hospital room waiting for the nurse to come back, I realized with a sinking heart I wouldn't be going home that night. Something was very wrong and there was no way I could leave her alone, not for a minute.

I had little time to feel too sorry for myself, though, as things started to move quickly when the specialist—a short, compact Asian woman—breezed into the room a few minutes later. Her authority was palpable in the small space and, spotting me in the corner trying to stay out of the way, she wasted no time with niceties.

"I want you to know I'm very good at what I do," she said, her voice clipped and heavily accented. "But it can be a painful procedure so better for you to wait outside."

I couldn't bear to leave Mom, but the doctor's tone left me little choice but to follow the nurse out of the room. She closed the door firmly behind me, the click of the latch loud and foreboding in the hushed silence of the brightly lit corridor. There was nowhere to sit, and the waiting area too far away, so I eased myself down to the floor, hugging my knees into my chest. Letting my head drop between them, I stared at the small patch of scratched linoleum beneath me, trying to focus on anything but what was happening on the other side of the door.

∽

Time moves differently when you're in the hospital, sometimes spiraling forward so fast it's hard to keep up, but other times creeping along so slowly it doesn't feel like it's moving at all. Waiting outside Mom's room, it seemed impossible that it was still the same day I'd woken up to. How could that be? It was like I was in some kind of strange time warp where the hours between morning and night were so fused together it was hard to tell when one had ended and the other began.

Even now, watching the gray dawn light inching its way through the window blinds, my memories of what else happened the night before are just blurry snippets in my mind, with no pattern or sequence. The aide came and went. The nurse came and went. Mom woke and slept, and I woke and slept next to her in the recliner I'd pushed up close to her bed so I could reach out and touch her when she cried out in pain. I'm relieved that it's finally morning, although anxious about what this new day will bring.

I let my gaze settle on Mom, resting peacefully now despite her strange conversation. The oxygen mask is so big it covers most of her face, its rubber edges pulling the skin on her cheeks and forehead so taut her wrinkles look like they've been ironed out. Even with the mask, my mother's face is so familiar I feel like I know it almost better than my own. How is it possible that one day, perhaps even today, it will be gone and I won't see it ever again? It's the only thing in my life that has always been there, and I can't imagine my world without it. I shift in my seat, the fact of my mother's inevitable, and perhaps even imminent, death scaring me in a way I'm not used to.

Because up until this moment I thought I was prepared for Mom to die. She'd had a good, long life with few regrets, at least as far as I knew, and lots and lots of love. And though her spirit was still strong, her body no longer was, making her feel old and tired. I felt tired for her. Did I want her to die? No, of course not. But in the years since my dad passed away, I'd come to believe that death was a transition rather than an ending, and our energy—the spark that makes us who we are—doesn't disappear when we die, but transforms to a higher vibration. I may not be able to see Mom anymore when she's gone, but I'll still be able to feel her, the way I did with Dad.

Up until his sudden death when I was thirty-three, I'd been terrified of dying, of disappearing forever into the deep, dark nothing I imagined death would be. I mean really and truly, panic-attack-inducing terrified. The first time it happened I was around ten years old. It was a regular night and I was reading in bed, waiting for Mom to come tuck me in and kiss me goodnight.

"Did you say your prayers?" she asked, sitting down on the edge of the bed. Taking my book, she marked the page and set it on the bedside table before turning off the lamp. Light from the hallway fell on her face as she gazed at me expectantly.

"Not yet," I admitted, clasping my hands together and closing my eyes. "Now I lay me down to sleep, I pray the Lord my soul to keep." The words were so familiar they tumbled out of my mouth without me even having to think about them. "If I should die before I wake, I pray the Lord my soul to take."

I'm not sure why on that particular night I all of a sudden understood what I was praying for. But as Mom kissed the top of my head and left me alone in the dark, it struck me for the first time that I might actually "*die before I wake.*"

I tried to push the thought away, but as I lay there staring into the darkness behind my eyes, I started to imagine what it would be like to never wake up, to be stuck in that darkness forever. Down, down, down my mind spiraled into its ominous depths, until it became so deep and black I was scared I might get lost in it right then. My eyes popped open, my heart racing so hard I could barely breathe, panic propelling my ten-year-old self right out of bed, through the door, and down the hall to my parents' room.

I didn't go in, though. Maybe I was embarrassed. Or maybe part of me just didn't want to give voice to the deep, dark nothing and make it more real. Standing outside the door, I listened to the muffled sounds of Mom and Dad getting ready for bed. A toilet flushed, a drawer closed, my mom's voice murmured something I couldn't make out.

Their reassuring presence on the other side of the door was enough to calm me down so I was able to turn away and tiptoe back to my room. Crawling into bed, I pulled the covers up tight around me, somehow finding a way to lull my thoughts away from the scary darkness and into the safety net of sleep.

That same paralyzing fear of death would follow me into adulthood, an insidious foe I learned to keep at bay by steering my thoughts away whenever they threatened to take me down into the deep, dark nothing. I wasn't always able to—sometimes when a dark thought crept in, especially when I was alone, I couldn't push it away, the ensuing panic making me, like my ten-year-old self, jump up to go find something, *anything*, to distract myself.

But the day after Dad died, it was like a switch went off in my head. The paralyzing fear that had been following me around like a shadow for so many years melted away as if by magic, leaving me with an inner calm I'd never experienced.

Not right away, of course. When Mom called to tell me Dad was gone—a heart attack from complications after abdominal surgery to remove a blood clot—the familiar panic immediately began squeezing at my chest, even as I spoke calmly with her on the phone, making sure she was okay and promising to be there first thing in the morning. But as soon as I hung up, I collapsed onto the bed with a howl so deep it sounded almost inhuman, even to my own ears. John came running from downstairs, and though he tried to comfort me—shushing me gently, trying to hold me close—I kept pushing him away, jumping up off the bed to pace the room, heaving great staggering sobs that seemed to come from the bottom of my soul. My dad was *dead.* The fear I'd kept at bay for so long was swallowing me into its deep, dark depths and all I could do was let it, finding a strange relief in finally allowing it to have its way with me.

But then, like a violent storm passing through, my tears stopped, leaving me shaken, but strangely calm.

Unsure what to do next, I was grateful to find that John, when he realized he couldn't help me, had gone back downstairs to call the airline and get me on the first flight to Ohio the next morning. Giving him a hug, I attempted to pack a few things while we talked about who we could get to help him with the kids, all under the age of five.

And then we tried to get some sleep. Exhausted in a way I'd never been before, my body melted into the sheets, but my mind wouldn't rest, bouncing around to all the things I needed to do before I left. Lying in bed, fretting and worrying, I began to notice a little niggly voice in the back of my head telling me I shouldn't take the early flight. "*You should wait,*" it kept saying, "*You should go later.*" I tried to ignore it, and when that didn't work, I tried to argue with it, going over all the reasons why I had to get to Ohio as fast as I could. *Mom's all alone. She needs me. The reservation is already made. I can get there the fastest.*

But the more I argued with the voice, the more insistent it became until I couldn't ignore it another second. Climbing out of bed slowly so as not to wake John, I padded down the stairs to the kitchen and paced the cold floor in my bare feet wondering what I should do. Finally, I realized I didn't have a choice. Whatever the voice was in my head—intuition, premonition, gut instinct—I knew I had to listen. So I did. Picking up the phone in the kitchen, I called the airline and changed my reservation to a later flight.

Feeling numb but a little less anxious, I went to stand at the living room window while I waited for some coffee to brew. The sun was just starting to peek its way over the horizon, the sky turning from pink, to silvery crimson, to the palest of blues. Lights came on in the house across the street, and the newspaper boy flashed by on his bicycle.

How is it possible, I wondered, watching the day wake up in front of me like it was any other day, *that everything's the same, but totally different?*

Upstairs, I heard John and the kids begin to move around, and I turned away from the window, taking a deep breath to steel myself for the day ahead. Changing my plane reservation turned out to be the right thing to do, because at the last-minute Mom decided she wanted all the grandchildren to come, too. Had I been on the earlier flight, it would have been next to impossible to get all our kids to Ohio without me.

I can't help but think the voice in my head that night was my dad. That somehow he knew, wherever he was, it would be better for everyone if I took the later flight, so he nudged me and nudged me until I did what he wanted me to do. Just like he always had, in real life.

Then, later on the plane, after a crazy morning getting myself and the kids packed, trying to keep my grief in check so I wouldn't scare them, the most amazing thing happened. I'd always been a white-knuckled flier—terrified not only of dying in a plane crash, but of *knowing* I was going to die as the plane plummeted to the ground—when I suddenly realized, sitting with my children thirty thousand feet in the air, that I wasn't scared anymore. Not of crashing, and not of dying. Looking out the window at the endless expanse of empty blue sky, I felt an unfamiliar sense of peace. It was like Dad was there in the seat next to me, reminding me, as he often had when we flew together, that planes rarely crash, so I should stop worrying.

And for the first time in my life, I believed him. Even if my worst fear came true and I fell to my death in a fiery ball of burning metal, the deep, dark nothing I'd been so afraid of my whole life didn't feel so scary anymore. Dad was there now, and wherever *there* turned out to be, I knew I'd be okay.

That experience—that deep knowing Dad was somehow still around me—sparked a spiritual curiosity in me I'd never had before, sending me on a journey into the metaphysical world I may otherwise never have gone on. It led me to books on spirituality, and science, and the connection between the two. I discovered energy healing and became a Reiki practitioner. I volunteered at hospice. I meditated, and journaled, and practiced yoga. I talked to psychics, and astrologists, and tarot card readers, which led to classes and webinars on how to become more intuitive myself. And everything I learned, everything I'm still learning, has only confirmed in my mind that death is not the end, but a transformation, and not something to be feared at all.

Mom coughs and reaches for her mouth, squinting her eyes open when her hand touches the oxygen mask covering half of her face. I lean forward to push it up, trying to keep its elastic bands from touching the line of staples crossing her head.

"Thank you," she murmurs, giving me a small smile before letting her eyes drift closed again. I wait a moment or two, then gently pull the mask back down, scared to leave it off too long and have her oxygen level drop. Watching her sleep, I remember a conversation she and I had about dying, not too long ago. We were just finishing dinner one night during one of my more recent visits when she looked across the table at me and said, out of the blue, "I wonder what death is like?"

For a moment I was paralyzed, the bluntness of her question catching me completely off guard. Taking a sip of wine, I tried to think what to say. "Wow, Mom—I'm not really sure," I finally ventured. "What makes you ask?"

"I don't know," she sighed, looking down at her empty plate. "I think maybe it might be just a big, dark nothing."

I stared across the table at her, thinking to myself how crazy it was that my mother and I would use the exact same words to describe how we pictured death. Should I tell her that? Did I dare try to explain my change of heart? Having never talked to anyone about my beliefs around death before (well, maybe John a little bit), I wasn't sure if I could explain it so someone else could understand. Wanting to reassure her, though, I decided to give it a try.

"Well, I don't think it's nothing," I said, going on to explain my (very) limited understanding of quantum science and how everything in the universe is energy, just energy vibrating at different frequencies. "Take a hummingbird," I proffered. "Its energy vibrates at a very high frequency so it's more nebulous, harder to see, right?" Mom nodded, so I kept going. "But this table is solid," I gave it a little knock with my knuckle, "so its energy vibrates at a much lower frequency, making it way denser." Mom nods again. So far so good.

"So if *everything* is energy," I reasoned, "then *we* must be energy, too. Right? How could we not be? And since science has also proven that energy can't be created or destroyed, it can only transform, then that means we *can't* disappear into a big, dark nothing when we die—we have to go somewhere!"

Mom nodded, but didn't say anything, so I forged ahead.

"You still feel Dad around you, don't you?" I asked, knowing she did because she'd often told me she still talked to him. Again, she nodded, taking a small sip of wine.

"What if it's his *energy* that you can still feel? That when he died, the energy that made him who he was—his soul, his spirit—didn't disappear, but transformed to a higher vibration? You aren't able to *see* him because his body's gone, but you can still *feel* him because his spark of energy is still there, vibrating around you."

"But where is *there*?" Mom asked, her brow furrowed.

"I guess maybe heaven?" I took a sip of wine, too, hoping I wasn't confusing her completely. "I don't know, Mom—maybe I'm wrong. But I hope I'm not. I hope when you get wherever *there* is, you'll laugh because you'll see I was right—that death isn't a big, dark nothing at all, just a change in vibration."

Mom smiled, pushing back her chair. "Well," she said as she stood up to clear her plate, "I suppose we're just not going to know until we know."

And, of course, she was absolutely right. How *could* we know? I'm embarrassed by that spiritually arrogant self who dismissed her mother's fears out of hand, and realize now, sitting in this hospital room wondering if she might die today, that I'd been dismissing my own fears, too. I'll never be ready to lose my mom, not ever. I don't want her energy vibrating anywhere but right here next to me, where I can see it.

∾

Later that afternoon, after hours of waiting for doctors who never come, the door to Mom's room pushes open and there are Sal and Lib, somehow managing to arrive at the same time though they've come from opposite ends of the country. They pause in the doorway, as if trying to decide if it's okay to come in.

Mom's asleep, so I scramble out of the recliner where I've been reading and throw my arms around them in a tight, silent hug, my eyes welling up in teary relief.

"Oh my god, I'm so glad you're here," I whisper, planting a kiss on each of their cheeks before letting them go, the three of us turning as one to look over at our sleeping mother.

"God, she looks so frail," Lib murmurs, moving over to the side of the bed. Sal follows and the two stare down at Mom, their faces etched with concern. Watching them, I'm struck by how much alike they look, which is funny because it's always been me and Lib who often get mistaken for each other, with our matching chin length bobs and blonde (well, gray now) hair. Growing up we were forever being called the other one's name by Mom's and Dad's friends, to the point that one time Paul, Sal's husband, jokingly made us name tags to wear to the annual Christmas Eve party—a little funny, I guess, but mostly annoying. No one ever called Sallie by the wrong name.

But now, standing side by side as they are, I can see a distinct similarity in the set of their mouths and angle of their chins, something I've never noticed before. A weight shifts inside me, the shared worry I see reflected in their expressions reminding me I'm not alone anymore. My sisters are here.

Mom stirs and opens her eyes, blinking up at the ceiling a few times as if trying to decide if she's really going to wake up.

"Hey there, Mom." Sal leans over and kisses her forehead, moving a step over to make room for Lib, who lowers herself down on the edge of the bed, smiling. Mom's eyes light up.

"You're here!" she says in wonder, looking from one to the other, then over at me. "I'm so sorry to do this to you girls, but oh, I'm so glad to see you!"

And once again, having us all in the same room animates Mom in a way I haven't seen since I arrived—she's actually trying to sit up for the first time in forty-eight hours. And as I watch Sal and Lib cajole a smile from her here, a soft chuckle there, I feel hopeful and grateful and relieved. The infusion of energy my sisters have brought with them feels almost tangible, like there's another living, breathing being in the room who's come to help get our mother through this.

Day Five

After almost two full days, though, Mom just isn't bouncing back the way we'd hoped, even with the three of us all there by her side. First of all, her oxygen levels keep dropping precipitously when they try to switch her from a full mask to a nasal cannula. Not a huge problem as long as she's in the hospital, but in order to be discharged, even to a skilled nursing facility, she has to maintain an oxygen level of ninety-five percent with *only* the nasal cannula, for a minimum of twenty-four hours.

On top of that, her mysterious leg pain is getting worse. None of the doctors who've examined her can figure out the underlying cause, and they won't prescribe pain medication on a regular basis until they do, which leaves it up to us to make sure Mom gets the medicine when she needs it. We take turns sitting with her, watching for signs that the pain is coming back, then when it does, rushing out to the nurse's station to ask for the painkiller, which they'll give, but then won't give the next dose in time to prevent the next spasm. It's a vicious cycle that has all of us, especially Mom, exhausted.

But even so, when a nurse gently suggests calling in the hospital's palliative care group, we're reluctant. It feels so final, like we're giving up. And though I know from my hospice experience that getting someone's pain under control can, oftentimes, extend their life, it's scary to admit that Mom has reached that point. But there's no way around the fact that she has and, not wanting her to suffer any more if there's a way to relieve it, we agree to make the call.

The palliative care doctor, a tall, attractive woman with a soothing voice and manner, listens attentively to Mom who, though clearly annoyed at having to go through it all *again*, is trying her best to be cooperative.

"Where do you feel the pain the most?" the doctor asks, lightly probing different areas on Mom's legs.

"No, no it's not my legs!" Mom shakes her head in frustration, and I look at her in surprise.

"But, Mom—you've been saying all along it's your legs!"

"Kay?" The doctor steps in, pulling a stool up next to the bed, and Mom turns her head toward her. "It would help me much more if you can tell me what the pain *feels* like?"

Mom hesitates, her brow furrowed over her oxygen mask. She looks like a worried little bird and it melts my heart. She's trying so hard.

"It feels, you know, like when you want sex and don't get it."

Wait—what? I stare at Mom in confusion, trying to make sense of what she just said. Sex is not something my mother ever talks about, at least around me. Growing up, the closest she ever got to it was when I was thirteen and getting ready to go away to summer camp. She'd come into my room where I was packing and handed me a giant box of Kotex and a garter belt. I'd stared at them uncertainly—having not yet gotten my period I only had a vague understanding of the actual mechanics involved.

"You may need these while you're away," she'd said in way of explanation. Flushing with embarrassment, I'd stared at the floor, unable to meet her eyes. "Getting your period is nothing to be ashamed of," she'd gone on, her tone matter-of-fact. "It just means that you'll be able to have babies."

And that was that. We'd never talked about it again as far as I could remember. To hear that same mother telling this doctor that the leg pain she's been having isn't leg pain after all, but rather some kind of unsatisfied sexual urge, is so unbelievable it almost makes me laugh. Almost.

But the doctor is nodding, explaining to Mom that she is probably suffering from something called RGS—Restless Genital Syndrome. Similar to the more common Restless *Leg* Syndrome, it starts with a strong, unpleasant urge to move, and, in some cases, can be quite painful, especially if you *can't* move. Listening to the doctor, I try not to squirm, but inside I'm cringing like an adolescent who's just realized her mother has sex.

"Is this something you've dealt with in the past?" she asks Mom.

"Oh, yes," Mom replies, nodding her head, surprising me again. "But it would always go away as soon as I got up. It was never like *this* before."

"Well, I can't say for sure why it's gotten so bad, although the loss of blood from your cut may have somehow exacerbated it. And, of course, you can't get up, which doesn't help." The doctor pushes the stool back and stands up. "The good news is there's a new medication I think will help, so we'll start that up right away."

She pats Mom on the shoulder and turns to me. "Not to worry," she murmurs, taking my arm and leading me out into the corridor, away from Mom's hearing. "This condition has nothing to do with someone's sexual *desire*. It actually occurs more often when there's an *absence* of desire."

I nod and thank her, my inner teenager heaving a deep sigh of relief that her eighty-eight-year-old mother isn't, on top of everything else, sexually frustrated. At the same time, my grown-up self is relieved that maybe we've gotten to the bottom of Mom's pain, discomfiting as it may be, because with that under control, maybe her oxygen levels will improve.

And if her oxygen levels improve, maybe, just maybe, there's still a chance we can get her home.

When the physical therapist arrives later that day to try and get Mom up and walking again, we're all feeling hopeful, especially as it seems the new medicine is already starting to work. She hasn't complained about 'leg pain' since getting the initial dose a few hours before and is, in fact, sitting up in a chair for the first time in four days. Her eyes are alert, darting from the therapist, who's explaining what they'll be doing, down to Lib who is putting on Mom's shoes and socks.

God, how her sneakers crack me up. Since I was a little girl, Mom had always worn shoes that were sturdy and sensible, a rule that also applied to the shoes she bought for me. All through grade school she made me wear ugly, red leather tie-shoes, insisting they were best for growing feet, and I would thank her one day when I was older. I *hated* those tie shoes, especially in fifth grade when my best friend, Carrie, showed up one morning in a brand-new pair of shiny, brown penny loafers. I was so jealous, begging Mom when I got home that afternoon to please, *please*, let me get a pair, too. But she was adamant and wouldn't budge, decreeing there would be no penny loafers for me until middle school.

So you can imagine my surprise when that same mother went out and, after eighty some odd years of practical, boring footwear, bought herself a flashy new pair of running shoes. Electric green with purple trim and bright pink laces, Mom's new shoes almost glowed in the dark.

"Mom!" I cried when I first saw her in them, "I can't believe it! You look so hip!"

"They're the only thing that would fit over my hammer toes," she'd lamented, looking down at her brightly clad feet. As she'd aged, Mom's toes had been getting more and more crooked, to the point that they literally crossed over each other. It was hard to understand how she was even able to walk, let alone get shoes, *any* shoes, on over them.

"But you know what?" she'd said, looking up in wonderment. "They're so comfortable! I can't remember when shoes didn't pinch my feet!"

Now, watching as Lib ties those same neon pink laces, I feel a tug in my heart at the stark contrast of those colorful sneakers beneath the drab blue hospital gown hanging almost to Mom's ankles. I have to look away.

"We'll go as slow as you want to go," the therapist is saying, interrupting my bleak thoughts.

"Even if you can just stand up for a minute or two," she reassures Mom, "that will be a good start."

Mom gives a quick nod and pushes herself forward to grab onto the walker the therapist has positioned in front of her. Looking sideways at Lib, who's still kneeling down next to her, she offers a grim smile and tries to pull herself up off the chair. Nothing happens.

"Take your time, Mom," Lib says, sitting back on her heels to give her a little extra space. "There's no rush."

Mom tries again, gripping the walker more tightly, straining to lift her body up to stand. Again, nothing. She slumps back in the chair.

"I'm sorry," she sighs, shaking her head. "I just can't."

Poor Mom. Lately it seems that everything she has to do is a struggle. Sitting up. Eating. Going to the bathroom.

Breathing. And being in the hospital has made all those things that much harder because it's almost impossible to get the one thing she needs most—sleep. No sooner will she have dozed off than a doctor, or aide, or nurse, or janitor, or volunteer, or dietician, or therapist will come into the room and startle her awake. We've begun to take turns standing guard outside her door to keep them all out so she might get some uninterrupted rest.

Not that it's helped much. Mom is still exhausted, and so are we.

The therapist is kind, murmuring something about trying again the next day as she gathers up her equipment, but her behavior is disconcerting. In my experience, physical therapists are pushier, and I worry that her hasty departure is a sign the hospital is giving up on Mom. Is this what happens when you call in palliative care? Do they not try as hard?

I suppose that makes sense in a way. The fact that we *had* called in palliative care, combined with Mom not improving in any meaningful way, puts the hospital staff in a tricky situation. Their job is to get patients better, after all, and if someone isn't progressing, despite their best efforts, what else can they do? And when there also happens to be a glaring purple Do Not Resuscitate bracelet on that same someone's wrist, it's no wonder the nurses' attention may be starting to lessen.

I hate the purple bracelet. It's like having a giant neon sign flashing *"your mother is going to die!"* every time I see it. And even though I know having a DNR is the right thing for Mom to have at this point, it's so final. So unalterable.

I'm reminded of the time, a few years before, when Mom and I had our first DNR conversation. She'd been rushed to the hospital for what turned out to be pancreatitis, but at first we didn't know what was wrong with her. She was so sick, moaning and vomiting into a plastic tub in a curtained off cubicle in the emergency room when a nurse came in with a clipboard and a pen.

"I know this isn't the best time," she'd apologized, glancing from Mom to me, "but I need your mom to answer a couple of questions about her wishes."

"Her wishes?" I asked, confused.

"Do you know if she has a living will?" the nurse clarified.

"Oh, right, I see." My heart fluttered as I looked down at Mom. "Yes, yes, of course she does."

"Mrs. Ball?" The nurse turned to Mom, her voice loud and jarring in the small space. "We just need to know if your heart should stop..."

Mom blinked up at her, then over at me, a worried frown furrowing her brow.

"No, no—don't worry!" The nurse pasted a reassuring smile on her face. "No one is saying it *will*. But if it *should*, we need to know if you want us to do everything we can to try to resuscitate you, or would you rather we just make sure you're comfortable?"

Mom stared at her for a moment, then looked over at me again. "Does she mean should they let me die?" she whispered, her eyes wide in her pale face.

"Um—well, I guess she's asking *if* that's what you want," I explained as gently as I could. "So *if* your heart should stop, do you want to let nature take its course, or do you want them to try and get it started again?"

Mom was quiet, gazing up at the ceiling, and I wondered what was going through her mind. But then, with maybe the tiniest, mischievous glint in her eye, she looked over at the nurse and asked, "Couldn't they try just a *little*?"

Choking back a relieved laugh, I leaned down to hug her. "Of course, they'll try, Mom," I told her, smiling over at the nurse. "Don't you worry about it one more second."

This time, though, Mom hadn't been able to make the decision about a DNR when the ER nurse came in to ask. It was up to me to decide. And as I checked the box to withhold intervention if Mom's heart should stop, I found myself wishing there *was* a third choice 'to try just a little'.

Now, watching the physical therapist hurrying out of the room, it's clear we've reached a crossroads. Mom can't stay in the hospital indefinitely, not when there isn't anything more they can do for her, but she can't go home either, not with her heavy oxygen needs. So where *does* she go?

"I'm afraid there aren't many places that can provide the level of oxygen support your mom requires," the hospital's social worker explains to us later that day. "There are the two hospice facilities in the area—Toledo and Perrysburg—and then possibly the skilled nursing at Sunrise Crest could take her, but you'd have to speak to them directly to make sure."

Staring at my hands folded tight in my lap, I wonder how in the world we'd gotten here. Hospice? Have we really reached that point? Images of the people I've sat with as a volunteer over the years blink through my mind like so many slides in a projector—Richard, Rosemary, Frank, Ida, Martha, Dorothy—their faces all gray and drawn, their bodies failing, their spirits waning.

My gaze turns toward Mom, now dozing in the recliner under a mountain of blankets, and my heart sinks further. She looks just like them. And though I want her to keep fighting, I want her to be free of fighting, too. My body feels heavy under the weight of this paradox, and I worry my own exhaustion might be stronger than my will to help her keep going.

"Well, I guess we have some decisions to make," Sal says, snapping me back into the room, and I'm grateful for the resolve I hear in her voice. "We'll go check out those places this afternoon," she tells the social worker, glancing at me and Lib before pushing her chair back to stand up. "We'll let you know first thing in the morning what we decide."

"Sounds like a good plan," the social worker agrees, gathering up her files. "I would also recommend meeting with the hospital's hospice liaison this afternoon, as well," she adds, her eyes darting over at Mom. "It's a bit of a process and will speed things up if the papers are signed ahead of time. *If* that's what you decide, of course," she says quickly as Sal, Lib, and I exchange uneasy looks. "Nothing's definite until you say so," she reassures us. "It's really just in case."

∽

So, while Sal and Lib go check out the different facilities a little while later, Mom and I meet with the hospice liaison to get the paperwork started, *just in case*. At least that's what I keep telling myself because, as it turns out, it's really hard to tell your mother that hospice may be her only choice. Not just hard. Surreal. It's like there are two of me in the room that afternoon—the me who's in control, and the me who is absolutely not.

There is the calm, matter-of-fact me who ushers the liaison into the room, offering her a chair before pulling my own up next to Mom, who is now sitting with her feet up in the recliner, though still under a mountain of blankets.

The me who makes pleasant small talk to break the ice, and then, wanting Mom to take the lead, sits by as she struggles through her oxygen mask to answer the liaison's myriad questions.

The me who, when I see a tiny flicker of fear flash in her eyes, squeezes her hand reassuringly and says, "Don't worry, Mom—nothing's set in stone. If you go to hospice it might be a kind of an interim step until you get stronger."

"Of course, of course," the nice liaison pipes in. "We see that quite often. Some patients rebound surprisingly quickly after they've had a few days to rest."

The me who's sitting there, smiling and nodding, pretending this is no big deal. That it's all *just in case, Mom. Really.*

But then there's the other me. The scared-out-of-my-wits me. The me who doesn't believe for one second that it's *just in case*, and is screaming to herself, *"No no no! This can't really be happening!"*

The me whose heart is racing a million miles a minute because, *oh my god, this* is *happening.* There is a real lady sitting here, with real papers that will set the wheels in motion for Mom to go to hospice. Hospice!

I'm not sure what I expected the end of my mother's life to look like, but somehow this is not it. I guess I always imagined it would be sudden, that one day the phone would ring and there would be a stranger's voice on the other end saying, "I'm so sorry, but we found your mom in her apartment this morning. It seems she died in her sleep."

Or maybe it would be a worse scenario, where she was rushed to the hospital but died en route, or in the emergency room, so a kind nurse or doctor would make the call, their subdued voice on the other end of the phone saying, "I'm so sorry, there was just nothing more we could do."

It never occurred to me that Mom would end up in hospice, her body slowly withering away as my sisters and I sit helplessly by her side watching her die. I can see the scene unfolding so clearly in my mind it's as though it's already happening, and I feel the pain of my mother's impending death wash through me like burning ash, making it hard to breathe. Somehow, despite all the good things I know about hospice, I'm inexplicably terrified of my mother going there, and as the liaison holds the papers up for Mom to sign, the scared-out-of-my wits me wants to grab them away and tear them into pieces.

But, of course, I don't. The other me, the calm, matter-of-fact me, sits by watching as Mom leans forward in the recliner to sign them one by one, her hand so weak her signature is unrecognizable, so faint and illegible it's like a ghost's. Handing the pen back to the liaison hovering by her shoulder, Mom looks at me and offers a feeble smile, then leans her head back, staring up at the ceiling for a moment.

"Maybe what I'm going through will help someone else someday," she murmurs, letting her eyes drift closed.

"Maybe," I tell her, leaning in to give her a quick squeeze. "I hope so."

Watching Mom rest, I wonder if I'd be as brave if I was going into hospice—it's hard to imagine facing my own imminent death. But I suppose at age eighty-eight maybe there's a certain relief in surrendering to its inevitableness.

A little stab of guilt pricks at my conscience as I become aware of a third me in the room—a me who may be just a little bit relieved, too. Because, by signing those hospice papers, Mom has set the wheels in motion toward a point of no return and, come what may, there's nothing more for me to do than go along with her on the ride.

Later that afternoon—just after Lib and Sal have arrived back from their scouting excursion and are filling me in on what they'd learned—the nurse comes bustling into the room and announces that Mom is being transferred to a private room. Part of me is happy about this new development as up until now Mom's been in a small, semi-private room where there's always been a nagging worry she might get a roommate. But another part of me is confused—why would they go to the trouble of moving her when they know we're actively looking at other options?

We start gathering up all the things that have accumulated the past four days: Mom's yellow floral toilet kit from home, the bulging plastic bag of clothes and shoes she'd worn into the ER, several copies of the local newspaper, though she hasn't so much as glanced at it since she's been in the hospital. Somehow, whether from habit or hope, we keep bringing it with us every morning. What would we give to walk in and find Mom sitting up in bed, reading glasses perched on her nose with the newspaper spread out around her, eyes spitting fire over something going on in the world she's not happy about? Amazing the things we take for granted.

Lastly, there's the basket of beautiful spring bulbs—tiny yellow daffodils, lavender hyacinth, and dark purple violets—that Mom's driver, Trish, had dropped off the day before. Such a perfect choice for Mom who, though she loves flowers and has been a member of a garden club for over fifty years, has a curious disdain for big bouquets of cut flowers. Especially when someone is sick or in the hospital. And especially if that someone is her.

Mom has always preferred small bouquets, in equally small vases. Whenever we come home for a visit there is always a little 'posy' on our bedside table, just a small bloom from her garden or, if it's winter, a snip of evergreen and berry. Maybe once in a while she'll have a vase of tulips on her kitchen counter, or some sunflowers or hydrangeas, but rarely would there be anything more elaborate, unless someone who doesn't know her very well has sent something.

I smile to myself as I pick up the basket, remembering when I first met Trish how I'd had to coach her on the best way to handle Mom, who was a bit peevish about needing a driver at all. Trish had sent me a text the day before she started, saying how much she was looking forward to getting to know Mom, and that she was sure they would be best friends before too long.

I didn't waste any time and texted her right back.

"Whatever you do, DO NOT try to be friends with Mom! She doesn't think she needs you so she's going to act more like a sullen teenager than a grown woman! Less is definitely more with my mother," I warned. *"Way safer to let her make the first moves."*

Pushing the send button, I hoped Trish would get the message so she wouldn't go the way of Deb, the first driver we'd hired, who made the big mistake of thinking she knew better than Mom what Mom needed. Deb had tried to be more of a caregiver than a driver, following Mom into the grocery store and doctor's appointments despite repeated requests that she wait in the car.

"She's awfully pushy," Mom would say when we asked her how it was going.

"It's not like I need another daughter," she'd complain after a doctor's visit.

"I don't know, there's just something about her," was her vague response when pushed to explain what exactly she didn't like about Deb.

Giving up driving was one of the hardest things Mom ever did and, true to her nature, she didn't give it up without a fight. At first she kind of tricked us, agreeing without much resistance to stop driving at night. She hired Jim, the nice gentleman who drove her to and from the airport, to take her to the club for dinner, or the museum for a concert.

But when it came to giving up her daytime driving, Mom dug in her heels, and somehow, no matter how strongly we all felt about it, Sal, Lib, and I couldn't find it in ourselves to put our collective foot down and take away her keys. We *tried* reasoning with her. We *tried* explaining that if it was just *her* safety at stake, we wouldn't be so worried, but what if she hurt someone else?

"You'd feel so bad, Mom!" we warned her time and time again. But no matter how much we pleaded and cajoled, no matter how many good reasons we came up with that it was time to hand over her keys, she wouldn't budge.

"I'm very careful," she would insist. "I don't go very far."

Incredibly, and in hindsight perhaps irresponsibly, we couldn't even bring ourselves to take away her keys after she drove her car into a bank—yes, a literal brick-and-mortar bank—when she was up in Maine one summer. Mom was in her early eighties, just before her health started to decline, when she got flustered at the drive-up ATM. It's still unclear what had flustered her—either too much cash had spewed out, or possibly not enough—but whatever it was, she wanted to get it cleared up inside with a teller. When she pulled into the parking space in front of the bank, though, she stepped on the accelerator instead of the brake, propelling her car forward through the double glass doors, straight into the lobby.

It's a miracle there were no other customers there at the time, but the poor tellers, though safe behind their counter, must have been scared witless when an old, white Dodge minivan, driven by an equally old, white-haired lady, plowed through the doors.

Mom was pretty shaken up afterward, vowing to all of us that she wouldn't be driving anymore that summer. Relieved that she'd made the decision on her own, we all thought maybe the accident had been just the wakeup call she needed to give up driving for good.

Unfortunately, Mom's resolve didn't last long, and once she was home in Perrysburg with her old, familiar Honda sitting temptingly in the garage, she was back behind the wheel, promising us that *really*, she would be *so* much more careful from now on.

I'm not sure how we finally convinced her to hire someone to help with errands. I'd like to think it was after her stroke the following fall, but I know for sure it *wasn't* then because I'd asked her neurologist, out of Mom's earshot, if *he* might tell her she shouldn't drive anymore. "No," he'd said without hesitation, giving a quick shake of his head. "I find it's better for my patients if I don't get involved with decisions like that."

Her cardiologist and primary care doctor both said the same thing when I asked each of them, leaving me frustrated and wondering why physicians aren't more willing to step in when adult children ask for their help persuading elderly parents to give up driving. How easy would it have been for one of them to have said, "So, Mrs. Ball, given your condition, driving is not recommended at this time"? Mom wouldn't have liked it, and would have made sure they knew she didn't like it, but I think she would have listened.

So, it must have been after she fell down the stairs and fractured her back a couple of years later that we were able to convince her it was time to hire a driver. Hard for even the most stubborn of mothers to argue with her daughters about driving when her entire torso was Velcroed into a hard-shell brace for several months. But though Mom agreed to hire a driver, she did so only on her terms, insisting that she get to keep her Honda.

"If I have to be driven around, at least I want to be in my own car," Mom pouted, like she was the aggrieved teenager and Sal, Lib, and I the unreasonable parents. And though we didn't trust her true motives, we gave in, reasoning that it would be easier for us to have the car there when we were visiting.

Of course, we were right to worry and shouldn't have trusted her for a second, because before too long Deb was reporting that the driver's seat in Mom's car was often in a different position than how she'd left it.

"I think your mom may be driving on the days I'm not there," she told us, her tone reproachful, as if we were responsible for our recalcitrant mother sneaking the car out behind our backs. But not wanting to throw Deb under the bus—Mom was already starting to complain about her—we made a unanimous decision to let it go, crossing our fingers that nothing bad would happen. We did, however, have Libby, who handled Mom's insurance, call to get the liability coverage on her auto policy increased, just to be safe.

Mom must have started to have a guilty conscious, though, because one Sunday morning a month or so later, we received an email from her with the subject line, "Confession":

> On Nov, 10, 2013, at 9:56 AM, Kay Ball
> <kball84@bex.net> wrote:
>
> I drove my car to church this morning at 7:45.
> There was no traffic. It gave me some time to
> get use to our new Minister.
> It felt wonderful to drive.
> I will not use the car for anything else.
> I promise
> Love you
> Mom

Reading my mother's email, I wasn't sure if I should laugh or cry. How many times as a teenager had I written my parents such a note after doing something I knew I shouldn't? Sneaking the car out in the early dawn to go to the airport and kiss my boyfriend goodbye; getting pulled over up in Maine for speeding when I was sixteen, barefoot and without my (brand new) driver's license; leaving Mom's and Dad's surprise twenty-fifth anniversary party early to go to another party.

"*Peggy,*" Mom and Dad would implore after each transgression, "when will you start using your better judgment?"

Oh, the circle of life. It wouldn't be until she moved into Sunrise Crest that Mom would finally use better judgement and hand her keys over to Trish for good.

Now, arms laden with Mom's things and our own tote bags, purses and coats, Sal, Lib, and I make our way up the elevator to her new room. Passing by the nurses' station, I feel a twinge of concern when I see Mom's gurney being turned into a room at the far end of the long corridor.

"I guess it will be nice and quiet," I whisper to Sal and Lib, trying to mask my worry that Mom will be so far away from her nurses.

The new room is enormous. Triple windows span one whole wall with a built-in couch underneath, giving us plenty of space to drop our things. The bed is centered in the middle of another wall, with a small nightstand next to it, along with a recliner and a couple of straight back chairs scattered around. And though we're excited at first to have so much more room, once the gurney is gone, we realize it might be too big. Settled in her new bed, Mom looks even smaller and frailer than before, like she's been set adrift in a rowboat in the middle of an ocean, helpless and alone.

And she's *so* pale. Automatically looking to check her oxygen level, I realize there isn't a vital sign monitor anywhere in the room, giving me a moment of panic. After four days of hardly taking my eyes off those flashing numbers, it's unsettling not to have the visual reassurance that Mom is getting enough oxygen.

Pointing out its absence to Sal and Lib, we're debating who should go ask how to get one brought in when a nurse pops his head in the door.

"Just want to say I'll be in as soon as I can. We're a little understaffed this afternoon."

"Where's the monitor?" Libby asks, her tone brusque, demanding. "You know she's having trouble with her oxygen, right?"

The nurse pauses, his eyes darting over toward Mom, then back to Lib. "We don't generally have those on this floor, but let me see if I can find a portable one. Give me a few minutes."

He disappears, and the three of us look at each other in disbelief. What is happening? Is this where they send sick, old ladies to die when you've called in palliative care?

"Maybe we shouldn't have moved her," Lib frets. "I don't like this at all."

"Let's give him a chance," Sal says. "Maybe it will be okay."

True to his word, the nurse returns a few minutes later with a small, portable monitor that he sets up on the bedside table. But somehow, though I'm relieved when it begins to flash out Mom's oxygen levels in a steady pattern, it doesn't seem as official as the one in her old room, and I don't trust it. In fact, I don't trust the whole situation.

Our dad taught us at an early age that when we're faced with a big decision and not sure what to do, we should pull out a sheet of paper and make a list of pros and cons, taking our time to come up with as many as we could under each heading.

"The key, though," he instructed, "is to be honest. Don't be afraid to write down everything that pops into your head, good or bad, silly or important. The right decision will become clear, I promise."

The first time I made such a list was when I was fourteen and deciding if I should go to boarding school or stay home and continue at the same school I'd been going to since first grade. I was so torn—a few of my close friends had decided to go away, but a lot of other friends were staying. Sallie had gone away and, in fact, had just graduated the year before from the same school I was considering. And I knew Mom wanted me to go there, too, whether to broaden my horizons, as she insisted, or to get me out of her hair, I'm still not sure. Dad, on the other hand, didn't seem to have an opinion one way or the other, a bit disconcerting to my young teenage self as normally my father was very quick to let us know what he thought.

Like Mom, I'm not sure Dad ever second-guessed himself—if he did, he certainly never let on to me. An Ivy League educated engineer, he was so pragmatic and sensible, always looking at things from different perspectives before giving advice or making a decision. He was strict, though—perhaps from his years as a pilot in the second world war—and brooked no nonsense, especially from his daughters. At the same time, he was also the sweetest, most sensitive man in the world, the kind of dad who watched *Little House on the Prairie* with me, never failing to tear up at the end of every show.

"It's your life, Peglet," he told me when I asked him what I should do. "Only you can decide this one."

At first, I resisted his suggestion to write down the pros and cons, choosing instead to wallow in the angst of my indecision. But as the deadline for accepting the boarding school's offer crept closer, I finally relented. The cons came easily; leaving my boyfriend, my friends, my dog, my bedroom, and even Libby, who at that point was still a fairly annoying eleven-year-old sister. The pros were harder, though, and I was only able to come up with a few; meeting new friends, getting out from under my parents' scrutiny, 'broadening my horizons' the way Mom kept telling me I would.

When I couldn't think of any more, I studied the two columns side by side and, at first glance, thought I had my answer, as the cons far outnumbered the pros. But as I contemplated staying home for the next three years, I was surprised by a little pang of regret at the prospect, and realized that the pros, though fewer in number, held more weight. And just like Dad had promised, it became clear what I wanted to do. I went to boarding school.

So doing a pros and cons list has become second nature to me over the years, and something that has helped me make countless decisions, both big and small, not just for myself, but for my family, too. And in the past few years, as Mom's health has declined, it's been particularly useful helping her navigate some of the big decisions she's had to make. Of course, Mom being Mom, she hasn't always agreed with the results of the pros and cons we've done on her behalf, having already made up her mind about what she wanted to do, or *didn't* want to do. She just hadn't told her daughters yet.

A few years back, for example, we thought we'd convinced her to move to Saybrook Ridge, an independent living facility in Connecticut, not too far from where I live. We thought it was the perfect spot, not only closer to me, but closer to Sal and our family's summer camp in Maine. Mom also knew a few people who lived there already, old friends from Perrysburg who had made the move to be closer to their own families.

We were thrilled when Mom finally agreed to go look at it, and even more thrilled when she seemed to like it, at least enough to put down the deposit to hold a two bedroom apartment until she could sell her house. She even agreed to have her financial and medical records forwarded—part of the three-step review process all prospective residents had to go through.

"Now there's just one more thing we'll need," Beth, the nice lady conducting the interview, told Mom, who was sitting between Sal and me like a dutiful child. "There's a short cognitive assessment that all our residents need to take prior to final approval. Don't worry," she added, seeing Mom start to shake her head. "It's just a formality. We do it right here, and could even arrange for you to take it today if you'd like to just get it out of the way?"

Mom glanced at Sal, then at me, and seeing the defiant set of her mouth, I knew right away she didn't want to take the test. I didn't know *why* she didn't want to, but I'd seen that same look on my mother's face enough times to trust it wasn't worth arguing.

"That's so nice," I smiled, trying to defuse the awkward pause when Mom didn't respond right away. "But I'm a little worried about running into traffic if we don't get on the road soon. Maybe another time would be better, if that's okay?"

"Of course, of course. That's just fine. Here, let me help you with that," Beth jumped up, moving quickly around the desk to help Mom, who was already putting on her coat. Taking our mother's not-so-subtle lead, Sal and I stood up as well, exchanging baffled looks with each other before following them out to the lobby.

Mom could not get out of there fast enough. She paused at the front entrance to shake Beth's hand, but then pushed her way out the door, leaving Sal and me to apologize for our mother's rather rude behavior.

"Don't worry about a thing," she assured us. "We see it all the time. Can't take these things personally! I'll be in touch to set up another visit once we get all the forms back."

Thanking her for her time, Sal and I hurried out to catch up with Mom, who was standing in the small garden in the middle of the driveway circle, frowning at one of the plants. Not sure if I wanted to hug her or strangle her, I walked over to where she stood while Sal went to bring the car around.

"What the heck, Mom?" I crossed my arms, feeling more like an aggravated parent than a daughter. "Why wouldn't you just take the test and get it over with?"

"I'm terrible at tests," she declared. "I always have been. I'll take it when I have to."

Halfheartedly agreeing that it might make sense to wait until she'd passed the financial and medical reviews anyway, we didn't talk about it again until Beth called a few weeks later to tell us that Mom was, indeed, eligible to join their community, as long as she passed the cognitive test.

"Now I know she's nervous about it," she said when we spoke on the phone to schedule the next visit, "and I don't do this very often. But I like your mom, so I'm going to send you a link to the kinds of questions she'll have to answer, in case she'd like to practice."

Relieved by such a nice offer, I assumed Mom would be, too, and was surprised when she refused to even look at the questions.

"Come on, Mom," I urged the evening before the test, my laptop open on the table between us, ready to go. Having looked at some of the questions beforehand, I'd picked out a couple that I thought might be the most challenging—drawing a clock and putting in a specific time, for instance, and naming as many animals as possible in one minute. I knew Mom could do both things if she had enough time, but under pressure I could see her freezing up.

"It might help you feel less worried if you know what they're going to ask you," I reasoned, my fingers hovering over the keyboard.

"I'm not worried," she insisted. "I'm just terrible at tests. Practicing won't change that."

"But Mom—that doesn't make any sense!" It was like talking to a difficult child and I had to force myself to take a deep breath. "Of course practicing will help! *Especially* if you're not good at tests!"

But no amount of logic would change her mind so, shrugging my shoulders in exasperation, I gave up trying. I suppose I could have kept pushing. I suppose I could have treated her like one of my kids and made her sit at the kitchen table until she did what I said. But she was my mother, and I just couldn't.

As it turned out, though, I guess I should have been more insistent, because Mom did not, in fact, pass the test the next day. I'm not sure I've ever felt as humiliated as I did when Beth came into the office where they'd put Mom and me to wait and gave us the bad news.

"We *so* want you to be part of our community," she said to Mom, who was sitting like a statue next to me, seemingly unfazed by this mortifying development. I, on the other hand, was painfully embarrassed, my face flushing hot and red, the blood rushing in my ears so loud it was hard to concentrate on what Beth was saying. I couldn't believe this was happening.

"Unfortunately, we can't offer you a spot here unless you're able to pass this test," she reiterated, looking from

Mom to me, then back to Mom. "We're willing to let you try again because we understand you may have been nervous, but it would have to be today. Right now, in fact."

"No." Mom sat forward in her chair, her hands gripping the arms tightly, her white head shaking back and forth slowly. "I'm just not going to do that. I could take that test ten times and it wouldn't change anything." She glanced at me, her eyes flashing with indignation, like this was somehow *my* fault. "I told you I'm just not good at tests. I never have been!" Her voice shaky with frustration, she looked back over at Beth, who seemed as confused as me by Mom's reaction. "And I don't understand why you need a test to tell you I can take care of myself! I am doing perfectly fine on my own!"

I didn't know what to do. Part of me wanted to grab Mom's arm and march her right back into the other room and make her take that test until she passed it. *If only she'd f...ing practiced,* I couldn't help thinking. But she genuinely didn't seem to care. Indignant, yes, but not upset, or even embarrassed, the way I would expect. The way *I* was.

Wait a second, I thought, a flicker of suspicion growing in my mind. *Could she have failed it on purpose?* I looked over at her, not wanting to believe my mother could be so duplicitous as to waste all of our time intentionally, but I also couldn't totally put it past her either. Not that Mom was manipulative, but she *could* be quite headstrong when she'd made up her mind about something.

Another thought, a little more worrisome, flashed through my mind. What if the stroke she'd had a couple of years before had done more damage than we knew, and her cognitive ability *was* actually impaired? What if she didn't pass the test because she *couldn't* answer the questions? Except, no. Sal, Lib, and I had been keeping close tabs on her the last year or so and Mom was doing a good job taking care of herself. She managed her medications, she paid her bills, and she got where she needed to be when she needed to be there. Except for the driving, we hadn't seen any red flags at all.

Of course, maybe Mom just *wasn't* good at taking tests, like she kept insisting. It occurred to me that though she spoke often of her two years at Ogontz Junior College and the friends she met there, I had no idea if she was a good student or not—she had never mentioned her grades. She'd spent her junior year at the University of Arizona, but then never graduated, choosing instead to marry Dad the following year. I know she had regrets about not getting her degree, but this whole being bad at tests had never come up once when I was growing up, even when I was a struggling math student flunking tests left and right.

Whatever the reason, though, it was clear this wasn't the place for Mom. Even Beth seemed less friendly, a bit arrogant, in fact, and I found my embarrassment turning to anger as I listened to her suggest that perhaps the assisted living facility on the other side of town would be a better fit?

Now it was me who couldn't get us out of there fast enough. Grabbing our coats and Mom's arm at the same time, I thanked her for the suggestion but that, no, we'd figure something else out, all the while propelling Mom toward the door.

"Let me walk you out," Beth offered, but I couldn't bear to be around her one more second.

"No, that's okay, we know our way." I knew I was being rude, but I couldn't help it. Adrenaline was rushing through my veins and I was in full fight or flight mode. "We'll be fine. Thank you."

Somehow, I got Mom through the lobby and out to the car, my mind racing, trying to decide what to do next. We'd made plans to stop by to see her friends from Perrysburg after the test, but I wondered if maybe we should just head home. Glancing sideways at Mom in the passenger seat, I tried to gauge her mood, but she was staring out the window, her jaw set, her mouth drawn tight. Thinking it might be wise to let her be, at least for a couple of minutes, I stared out the window, too.

The shame and anger I was feeling took me a little by surprise, reminding me of the time Bill didn't make the travel hockey team when he was ten years old. His two best friends *had* made it, and because I was good friends with both their moms, my first thought was, sadly, not about Bill, who would be crushed by the news, but how hard it was going to be for me that he wouldn't be on the same team. And now there I was, twenty years later, feeling the same way about my mother, who we'd just found out hadn't gotten into the top-notch retirement home that her friends had. The last thing in the world I wanted to do right then was go face them in person and have to explain what had happened.

But though I wanted to drive away from Saybrook Ridge and never look back, I knew that wasn't the answer. If there was one thing I'd learned from my mom over the years, mainly by her own example, it was that Ball girls did not run away. Not from a mistake, or a failure, or an embarrassment, tempting as it may be to turn tail.

Like now. I started the car. "Okay, Mom," I said, turning to look at her. "We told the McNichols we'd stop by, so

I guess we still need to do that. Unless you'd rather...?" I let my voice trail off, half hoping that maybe just this once she wouldn't make me do the thing I didn't want to do.

"Yes, of course. They'll be expecting us." Mom paused, looking down at her lap. "I'm sorry I didn't pass the test."

"Oh, Mom, it's okay." I put the car in reverse and started to back up. "I don't think you wanted to move here anyway."

She was quiet for a moment then, sighing softly, whispered, "No, I really didn't."

And she *really* didn't. Not just to Saybrook Ridge, but to anywhere that wasn't her house in Perrysburg. It took another four years, and a few more pros and cons lists, before Mom finally decided it was time to move to something smaller. But, true to her nature, once she'd made up her mind about it, she moved on with grace and determination, never second-guessing her decision, at least as far as her daughters ever knew.

Now, just over a year since *that* big move, Sal and I are sitting in Mom's living room, sipping our cocktails and contemplating her next one. Lib decided to stay at the hospital for the night, leaving us to narrow down the limited choices before us by making yet one more pros and cons list for our mother. This one is turning out to be harder, though, and we find ourselves going around in circles with all the unknowns and 'what ifs' of Mom's current situation.

Finally Sal, a business consultant by trade, takes out a clean sheet of paper and tries a new tack. Instead of looking at the pros and cons of the different options—skilled nursing, hospice, moving Mom in with John and me, or Sal and Paul—she makes a flowchart by listing all the potential scenarios we have to choose from and then takes each one to all of its possible outcomes.

When she's done, at first all I can see is a crazy mishmash of arrows pointing this way and that, and I have to choke back a laugh because it looks exactly the way the inside of my head feels. But then, despite the many variables of the different situations, I see that, because of her oxygen constraints, they all eventually end up in the same place. Hospice. Sal and I look at each other.

"Okay, wow," I murmur, more to myself than to her, surprised, but not surprised, that we've reached this conclusion. The specter of hospice has been hovering on the edge of my awareness like a dark shadow all day, and

I've done everything I could to ignore it. But now here it is staring me straight in the face from the sheet of paper before me, and I can't push it away any longer.

Looking around the living room at so many familiar things, it seems impossible Mom will never see them again. That she'll never sit in this room reading the newspaper after breakfast, or watching the evening news as she sips a small glass of wine. She'll never shuffle over to the big bay window to check if the spider plant needs watering, or doze off in the afternoon while reading a book on the loveseat.

My gaze wanders from one thing to another, all so *mom*-like, it's hard to imagine they can exist without her. The wing chair from Dad's college years at Cornell, its graceful lines still solid and sturdy despite decades of use; the butler coffee table that had been a wedding present almost seventy years before; the wood casement clock Dad had made in his early retirement, sitting prominently atop my grandmother's mahogany desk, its four weighted brass balls mesmerizingly spinning, first one way, then the other.

It still amazes me how all the things Mom brought with her from the old house fit so perfectly into this new, much smaller space, transforming the sterile, nondescript apartment into a tiny replica of the home she'd just left.

God, what an experience *that* had been. Sorting through thirty-five years of belongings is hard enough to do when it's your own things, but when it's your eighty-seven-year-old mother's, and she's still very much alive, well, let's just say at times it had been a bit trying. Mom did her best to let us take the lead, picking the things she wanted to take with her, then leaving the rest of the clearing and packing to Sal, Lib, and me. One time, though, I caught her in the basement taking things out of the pile we'd started for Goodwill and putting them aside in a new pile.

"Mom!" I cried when I saw what she was doing, and she looked at me in surprise. "You said you didn't want any of this stuff!"

"But don't one of you girls want *this*?" She held out a ceramic cachepot, one I had a vague recollection of seeing before, but certainly not something of any value, sentimental or otherwise, at least to me. "Tibble gave it to me for my birthday years ago," she murmured, setting it back down with a sigh when she saw me shake my head. I tried to be patient as she wandered around the pile, eyeing each of the castoff items with a forlorn frown, but quickly decided if we were ever going to get through this I had to get these things out of her sight.

So when she went up to take a rest, I didn't waste any time. As stealthily as I could, I carried the whole pile up from the basement to the garage, loading what would fit into the car and driving it over to Goodwill. It took me several trips, but by the time Mom was up from her nap, everything was gone and, just as I suspected, she never mentioned any of it again.

And now somehow, not even two full years since Mom settled in here, we're facing another momentous move, so final it's almost paralyzing to contemplate. Less than a week ago Mom had been sitting in this living room, perhaps having some dinner as she watched the nightly news, with no idea it was the last time she would.

I look over at Sal, who stares sadly back at me. As long as Libby agrees with the decision, we're going to have to tell Mom she won't be coming back here—she'll be going to hospice, instead.

Day Six

"Okay, Dad," I whisper to the empty space around me, driving to the hospital early the next morning. "Can you please send me a sign that hospice is the right place for Mom?" Pulling up to a stop light, I let my eyes scan the busy intersection, looking for some kind of spiritual reassurance from my long-deceased father to ease my anxious mind. And though I'm not sure what it is I'm looking for exactly, I trust I'll know it when I see it.

Because, well—I believe in signs. I believe in angels, and spirit guides, and that our loved ones who have passed are still around us, supporting and guiding us whenever we remember to ask them for help. I didn't always believe these things and, in fact, had never even heard of a spirit guide until after my dad passed away.

One of the first books I read after his death—and the one that would introduce me to the metaphysical world—was called *Embraced By The Light*, written by a woman who claimed to have had a near death experience, something

I'd never heard of before. After undergoing a routine surgery, she found herself looking down at her body in the hospital bed, before being pulled through a dark tunnel toward a bright light where she was met by her angels and spirit guides. They reminded her that rather than being a human being having a spiritual experience, she was a spiritual being having a human experience; that, as souls, we come into the world to learn certain things, and once we've learned them, we return to where we came from, still very aware of who we are.

The author's words, though hardly scientific and impossible to prove, washed over my grieving heart like a balm. I wasn't crazy! Dad *could* still be out there somewhere and, at least according to this woman, as aware of me as I was of him. The book offered me an enormous amount of comfort and reassurance.

It wasn't long, though, before I found myself wanting more—more stories, more answers, and above all, more proof. Through a friend, I discovered the existence of psychics—people who could purportedly speak to the dead—and I became a bit of a junkie, going from one to the next, searching for an elusive something I couldn't even articulate in my own mind. I just knew I would know it when I found it.

One day, almost twenty years after Dad died, I was leafing through our local newspaper when I saw an article about a new book called *Talking To The Dead in Suburbia*. The author happened to live in Wilton, and being the psychic junkie that I was, I couldn't resist the temptation to go see her for a reading.

For me it was love at first sight. Pretty and petite, almost sprite-like with her short dark hair, Anna opened her front door with a wide, inviting smile, ushering me into her living room like we were old friends. Pointing me to her couch, she sat down in a chair opposite, and without preamble, began to talk about things no one else in the world knew but me. There were no tarot cards, no crystal balls, no incense burning, just an everyday person—someone I might run into at the grocery store, or in the school pick-up line—sitting across from me, head cocked to one side like she was listening to something.

"Your father has passed, right?" she asked, but didn't wait for me to respond before quickly adding, "Oh he's funny! Your dad is funny!"

She paused, then looked across at me. "He says you have something of his. Something small and shiny. Do you know what he's talking about?"

Tears welled up in my eyes. Was my dad really talking

to Anna? Could she really hear him? Oh my god! I tried to focus, tried to think what shiny, small thing I had of his, but my mind was blank, like a chalkboard wiped clean. I shook my head.

"That's okay," Anna said, flashing me a reassuring smile. "Maybe it'll come to you later."

She started to say something else, but just then it hit me. "Oh wait, I know!" I cried out, interrupting her. "I have his gold money clip in my jewelry box!"

"Okay, let's see if that's it." Anna paused, then nodded slowly. "He's saying you were supposed to give it to someone and you haven't. Does that make sense?"

I didn't dare laugh, but I wanted to. I mean, how typical of my father to find his way through the ether to remind me that he'd left me his money clip to keep until Bill, his eldest grandson and namesake, was old enough to take care of it. I just hadn't gotten around to it yet because, well, Bill was maybe not the most responsible twenty-one-year-old in the world, and I was scared he would lose it.

"He says it's time," Anna reported. "And not to worry so much. He's looking after your son."

I don't know. Was I too gullible? Was I too quick to believe that Anna was actually communicating with my dad? Maybe a little, but the feeling of comfort I had that afternoon was so real it had to count for something. The idea that Dad was still watching over me, still aware of the things I was, and *wasn't*, doing was incredibly reassuring. I *wanted* to believe.

And ever since that day, I talk to Dad a lot, especially when something is troubling me. Like right now, on my way to the hospital to tell my mother she's going to hospice. I'd give anything to hear his calm, reassuring voice telling me to trust myself, that we'd made the best decision we could, given the situation Mom is in, and to stop second-guessing it.

Now, sitting in the car waiting for the light to change, hoping to see something, *anything,* that will put my mind at ease about Mom and hospice, my eyes come to rest on a billboard across the intersection. It's the kind that changes ads every few seconds and as I'm looking, it switches to one for Hospice of Northwest Ohio—the exact same hospice we're about to take Mom. Bright and colorful, it's a picture of a happy, smiling nurse standing over an equally happy, smiling patient.

Of all the signs I've ever gotten, none has *ever* been as clear as this one. Laughing out loud in absurd relief, I move forward with the traffic as the light turns green, thanking Dad over and over as I make my way to the hos-pital and the impossible day that lies ahead.

∾

Mom and Lib are sleeping when I poke my head through the door a few minutes later. Trying not to wake them, I tiptoe across the room to the built-in couch under the window, settling myself as softly as I can on its narrow seat, the maroon vinyl cushion stiff and a bit slippery underneath my leggings. Behind me, the vertical blind is closed against the early morning light, and I have to sit up straight so as not to jangle it, making it even harder to get comfortable. Sighing, I bend down to get my phone from my bag and see Lib peering at me from the recliner.

"Shoot, sorry!" I whisper. "I was trying to be so quiet! Go back to sleep!"

"It's okay," she whispers back. "I wasn't asleep—just too exhausted to keep my eyes open."

"Bad night?"

"Horrible. I don't think either of us slept at all." Lib stretches her legs, then curls back up under the blanket she's buried herself under. "Mom kept thinking she had to go to the bathroom, so the nurse would come put her on the bedpan, but then nothing would happen. We must have tried a dozen times."

"Why don't you take the car and go back to the apartment for a while? Sal's there—you and she can come back later after you get some rest."

"I'm too tired to drive. I think I'll just stay here."

"Okay…I'll be extra quiet. One thing, though," I pause and glance over at Mom, her pale face sunken and drawn under the oxygen mask. "Sal and I talked last night and are thinking hospice is the best place for her right now—are you okay with that?"

Lib looks at me, then over at our sleeping mother, the hiss of the oxygen machine the only sound in the room. "She's so tired," she finally murmurs, "And so sad. I think, yes, we have to do something."

I want to tell her about seeing the sign on my drive over, but her eyes are already starting to close so I decide to hold off. Maybe it will be a better story to share later when we're all together, I think, putting my phone back in my purse as I stand up.

"I'll go talk to the nurse then and see what we have to do. Try to sleep—I'll make sure no one comes in."

Slipping out into the hall, I close the door gently and walk down the corridor to the nurse's station. An attractive young woman looks up from her paperwork as I approach the counter.

"Can I help you?" she asks, closing the file in front of her.

"I'm not exactly sure," I reply hesitantly. "I'm Kay's daughter? In room 609? We…well, we spoke to the hospice liaison yesterday and umm…we think it's time." Pausing, I take a breath to steady myself. I can't believe I'm going to say what I'm going to say. "We'd like to go ahead and see if we can get Mom into hospice. Do you know what we need to do?"

My words seem to hang in the air, their weight so heavy it's hard for me to breathe.

"I'm so sorry," she murmurs, reaching out to touch my hand. My eyes immediately well up and I blink rapidly, trying not to cry. "I can definitely make that call for you. Are you okay? Can I get you anything?"

"No, no I'm fine. Thank you though." Pushing back the tears, I offer her a forced smile. "So I know from the liaison there's no control over this, but if we could get her into the one in Perrysburg that would be our preference."

The nurse nods. "I'll make sure to tell them. But just so you know—it can take a little while to make the arrangements, so don't worry if no one gets back to you right away. I'm here all day, though, so I'll try to keep you in the loop."

Thanking her, I turn and wander back down the corridor, oddly silent except for the fall of my footsteps on the speckled linoleum floor. Where is everyone? It's such a difference from the hustle and bustle outside Mom's old room it occurs to me again that maybe this is where they send all the sick, old people waiting to get moved someplace else. Or to die. A quick wave of lightheadedness slows my steps, and I have to take a couple of deep breaths. I don't want Mom to die here, in this cold, sterile hospital, and I don't want her to die in the Toledo hospice, somewhere she's never been before. I want her to die in Perrysburg, a place she knows and loves, and my sisters and I know and love, too.

A small Ohio town on the banks of the Maumee River, Perrysburg is about as idyllic a place to raise a family as Mom and Dad could have found. Sidewalks line every street, so growing up we could ride our bikes everywhere—a friend's house, the library, the corner drugstore—giving me a sense of independence from an early age. I remember the first time I was allowed to ride my bike around our block by myself, pedaling my two-wheeler as fast as my six-year-old legs could go, exhilarated and nervous, but not scared. Everyone knew everyone else in Perrysburg, so no matter where I went, I felt safe.

As a teenager, though, that same sense of security became a bit stifling, and rather than making me feel safe, I felt trapped. I couldn't bear the place. It was like living in a giant fishbowl with not only my parents' eyes watching my every move, but all my parents' friends' eyes watching me, too.

One time, when I was about seventeen, I got home from spending the afternoon at my boyfriend, Chris's, house—a bit of a bad boy who neither of my parents liked very much though we'd been going together since we were fourteen—to find Mom waiting for me, fire spitting from her eyes.

"I hope you know the whole town's going to be talking about you," she fumed as I walked into the kitchen.

"Talking about what?" I asked, not sure what I'd done, but knowing from the tone of her voice it must be bad.

"Mrs. F saw you and Chris all over each other just now. In the middle of the day! Right in front of the window! What were you thinking?" Hands on hips, mouth set in a line, my mother was as mad as I'd ever seen her. At least with me.

I stood there frozen, my face flushing hot as I imagined Mrs. F watching Chris and me making out on the couch next to the large picture window in his family room. Cringing inside, I didn't know what to say, my mind spinning, looking for a way out.

"I hate this stupid town!" my indignant seventeen-year-old self finally spat out, stomping past Mom and up the stairs to my room. Slamming the door behind me, I vowed I would move as far away from Perrysburg as I possibly could, as *soon* as I could.

It took a few years but, true to my word, I did just that. Practically the minute I graduated from college, I kissed my parents goodbye and moved to New York City, without so much as a backward glance. It wouldn't be until I was raising my own family years later that I'd begin to see Perrysburg the way my parents must have. Not a fish bowl after all, but a safe haven where friends looked out for each other, and each other's kids. As an adult, my memories of growing up in Perrysburg make me feel part of something bigger than myself, and I wish I'd given it more of a chance.

I come to Mom's closed door and, sinking down in the chair next to it to keep guard until Libby wakes up, I send out a silent prayer that there will be a bed for her at the Perrysburg hospice. Because if there is one thing that could make this whole wretched situation more bearable, it would be to bring our mother full circle—back to where she belongs.

∞

A little later that morning, Sal, Lib, and I are watching helplessly as the nice nurse tries, again, to get the bedpan under Mom, who is moaning from the effort to lift up her hips. After the long, sleepless night, she is exhausted, both mentally and physically, spiraling downward so quickly we aren't sure she's even going to make it to hospice.

"I can't, I'm sorry," Mom finally murmurs, laying her head back on the pillow.

The nurse looks across at us, her forehead creased with concern. "Perhaps a brief might be something to consider?" she suggests gently. "I worry about the risk of infection if she keeps holding it in."

Sal leans down. "What do you think, Mom?" she asks. "Want to give it a try?"

Now if anyone had told me my mother would ever agree to wearing a 'brief'—hospital code for adult diaper— even on her deathbed, I would have laughed out loud. *No way*, I would tell them. *If there's one thing I know for sure about Kay Ball, it's that she would never, ever give up like that.*

When Mom started having a little bladder problem a few years before, she wouldn't even buy the pads that were specifically made for leaks of that nature. She insisted on using the pads meant for younger female issues, and no amount of reasoning would change her mind. Maybe it was vanity. Maybe it was Mom trying to exert some kind of control over a body that was beginning to let her down. Maybe she was embarrassed to walk down the adult incontinence aisle. But every time I suggested that a more appropriate pad might work better, she would shake her head and say, "No, Peg. I like the ones I like."

So when Mom gives a weak nod that yes, she'll try the brief, it's as though a death knell begins tolling in the corners of the hospital room. Sal, Lib, and I hear it clear as day, and look at each other in despair.

Mom is giving up.

"Maybe we can hijack the ambulance and have it go to Maine instead," I joke, breaking the worried silence in the room as we wait for the EMTs to come transport Mom to the Perrysburg hospice. I'd been so relieved to find out earlier that a bed had opened up for her there, but now with the moment getting closer that she's going to *go*, I'm filled with dread. How can this be happening?

"I'd give anything to take her to Maine," Libby sighs, and Sal and I nod in unison. We all would.

Because as much as Mom loves Perrysburg, she loves our family's summer place in Maine even more.

Built by her grandfather in 1917, the rustic camp sits on a rock cliff overlooking the St. Croix River in Robbinston, a small, remote town in downeast Maine. It's nothing fancy—in fact, up until my sisters and I started having children, there wasn't even plumbing, or a phone. We filled buckets with water from a hose that was fed by a stream, and if we needed to make a call we had to go to our neighbors across the street, or the payphone a mile up the road.

Standing on wooden stilts to withstand the twenty-foot tides that go in and out twice a day, the camp is one big open room centered by a thick chestnut post that supports the ceiling rafters, like the inside of an enormous wooden umbrella. The large space is loosely divided into three main areas—a living room filled with century-old wicker furniture circling a large, brick fireplace, a kitchen dominated by a heavy, old-fashioned soapstone sink, and a dining area with a table long enough, when all its leaves are in, to fit the whole family—eighteen and growing—when we're all there together. French doors lead out to a wrap-around porch that hangs, somewhat precariously, over the rocks and river below, while an old boat house and tool house serve as bunk rooms.

When grandchildren began to arrive, Mom and Dad decided it was time for a few upgrades. They put in a phone and some plumbing, building a bath house with flushing toilets and running hot water, things my sisters and I could only dream about growing up as we shivered under the cold hose water washing our hair, and plugged our noses emptying the chemical toilet into an oil drum buried in the ground. Sadly, Dad would only get to enjoy these modern conveniences for a few years before he died, but for Mom, having them would make all the difference, allowing her to be in Maine by herself after he was gone.

And since Dad died, being by herself in Maine was something Mom loved more than anything.

"Don't you get lonely?" I'd often ask, trying to imagine myself there without anyone else. Maybe I could see it for a couple of days, but Mom would stay for weeks on her own every summer after the rest of us had come and gone. I suppose it offered a nice respite from her busy life in Perrysburg with the many volunteer and social activities that filled her calendar the rest of the year. In Maine she didn't need a calendar, because for the most part she kept to herself. She gardened, and read, and watched the tide go in and out. And, I think more than anything else, she *remembered*—the generations of memories wafting around the rafters and beams keeping her company whenever she was there by herself.

"Oh, Peg, no," Mom would always answer, shaking her head as if I've just asked the silliest question. "I could never be lonely in Maine."

If we can have soul places in this life the way we have soul mates, then Maine is my mom's. And my sisters'. And mine. Maine is, and always has been, our family's constant, where we gather in the summer to be with each other and most importantly, with Mom. It feels impossible she won't ever be there again.

An idea pops into my head as Sal, Lib, and I fantasize, half-jokingly, about hijacking the ambulance. Maybe it's not possible to get Mom to Maine again, but maybe we could bring a little bit of Maine to her.

"Remember that picture Kit took last summer?" I ask them. "The one of the view from Mom's room?" They both look at me and nod, their expressions curious. "Maybe we can have it blown up into a poster and hang it on the wall in her new room!"

The summer before, Mom had to spend quite a bit of time in her bedroom due to her oxygen constraints, so Paul had trimmed the branches outside her window to give her a bigger view of the river. Lib's husband, Kit, a professional photographer, had taken a picture of it because, well—it's such a beautiful view.

"That's a great idea!" Sal exclaims, pulling out her laptop to find the fastest place to do it.

Lib jumps up. "I'll go call Kit and have him email me the file," she says, heading out to the hall.

I pull out my phone and start scrolling through my own photos to see if I have the picture, in case Lib can't reach Kit. Infused with a sense of purpose, the three of us latch onto this little project like a lifeline, if only for a few minutes.

Because the next thing we know, the nurse and aide are bustling through the door, followed closely by two uniformed EMTs pushing a gurney between them, and things start to move very fast. The nurse and aide busy themselves around Mom, who's now awake, her eyes watchful as they disconnect her from all the various apparatus. The EMTs position the stretcher next to her bed, and the one nearest her head squats down beside her.

"Mrs. Ball?"

Mom turns toward his voice, her oxygen mask pushing taut against her cheek. "I'm Howard, and Frank here," he motions to the other EMT at the foot of the bed, "we're going to lift you up now. You don't have to do a thing."

Mom nods and turns her head back, closing her eyes. I can't imagine what's going through her mind. We'd explained as gently as we could about moving her to hospice, and she'd seemed okay about it and, again, maybe even relieved. But still.

"On my count," Howard says, and the two men gather Mom into a cocoon of bed sheets, counting to three and then lifting her up and over onto the stretcher. They are so gentle I have to turn away, staring out the window as I try not to cry.

Outside, the world looks stark and gray in the late afternoon winter light. People and cars are coming and going in the parking lot below as if it's just another day. I'm trying hard to be strong, but the shadow of the deep, dark nothing I was so scared of as a child is creeping along the edges of my consciousness, and I want to crumble into a sobbing heap. I don't want to be strong. I don't want my mother to go to hospice.

When my children were little, they loved to build towers with their wooden blocks, piling one on top of another as high as they could go without the whole thing falling over. The taller the tower got, the more careful they had to be that the next block was balanced before they took their hand away. If they moved too fast, or let go of the block too soon, the whole thing would collapse, crashing down around them.

Right now, watching the world go on below me, my throat so tight with unshed tears it hurts, I feel like I'm holding up the last block on a teetering tower and if I'm not careful, if I let myself lose control for even a second, the whole thing is going to topple over.

So I take a deep breath and turn away from the window, pushing the shadow back as far as I can. The EMTs have Mom strapped into the gurney and are rolling her toward the door. Sal and Lib are gathering their things, so I do the same, slipping into my coat and hefting my bag over my shoulder, my heart thudding hard inside my chest, whether from exertion or trepidation, I'm not sure. I glance around the hospital room to make sure we have everything, then follow my sisters out into the hall. Not for the first time, I'm grateful for their solid presence, reminding me I'm not alone trying to hold up that last block. They're both trying to hold it up, too.

∞

"I love you," Mom whispers as I bend down to give her a kiss while we wait for the elevator to arrive.

"I love you, too, Mom. I'll see you in just a bit."

I give her hand a quick squeeze and step back from the stretcher, forcing a smile. Her cloudy blue eyes, though heavy with fatigue, look into mine with an intensity that makes me lean back over to give her another kiss.

"Don't worry—Lib's going with you. Sal and I will be right behind. Next time I see you we'll all be back in Perrysburg!"

She gives a slight nod and closes her eyes as the elevator doors open. I move back to let the EMTs push the stretcher past, giving Lib's arm an encouraging pat as she follows behind. Watching the doors slide shut, I stand for a moment, remembering another time I'd seen a similar look to the one Mom just gave me, and my chest tightens. It was the last time I'd kissed my father goodbye.

He'd been sitting in a wheelchair, just out of ICU after his blood clot surgery, and waiting to be taken to his new room. I'd flown out to be with Mom for a few days, but now that he was out of the woods I was heading home. Bending down to give him a kiss goodbye, his pale blue eyes caught mine, and something in his look gave me pause. It was so fleeting I thought maybe I'd imagined it, though I hugged him again a little tighter.

He's fine, I told myself as I walked toward the elevators. *He was just saying goodbye, Peggy, stop making something out of nothing.*

But I guess I hadn't been making something out of nothing—he died two days later.

Even now, some twenty odd years later, I can still see that look. Maybe he had some sort of inner knowing that we wouldn't see each other again, that our goodbye was a big one. Or maybe it was *my* inner knowing. In hindsight, though, it was almost as if Dad had been saying "Pay attention, Peg! Look at me! This is important!"

And though the circumstances with Mom are quite different, as I walk out of the hospital, I promise myself that I will do my best to pay attention to every moment I have left with her.

But in order to have *any* more moments with her, I have to be *with* her, so hurrying to my car I make a mental checklist of the things I am going to pick up at her apartment before heading over to hospice. We had decided earlier that while Lib went with Mom in the ambulance, I would go to the apartment, and Sal would head to Walgreens to pick up the poster of 'Mom's View.'

I'm feeling a bit jealous that Lib's with Mom, even though it had been *my* idea for her to go in the ambulance. What if Mom dies on the way? What if that look she gave me was, in fact, her way of saying goodbye and I never see her again?

The closer I get to the apartment, the more worried I am that Mom might die without me. In an ambulance. On her way to hospice. With just Libby. That isn't how I've pictured it at all! In my mind, we're all together—Sal, Lib, and me—sitting by Mom's bedside as she peacefully draws her last breath. I'm not sure I can handle it if one of my sisters gets to be with Mom at the end, and I don't. Even worse, what if they *both* are, and I'm the only one not there?

As the middle daughter of three girls, I often felt like the odd one out when we were growing up. I was born in January, for instance, while Sal and Lib were born in June. They both had Elizabeth in their name—I'm still not sure why they did and not me. Their bedrooms were on one side of the hall, mine on the other. While they sat next to each other at the dining room table, I sat across from them, by myself. Silly things, but important enough to imbed in my younger self's psyche a real insecurity that I was somehow separate from my sisters. That they shared things apart from me.

A sense of urgency to get back to Mom takes hold, and I drive into Sunrise Crest maybe a little faster than I should. Grateful to see a parking spot right near the main entrance, I pull in, then hurry through the sliding glass doors into the lobby.

Too late, I realize it's almost five o'clock and nearly every resident of Sunrise Crest is making their way to the dining room for dinner. The lobby is a sea of gray hair flowing in the same direction, the vast majority pushing walkers, which they take turns stowing side by side across from the dining room entrance, like so many cars in a parking lot.

And just like cars, each walker is a little different. Some are big, some small. Some have baskets, others have decorated name cards hanging from the handle bars. Red, green, blue, black—no two are alike, though they all look the same, much like their owners.

When Mom moved to Sunrise Crest, she had scoffed at the idea of needing a walker, taking great pride in the fact that she could still get around well enough on her own.

"Oh, I don't need one of those yet," I overheard her tell a new neighbor a few nights after she'd moved in.

"Give it a month, dear," the neighbor replied. "Everyone here gets one sooner or later."

And the neighbor was right. I don't think it took more than a month before Mom became the proud owner of a small, metallic maroon walker, with hand brakes and a pull-down seat she could use if need be. She loved that pint-sized walker the way I remember loving my first Schwinn bicycle—proudly and possessively.

I'm buzzing with nervous energy as I weave through the throng of dinner-goers, my mind more focused on where I want to be than where I am. Maybe there's something in my aura that keeps people from approaching me, but somehow I make it to the elevator and up to Mom's apartment without being sidetracked by any of her well-meaning friends.

Wasting no time, I grab a bag from the hall closet and start stuffing: her favorite nightgowns, a well-loved blanket she keeps folded at the end of her bed, some family photos.

Okay, I think, glancing around the quiet apartment. *Anything else? Hmmm—I wonder how hospice feels about wine?*

Deciding I don't care, I grab a bottle of chardonnay and tuck it into the bag. I'm sure we won't be the first ones to sneak a drink into hospice, I reassure myself as I head back out to the car. God knows, if there was ever a time for a drink, this has to be it.

∞

The drive from Sunrise Crest to the Perrysburg hospice is, in a bittersweet irony, the same route we'd taken to get to school every day, stirring up so many memories it's like my younger self is sitting next to me pointing out the familiar landmarks she'd stared out at from the carpool window.

Things have, of course, changed a lot in the passing years—gas stations and strip malls have sprouted up where once there was only open space. I remember watching, with great adolescent excitement, the Southwyck Mall being erected in the early seventies. The behemoth structure emerged from the acres of empty cornfields like a magical wonderland, promising trendy new shops, arcade games and *seven* movie theaters—a preteen paradise. It had ended up going bankrupt a few years back, and the immense building recently demolished, leaving in its wake a desolate vista of crumbling asphalt pockmarked with tufted weeds and grass, making me sad every time I drive by.

But some things haven't changed at all, like the three gigantic grain silos that tower over Reynolds Road, dwarfing in their shadow the railroad crossing that we'd sometimes get stuck at as a mile-long train snaked its way past, making us late for school or, even worse, late for getting home from school. Then, just on the other side of the tracks, McDonalds—one of the originals to open near us—where I'd been excited to try fast food for the first time with my friend Lock and his nanny. There's Dr. Lindsey's office, our orthodontist, and the red brick elementary school on the corner, with its gigantic liberty type bell in the middle of the concrete playground that always intrigued me. How did it get there?

Then across the bridge into Perrysburg, the river below muddy and high on this first day of March, and down West Front Street, past the Smith's house where we'd go every year to their annual Christmas Eve cocktail party, and the Harts, where the same families would congregate again on Memorial Day to watch the parade go by. Just beyond that is where the old Houck's corner drugstore used to be—a real old-time pharmacy with its soda fountain, comic book rack, and family charge account. There's the Commodore Perry statue standing guard at the top of

Louisiana Avenue, the hub of 'uptown' Perrysburg with its small shops and restaurants, where West Front becomes East Front, the street I grew up on.

Then block after block peppered with the homes of more family friends, their names running through my mind like a litany as I drive past each one—Welles, Giffords, Williams, Harris, Orser, Fauvers, Millers, Jones, Menton, McKelvy. And then my childhood home, its white clapboard, black shutters, and red tiled roof so familiar I feel a sharp pang of nostalgia every time I pass by.

With a nervous flutter in my heart, I pull into the hospice parking lot. Despite being a volunteer for many years, I've never spent time in an actual hospice facility, always having visited patients in their homes. Sitting in the car, I stare at the building—an aesthetically pleasing combination of wood, brick, and glass. Its peaked roof lines and wooden beams above the front entrance remind me more of an upscale ski lodge in the mountains than a place for the sick and dying.

A few years before, when this facility had just opened, Mom had insisted on bringing me here for a tour, mostly I suppose because I was a hospice volunteer, but also because she'd played a small part in the fundraising effort to build it. I didn't want to go, but Mom could be insistent when she got an idea in her head, so I ended up giving in. As soon as we walked through the door, though, I wished I hadn't. The sorrow in the building was palpable and I felt like an intruder, so self-conscious of my own non-dying status I don't remember a thing.

Staring at that same building now, it seems incredible that so much sadness can be contained within its walls, that it isn't oozing out of the bricks and glass, leaving dark puddles of grief scattered around the neatly landscaped grounds. Somehow, the place looks welcoming. Taking a deep breath to steel myself, I gather my bags and head toward whatever it is that's coming next.

∾

Walking through the heavy wooden door, I'm greeted with a warm smile by a receptionist behind a counter and, much to my immediate delight, the wagging tail of an enormous golden retriever sitting in the middle of the hall.

"Oh my goodness!" I croon, extending my hand as I walk toward him. "Hello! Who are you?"

"That's Juno," the receptionist tells me. "He's a volunteer."

I bend down to pat his big yellow head, and Juno rolls onto his back, his tail thumping the floor as I scratch his belly.

"Oh, you are so beautiful!" I murmur, grateful for this momentary reprieve. I love dogs, and having one greet me this way, when I'm feeling so anxious and unnerved, calms my whole being right down.

"He's a bit of a character," the receptionist adds. "But with a heart of gold. We all love him."

Giving Juno one final scratch, I stand up and walk back to her desk.

"I'm here to see my mom. Kay Ball? I think she may have just been brought in."

The receptionist nods and points to a notebook on the counter. "Sign in first," she says, and I obediently pick up the pen and scribble my name, glad to see on the lines above that Sal and Lib are already here. "Your mom is in room 102, which will be down the corridor to the right, past the nurses' station."

Thanking her, I head down the wide hallway, my footsteps the only sound on the highly polished wood floor.

Passing by a glass windowed cafeteria, I see a few people scattered among the tables, their faces pale and drawn, their expressions somber. *Oh, those poor people,* I think, before it hits me that now *I'm* one of those poor people, too. My chest tightens and, turning my head away, I pick up my steps.

I follow the receptionist's instructions, passing by what seems like an endless line of doors. Each one is marked by a small wooden plaque etched with a first name in colorful block letters and a little painted flower. They're tasteful and pretty, and just different enough to make them seem personal, as if someone put real thought into making them.

Up ahead two women are standing near the nurses' station, their heads bent toward each other in deep conversation. The one facing me—a nurse, judging from the stethoscope around her neck—nods her head, then reaches out to touch the other woman's arm.

"If you're meant to be there, you'll be there," I hear her say as I pass by, her words so clear and succinct it's like she's saying them right in my ear. Does she mean what I think she means? All afternoon I've been so worried about not being there with Mom at the end—could it be possible that it's not up to me?

If you're meant to be there, you'll be there.

I've tried so hard, for so long, to control so many things in my mother's life, to let go of the oars at this point seems counter-intuitive. But contemplating the nurse's words as I continue down the hall, I feel a certain weight lift off my shoulders, and decide to trust I was in that particular spot, at that particular moment, to hear those particular words for a reason.

Pausing in front of room 102, my heart quickens to see 'Kay' already on the nameplate. She only just got here! There's a little trail of ivy underneath that makes me smile a little, though. Mom loves ivy.

"Peg?" Sal and Lib are walking toward me, and for a moment I'm confused. How did they get behind me?

"The aide asked us to wait out here while she gets Mom settled," Lib explains, gesturing to a little alcove where they've stowed their things. "We just went to look around a little. This place is nice!"

Setting my bags down next to theirs, I pull out one of the folding chairs and sink into it. I should probably go look around, too, but my body is numb, my mind buzzing with a nervous energy I'm not quite sure what to do with. I can't believe I'm here, sitting in this hallway, waiting for my mom to get settled into *hospice.* The word almost hisses in my head.

Everything seems so normal, though. Serene even, despite the fact that people are dying behind every closed door. Nurses and aides move in and out of the rooms with slow, measured steps, their expressions soft. I marvel at their composure amidst so much pain and suffering.

Juno makes an appearance at the far end of the hall, padding softly in our direction before disappearing like a phantom into one of the rooms. Is he a harbinger of death, I wonder, or just a friendly dog looking for some attention? Either way, his presence is at once grounding and comforting, and adds to the pervasive sense of calm.

The door to Mom's room swings open, and the aide beckons us in with a smile.

"I think your mom is worn out from the trip over, poor thing," she tells us as we file past her into the room. "She's sleeping now, so make yourselves comfortable. The intake nurse will be by shortly to ask you a few questions." Glancing back at Mom, she offers us another small smile before pulling the door closed behind her.

Mom looks as peaceful as I've seen her since this whole nightmare began. She's tucked in beneath the crisp, white bedding, the sheet pulled up just under her chin. Her white hair has been brushed and swept back away from her forehead, the way she would like it, and the lines on her face seem less severe. She's sleeping so soundly, though, it makes me nervous.

"Do you think it's the morphine?" I whisper, pulling out the blanket I brought from her apartment and laying it over the end of the bed. In my hospice experience, I've learned that morphine can be a double-edged sword, especially at the end of life. It relieves the pain, but at a price. And though I don't want Mom to be in pain anymore, I also know I'm not ready for her to drift away in a drug-induced sleep—at least, not yet.

"Maybe," Sal says, "but I think it's mostly exhaustion." She looks at her phone. "I have to make a call—I'll be right back."

She steps out into the hall, and Lib and I busy ourselves putting away the things I'd brought from the apartment: nightgowns in the dresser drawer, toilet kit to the bathroom, family photos on the table. Having some of Mom's things scattered around warms up the otherwise generic room—an odd combination of hospital functionality and modern motel decor. Besides the standard hospital bed and rolling tray table, there is a large pine armoire housing a television and a set of drawers. A floral covered recliner is tucked into the corner facing the bed, and across sits a small laminate dining table with two matching chairs. Handmade quilts hang on the walls, along with a large, round clock, and a white board showing the date and the names of the nurse and aide on call.

The best part of the room, though, is the big bay window that looks out over a small pond and garden in the back. Trees, still bare of leaves, are scattered along an inlaid brick path that winds from one end of the building to the other, crisscrossing over a wooden bridge that divides the pond in half. Even on this dreary, gray afternoon, it is a beautiful, peaceful setting, and it makes me happy to think of Mom looking out at it, if—no, *when*—she wakes up.

A knock on the door interrupts my thoughts, and I turn from the window to see a man's head pop in.

"Hello," he says when he sees me, stepping into the room. "I'm Michael," he offers, glancing over at Mom. "I'm here to do your mother's intake form. Is this a good time?"

"Oh, yes, of course," I murmur, offering him a chair. Lib and I sit down as well and do our best to answer his questions, most of them the same ones we've been answering for the past week. I'm grateful Mom is asleep because she would be so annoyed—not only by the tediousness of the questions, but by Michael's overly solicitous manner. He is almost *too* nice.

"Would you like us to keep giving your mom her heart medications?

His question takes both Lib and me by surprise and we exchange a wary look. What exactly is he asking? The medicine Mom takes is what has kept her alive the past six years. If she stops taking it, her heart will go into A-fib, which will raise her blood pressure, and, I'm fairly certain given her current condition, kill her pretty quickly.

Oh my god, I think, my mind racing, trying to understand what is happening. *Is that why they're asking? Do they* want *to speed things up?*

"She's been so conscientious about taking them all these years," I tell him, "it might scare her if we tell her she doesn't need to anymore." Pausing, I look over at Mom. "Unless *you* think it would be better for her to stop them?"

"No, no—it's fine either way," Michael quickly assures us. "We just have to ask. Sometimes patients have trouble swallowing and well, it can be one less thing. Has that been an issue at all?"

"I don't think so." I look over at Lib, who gives her head a quick shake. "But she was going downhill so fast at the hospital today," I feel compelled to add. "I guess I'm not totally sure now."

"She took them this morning," Lib interjects, leaning forward in her seat to rub Mom's shoulder. "Let's not give up on her yet, okay?"

Poor Lib. As hard as this is on Sal and me, I think it might be even harder for our younger sister. When her son, Henry, was born with a rare genetic disorder called Angelman Syndrome, Libby and Mom formed a unique bond, and for the past twenty-two years our mother has been Lib's, and Henry's, staunchest supporter. With her unconditional love and unwavering support, Mom's been an anchor for Lib as she's navigated the turbulent sea of raising a child with a disability—she's not going to let go of that anchor without a fight.

"Okay, understood. We will keep her on them for now." Michael makes one last notation on his clipboard, then collects his papers and stands to leave. "We're going to take good care of her," he promises, pausing at the foot of the bed to gently pat Mom's leg on his way out. "Try not to worry."

The door closes behind him with a click, and Lib and I sit for a moment in silence. Well, almost silence. The soft hiss from the oxygen, combined with the gurgling of the water reservoir attached to it, and the steady tick, tick, tick from the large clock on the wall, fills the room with a soothing hum.

"Well, I don't know about you," I say to Lib, standing up to stretch my legs, "but I'm ready for a glass of wine!"

Still Day Six

"Mom??"

Like synchronized dancers, Sal, Lib, and I set down our drinks—the wine I'd smuggled in earlier camouflaged in plastic water cups—and stand up in a single motion, fanning out around the hospital bed where she's been sleeping soundly for the past hour. Her eyes are open and she's squinting over at the clock on the opposite wall. At the sound of my voice, she swivels her head.

"I think it's time for the news," she rasps through her oxygen mask, and the three of us stare at her, then at each other, in disbelief. Mom hasn't spoken a complete sentence other than 'I love you' for days, and certainly hasn't shown any interest in the news, or anything else for that matter. Just moments before, we were wondering if she'd ever wake up again, and now she's not only awake, but somehow knows what time it is.

Glancing at the clock, I laugh when I see it's exactly six-thirty, almost to the second.

"Oh my gosh, Mom! It is!" Leaning over, I kiss the top of her white head. "Do you want to sit up a little?"

She nods, so while Lib fumbles for the control button on the side of the bed to raise her up, Sal and I busy ourselves adjusting the pillows and bed covers like so many nervous nannies.

"Are you feeling better?" Sal asks. "Are you hungry?"

"Maybe I'm a little hungry," she answers, her voice weak, but clear. "I think I just mostly want to watch the news, though."

Her insistence on watching the news is so typical Mom, we are giddy with relief, laughing and shaking our heads in bemusement. I'm reminded of the time this past Christmas when she'd interrupted a spirited conversation amongst the three generations gathered in our family room because, well, it was time for the news.

"But Mom," I'd pleaded, "we're having such a good time! Do we have to watch it tonight?"

"It's only half an hour," she replied. "I hate to miss it."

Even when her millennial grandchildren chimed in to protest, Mom wouldn't be swayed so, groaning in defeat, I turned on the television and we all settled in to watch the evening news with my intractable mother.

"I'll see about getting something to eat," I offer as

Sal grabs the remote from the cabinet. Lib nods, pulling her chair up as close as she can get to Mom, who is staring at the TV screen waiting for Sal to find the right channel.

Hurrying down the hall to the nurses' station, I can see Mom's nurse, Jenny, behind the counter.

"You're not going to believe this!" I call out as I approach the desk, and she looks up with a questioning smile. "Mom just woke up, and she's *hungry*! And she wants to watch the news!"

Jenny's reaction, or rather *non*-reaction, surprises me. I guess I expected her to be as excited as me, but she just nods, turning to the aide behind her to ask, in a calm, measured tone, if she would please go to the kitchen for some hot broth. Then, coming around the desk, she takes me by the elbow and leads me back toward Mom's room.

"We see this often," she explains as we walk back down the corridor. "A patient can sometimes rebound once we get them settled and their pain under control. In hospice lingo it's called a 'rally,' and it can last anywhere from five minutes to five days. Sometimes even longer."

"I just can't believe it," I murmur, pausing outside the door. "She's been going downhill so fast today, we weren't sure she'd even make it through the night. It feels like a miracle."

Jenny nods in understanding. "We like to think of these rallies as little gifts to the family—but there's no way to know how long one will last, so just try to enjoy them."

Following her into the room, I'm struck by the ordinariness of the scene before me. There are my sisters, clandestine cocktails in hand, sitting on either side of Mom's bed, all three turned toward the television as if it's the most natural thing in the world. Which of course it is. Or used to be. How many times have we sat with our mother like this, having a drink and watching the news?

It's so familiar. So normal.

And because this day has been anything *but* normal—a rollercoaster ride of emotions that have me still reeling—I know Jenny is right. This moment of normalcy *is* a gift, and no matter how long it lasts, five minutes or five days, I am just so grateful to have my mom back I could weep.

Day Seven

Mom's rally continues over the next couple of days which, depending on the particular moment we are in, is both a blessing and a curse.

She's eating again, which is a good thing, but the food that's going in is having trouble getting back out, causing Mom great discomfort and the nursing staff great concern. They've tried everything to make it happen naturally—suppositories, prune juice, laxatives—but nothing is working.

"Maybe if I could sit on a toilet?" Mom finally suggests, frustrated more than anyone by her uncooperative body. "It's just hard to go in my pants when I've spent my whole life trying not to."

"It's okay, Mom," I assure her, relieved to see a whisper of her sense of humor. "You're doing fine. How about trying the commode? It might be easier than getting you to the bathroom."

She nods with a tired sigh, so while the aide moves to set one up next to the bed, Jenny shoos us out the door to give Mom a semblance of privacy.

We head toward the sunroom down the hall—a little oasis where family members and friends can sit and chat, maybe have a bite to eat, or talk on the phone so as not to disturb whoever they're visiting. It's a pretty space, warm and inviting, with scattered seating areas and leafy, green potted plants dotted throughout. Light streams through the glass walls, brightening up even the dreariest of Ohio winter days, like this one.

Turning the corner to go in, we stop short when we see another family already there, talking among themselves in subdued voices. Not wanting to intrude, we start to back out when a woman, about our age, separates herself from the others and comes toward us.

"Are you Kay's daughters?" she asks, and when we nod that we are, offers us a bright smile. "I love your mother so much! I was heartbroken when I heard she might be here." Sticking out her hand, she introduces herself. "I'm Bridget D…maybe we've met before? Kay and I were in the Garden Club for years together. She's always been such an inspiration to me!"

One by one we shake her hand, murmuring our names. We're used to hearing things like this about Mom—especially from our friends who still live in Perrysburg. There's something about her no-nonsense approach to getting things done, mixed in with her enthusiasm for whatever it is she might be working on—the Garden Club, her church, the museum, her social clubs—that younger women admire and want to emulate.

"My husband's in room 101," Bridget explains, gesturing to the room next to Mom's. "My daughters and I are just having a little break."

Oh dear. Looking over at the women behind her, my heart constricts when I see how young they are—early thirties, I guess, the same age I was when my dad died. I feel sorry for them—it's hard to lose your father so young—and for a minute their impending loss puts my impending loss in perspective.

After all, Mom is about to turn eighty-nine. She's lived a long, happy life. Her death will be sad, but certainly not tragic. Not like losing your sixty-something-year-old father.

Except, no, that's not true at all. Losing my mom *is* tragic, and I don't want to put it in perspective, not for one second. In fact, standing there on the perimeter of the sunroom, listening to my sisters make small talk with Bridget, I resent these strangers for making me feel, even if unintentionally, that their loss somehow eclipses mine. I'm losing my *mom*, my last parent. Without her physical presence in the world to ground me, how will I ever find my way around it? She's never *not* been there.

Out of the corner of my eye I see Jenny poke her head out Mom's door and motion for us to come back. *Thank God!* I can't bear making small talk even under the best of circumstances, so murmuring my apologies, I head back to Mom's room, relieved to leave this other family to their tragic story so I can get back to my own.

∽

"Any luck?" Lib asks when she and Sal return. I shake my head.

"I'm afraid not," Jenny tells them, repeating what she'd told me a few minutes earlier. "Unfortunately, even with both of us helping, your mom didn't have the strength to get off the bed. Wore her right out."

We circle around our sleeping mother, none of us daring to ask what happens next. Mom looks so old. Mottled with age spots, bruises, and bulging blue veins, her crepey skin seems to be melting off her bones, hanging in loose folds on her small frame. Her fingers, bent and crooked from years of untreated rheumatoid arthritis, grip the edge of the tray table as if she's trying to keep it from rolling away. Underneath the hospital gown, her once ample bosom lies flat, like a child's.

"What happens next?" Sal asks, and we all look over at Jenny.

"Well, as much as I don't want to put her through it," she says as she glances over at Mom with a sorry smile, "I'm afraid we're going to have to go in and remove the blockage manually, so it doesn't cause more problems."

My heart sinks. I can't even think how painful that's going to be. But there's no way around it, so once again Sal, Lib, and I exit the room, leaving Jenny and Mom alone to do what needs to be done.

Though it hasn't even been a week since Mom fell, I feel like I've been in Ohio forever. It's as if I'm in some kind of bubble where time moves in circles, and it's hard to remember that time is still moving forward outside the bubble. And even when I do remember, I don't care. Every ounce of my energy is so focused on Mom and her well-being there simply isn't much left for anything or anyone else. Not my life in Connecticut. Not even John.

God, how many times in the past few years have I dropped everything to fly out to Ohio to take care of my mother? Yet he's never complained, never once made me feel, even for a second, that I shouldn't go. We've had a more traditional marriage than many in our generation, so things like cooking, cleaning, laundry, and grocery shopping are in my wheelhouse, not his. When we bought our first house, we literally divided chores into 'Girl Jobs' and 'Boy Jobs'—John taking charge of house maintenance, along with the yard work and landscaping, while I handled the more domestic things. In the early days, when we were both working, we took turns cooking and doing dishes. We'd even make weekend trips to the grocery store together. But once we started a family and I became a full-time mom, meal planning and kitchen duties became my department, and they've been so ever since.

So John's life changes quite a bit when I'm not there and, under normal circumstances, I feel guilty leaving him to fend for himself, even for a couple of days. Not this time, though. Right now there's no room in my hospice bubble for even the slightest bit of guilt or worry for anyone but

Mom, and thankfully John understands. I suppose it helps that we're at a stage of life where he's more able to step in: he's traveling less for work, and our three children are grown and out on their own.

"Stay as long as you need to, Peg," he always tells me at the end of our calls. "Don't worry about me. I'm fine."

I'm grateful for his support. I'm grateful for all the support I'm getting from everyone on the outside. But the thing is, I don't like getting pulled out of the bubble. More often than not, when my phone rings I find myself letting calls go straight to voicemail, or sending a quick text: *'Sorry! Can't talk now! I'll call later!"*

It's exhausting trying to explain what's going on *inside* the bubble to someone not in it. Even the simplest question like "How are you doing, Peg?" saps the strength right out of me.

"Oh, I'm doing okay. Hanging in there," I'll answer, trying to sound strong.

But what I *want* to say, and what takes a lot of my energy *not* to say, is: *"Are you f...ing kidding me? How do you think I'm doing? My mother is dying and it's horrible! I can't bear another day of this. But if there* isn't *another day of this then that means my mom will be dead, and I can't bear that either. I don't want to talk to you. I don't want to talk to anyone. Please just leave me alone."*

I'd give anything to not be in this bubble, but here I am. And I'm finding it takes much less effort to stay inside its confines with people who understand what's going on. Like my sisters. And the nurses and aides. Even the other family members who I exchange sad smiles with when we pass in the hall. None of them need to ask me how I'm doing. They just know.

Day Nine

The world outside continues to spin, though, and it doesn't make sense anymore for Sal, Lib, and me to all be here at the same time. Mom's rally seems to be holding, and having no way of knowing how long it will last, we decide to start taking turns.

Mom's eighty-ninth birthday is next week, so Sal and I decide to stay through rather than deal with the hassle of airline changes. Lib, on the other hand, has an important doctor's appointment with Henry she needs to get back for, so she makes plans to leave the next day, hard as it will be for her to go.

And it *is* hard. Not just for Lib, who has to say goodbye to Mom for what might be the last time, but for me *watching* her say goodbye. I can't believe how strong she is, perched on the side of the bed, holding Mom's hand, smiling and chatting like it's just another day. Like her heart isn't breaking, which I know it must be, because mine is.

Mom is so real, so *there*—her body still solid and tangible, despite its fragility. How is it possible Libby may never see her again? That between now and when she comes back Mom could be gone, her bed empty, her body—what? What will happen to her body when she dies? A wave of panic washes over me as an image of Mom being fed into a crematorium oven flashes through my mind.

Peggy, stop, I admonish myself, shaking my head to dispel the morbid scene. I know deep down Mom won't be in her body after she dies—that the part of her that makes her *Mom* will be swirling around us safe and sound, finally free of her physical self. But still—a shadow of doubt is hovering around the edges of my certainty and it frightens me.

When my dad died, I didn't go to the funeral home with Sal and Lib to see him. They tried to talk me into it, telling me I might regret not going, that it would help bring me closure. But I couldn't do it. Though his sudden death made dying a little less scary to me, I wasn't ready to come face to face with its physical reality by seeing his lifeless body on a table in a morgue. I wanted to remember him alive.

So the first time I saw the dead body of someone I loved, it wasn't actually a person. It was our dog, Nitro, who died a couple of years after Dad.

The vet, who had come out to the waiting room to break the news, asked if I'd like a moment alone with him. John was out of town on business and I was there on my own, so I wasn't sure I really did. But not knowing how to say no, I let myself be led into the examining room where, on a stark, metal table, lay our beautiful, dead Labrador.

"Oh, Nitro," I whispered, resting my hand on his big black head. His stillness was startling, and it was instantly clear to me that Nitro, at least the part of him that *made* him Nitro, wasn't there anymore. I was patting an empty shell, one that happened to be in the shape of a ninety-five-pound Labrador Retriever.

Well, this is silly, I thought, *this isn't Nitro.* I patted his head one more time and turned away, confident that I wasn't leaving my beloved dog behind. I wasn't quite sure *where* he was, but I was very sure he was no longer on that examining table.

Nitro's physical absence in the days that followed was palpable, and it took quite some time for the hole he left to fill back up. I hadn't realized until he *wasn't* there, how much he had *been* there. Always right behind me, following my every move, no matter where I was going—the bathroom, the basement, the laundry, the car.

Nitro's absence was much louder than his presence had ever been and it scares me to think, contemplating my mother's death, how deafening hers is going to be.

Later that evening, after Lib leaves and Sal heads back to the apartment, I'm walking down the empty corridor to check on Mom one last time, when I notice movement at the end of the hall. A stretcher is being pulled from Mr. D's room, and it takes me a moment to register what is happening. Mr. D. must have died, I realize with a start, and they're taking his body away. Watching the solemn procession head towards me, I'm not sure what to do, and I stand paralyzed, scared to draw attention to myself. As they draw closer, I press against the wall to let them pass, trying hard not to stare, but unable to tear my eyes away.

The body bag, dark and stiff, is secured to the stretcher with wide straps, their ends tucked neatly in place. Four attendants, one in front and three in back, are all dressed in dark suits, their focus intent on the task at hand. They pass by as if I'm not there, the soft swoosh of stretcher wheels on the wood floor the only sound in the quiet hush of the corridor. I watch, unmoving, until they disappear around the corner, not quite believing what I've just witnessed. It's like this hospice corridor has special powers to put in my path the exact thing that will help me feel better about whatever has been worrying me.

Seeing firsthand the dignity and respect Mr. D. was afforded, even in death, with no family around to make sure that he was, is as reassuring as it is comforting, and it eases my fear. Mom will be taken care of here. She'll be okay.

Day Twelve

A couple of days later, I wake up with a feeling of despair so heavy and thick I can't make myself get out of bed. Staring out the window at another gray, overcast March day, I wonder how in the world I'm going to get through it.

It's like I'm living in some morbid version of the movie *Groundhog Day*, where each day is the exact same as the one before, and the only way to break the endless pattern is, unbearably, for my mother to die.

Which, of course, I dread happening, even as I long for it, too.

Every night I put the phone on my bedside table, praying it will ring, while in the same breath praying that it won't. And every morning, when I realize it hasn't rung, my heart lifts and sinks at the same time. The good me, the daughter who is grateful for every minute she gets to spend with her dying mother, says to herself, "*Okay, well, even though I can't believe Mom made it through another night, I guess I'll just be thankful for another day with her."*

But then there's the not-so-good-me, the daughter who is overwhelmed and filled with self-pity, who is groaning, *"Oh my god...I can't believe Mom made it through another night! I'm not sure I can bear another day of this."*

The two me's are in a constant state of conflict. Where one is accepting, the other is despondent. Where one feels grateful, the other feels guilty. One is content to sit with Mom for hours, the other is restless and antsy. Most of all, there's the me who is scared Mom will die, and the me who is equally scared that she won't.

It's horrible. And as I lie in bed wallowing in self-pity, I feel horrible for thinking that it's horrible.

But the thing is, walking into hospice every morning *is* horrible.

First of all, the main entrance door is incredibly hard to open, at least for me. I dread going through it. Especially early in the morning when I have my computer bag on my shoulder and a cup of coffee in my hand, having to *pull* the heavy, wooden door open *toward* me is aggravating.

Whoever designed it this way? I grumble as I struggle to maneuver my way through without banging my shin or spilling my coffee.

Then, once I've managed to get inside, I have to face the receptionist behind the front desk. She's very kind, always greeting me with a warm, albeit sad, smile, as she wishes me a good morning in her hushed, hospice-y voice. Early on we exchanged pleasant small talk as I signed my name in the guest log, but as the days have started to pile up on each other, I find myself hoping she might be on the phone or away from the desk so I don't have to talk to her.

I'm so weary. So tired of smiling and being upbeat. Of making small talk with the same person, no matter how nice she is, day after day. I've found it's easier *not* to talk, awkward and unfriendly as that feels, so I've started to keep my eyes lowered as I scrawl my name in the book, shooting her a quick, apologetic smile as I hurry past the desk.

The worst part, though, and the thing I dread more than anything, is walking down the hall to Mom's room for the first time every day.

The morning after she was admitted I'd gotten there early, before the 8:00 a.m. shift change, and halfway down the corridor I noticed an empty bed in a room I was certain had been occupied when I'd left the night before. For a moment I was confused—had the person been moved to a different room? Then it dawned on me that no, of course they hadn't been moved. What was I thinking? The person had obviously died. This was hospice. That's what people came here to do.

But still, that empty bed gave me pause. At some point, in the middle of the night, the person who had been in that room just hours before had taken their last breath, and just like that, they were gone. They had been, and now they weren't.

The bed was neatly made, the sheets and blankets tucked in tightly, the pillowcase crisp and smooth. The nightstand was free of clutter, the tray table carefully pushed in at the end of the bed. There was a faint odor of disinfectant, not unpleasant, but different from any-thing I had noticed the day before. The nameplate was empty.

And so it's been almost every morning since then— one empty bed after another. I dread seeing them. I dread their reminder that death is hovering in every corner, and one day it will be my mom's bed that's empty.

Sal pokes her head in the door and, seeing me still in bed, stands at the end of it peering at me.

"Everything okay?" she asks, "You don't look so good."

I shake my head, tears spilling out the corners of my eyes.

"I'm just so tired," I whisper. "And I feel like a terrible daughter for wanting this to be over." Putting my head in my hands, I let myself cry.

"It's okay, it's okay," Sal murmurs, rubbing my back. "Don't feel bad, Peg...this is really hard!"

She sits next to me until my tears finally run dry. I'm grateful for her quiet presence and willingness to let me be sad without trying to fix it. Sitting up, I blow my nose and give her a wan smile. "I think I'm okay now...thank you. I feel better."

"Are you good to go over still? I can reschedule my call if you're not."

After Lib left, Sal and I have been tag-teaming whenever we can in order to give each other little breaks. Often, I'll take the early shift because Sal, unlike me, has a full-time job, and the mornings are a good time for her to make phone calls and catch up on emails.

"No, no—I'm fine. I can go," I assure her, pulling myself off the bed.

Getting dressed a few minutes later, I remember reading once in a self-help book that a good way to shift your perspective on something that you *have* to do, is to tell yourself that you *get* to do it, instead. So as I gather my things together to go spend another day with my dying mother, I decide to try it.

"It's not that I *have* to go see Mom today," I remind myself as I make my way to the elevator. "I *get* to go see her."

And that simple shift in mindset makes all the difference, lifting my spirits and allowing me to be grateful that I get to spend at least one more day with my mom.

∾

Later that afternoon, as Mom is dozing and I'm reading in a chair next to her bed, an unfamiliar woman pokes her head through the door.

"Oh, hello," she says when she sees me, her voice loud, slicing the quiet hush in the room like a knife. I'm immediately annoyed, wanting to shush her so she won't wake Mom, but she continues, seeming oblivious to my sleeping mother. "I'm Rita, one of the chaplains here. Just wanted to pop in to introduce myself and see if your mom might like to chat."

The other day, Jenny, our favorite nurse, had suggested that talking to a chaplain might be helpful to Mom and thought Rita, this woman, would be a good fit. We hadn't had a chance yet to run the idea by Mom, so I'm surprised she would come before getting the okay from us—it feels presumptuous. Rita's whole demeanor is, in fact, a little off-putting. Middle-aged with frizzy, dark blonde hair, she's dressed in varying shades of loose-fitting beige clothing that look more like pajamas than work attire. There's an edge to her presence I find invasive, and my guard goes up.

"Um, I'm not so sure this is the best time…" I start to say, but then Mom's eyes blink open. She looks at me, then over at Rita, who's now standing next to the bed.

"Oh, hey Mom," I smile when she turns back toward me. "This is Rita, a chaplain here. Jenny thought you might like to talk with her. What do you think?"

Mom peers at the chaplain, her cloudy, blue eyes sharper than usual. "Yes," she murmurs, nodding. "I think I would. How nice."

"So lovely to meet you, Kay." Rita pulls a chair up next to Mom and looks at me over her wire-rimmed glasses. "We'll be fine," she says in a pleasant, yet dismissive, tone.

"Oh, okay…" I stand up, not wanting to leave Mom alone, but not sure how to stay without being awkward. Picking up my book and phone, I lean over to kiss the top of Mom's head. "So I'll just be out in the sun room then—if you need me."

Pausing outside the door, I hesitate before pulling it closed, my urge to eavesdrop almost getting the better of me. But my higher self prevails and, letting the door click closed behind me, I wander into the sun room, hoping wherever their conversation might go, it will be helpful to Mom. I'm happy she wants to talk to someone—even if that someone rubbed me the wrong way—as she's been ministerless ever since she gave up going to church two years ago.

It's still inconceivable to me that she left St. Timothy's, the small episcopal church a few blocks from where we grew up—she was a part of its congregation for almost sixty years. St. Tim's was a mainstay in our family's life. Sunday School, confirmations, weddings and funerals, its walls are filled with so many memories it's like being with an old friend whenever I'm sitting in its familiar wooden pews. Snippets of past moments are etched in my mind; singing a solo in the annual Christmas pageant, my eleven-year-old heart racing as my turn got closer and closer; waiting in the narthex with Dad on my wedding day, his hand squeezing mine as we start our walk down the aisle; standing with Sal and Lib in front of a packed congregation reading a poem at Dad's memorial service, looking out on the sea of familiar faces in front of me, trying not to cry.

But as is true with many other small churches, St. Timothy's has gone through a bit of a downturn in the past few years, the once vibrant and growing congregation dwindling to the point where it's hard to find, and keep, a good minister. But through all its troubled times, Mom never gave up on St. Tim's, always staying positive and making an effort to get to know all the ministers who came through, even those who were just temporary. Often when I'd visit, she'd insist on stopping by the church to introduce me to the latest prospect, ever hopeful, I think, that they'd finally found the right one. I could never keep track of them, though, their names and faces forgotten as soon as I'd met them. All of them, that is, except for one—John Johannsen—an interim minister I met a few years ago when I was visiting Mom for Mother's Day.

Though Mom usually went to the shorter eight o'clock service, that particular Sunday we went to the later one at ten so we could go directly from church to brunch with friends. A little bored, I was staring out the stained-glass window, reminiscing about this or that, when Reverend Johannsen—a tall, handsome, white-haired gentleman—took to the pulpit to give his sermon, his deep, friendly voice catching my wandering mind's attention, pulling me away from my memories and back into the present.

He was talking to the congregation like we were his friends, regaling us with stories about mothers and the love they carry for their children, both in life and in death. He spoke of Mary's love for Jesus, and of his own mother's love for him and how, though she'd recently passed, he could still feel that love all around him. Sitting next to my own aging mother, it seemed he was speaking directly to me, and I was grateful for his reassuring words.

Reverend Johannsen's whole message that morning was so pure and simple—so *real*—it resonated with me for days afterward, so much so that I tracked down his email address and sent him a thank you note. There was just something about him, a familiarity so comforting it was as though I knew him, though we'd never met. A couple of months later, I saw him again when he came to visit Mom in the hospital after her fall down the stairs, and I felt the same rush of familiarity when he walked into the room. I think Mom felt it, too.

But sadly, he was an interim minister and disappeared from our lives as soon as St. Tim's found a permanent replacement. Mom didn't like the new one from the start, telling us when we pressed her for a reason that he was just too forward.

"He *hugged* me," she complained after she met him for the first time. "In the middle of the aisle, for heaven's sake."

"But Mom," we laughed, thinking she was being a bit dramatic, "is that really so bad? Maybe you should give him another chance?"

To her credit, she did try a couple more times, but things only got worse.

"He's just too showy for my taste," she sniffed, digging in her heels. "I don't go to church to be entertained."

It seemed crazy to us that Mom would give up St. Timothy's so easily, especially at her stage of life when, well—she might need a church and a minister in the not-so-distant future. Or her daughters might. But there was no arguing with her. Mom had made up her mind, and that was that. No more church. She never went to St. Tim's again.

The new minister did reach out when he heard Mom was in hospice, but she just shook her head when we suggested it might be nice to have him visit. "I don't think so," she murmured. "It wouldn't feel right."

"Maybe we could ask Reverend Johannsen to visit?"

I wondered out loud, feeling the need myself for some spiritual bolstering those first few days of hospice. "I think I still have his email address—I could send him a note."

"Yes, I think I'd like that," Mom agreed, so I went ahead and sent him an email explaining the situation. Within the hour Reverend Johannsen replied, saying he would be in the area on Sunday, the next day, and would be happy to stop by.

His visit was mostly a blur—it felt so final having a minister sitting by Mom's bedside, like she was receiving last rites, or at least what I imagined receiving last rites must be like, and part of my brain shut down. Listening to the reverend's prayers, I felt a certain detachment, like I was an extra on a movie set with no real role except to be in the room. It was calming, though, and nice to have the diversion of a visitor on that quiet Sunday afternoon. Since arriving at hospice, Mom has steadfastly refused to let any of her friends come by to visit, though they've all tried.

"Can't I just stop in for a minute?" they beg. "I just want to give her a hug."

"We're so sorry, we wish we could say yes," we tell them, sympathizing with their frustration.

We'd give anything for Mom to want to see them, if only to break up the monotony of the day for *us*. "Mom's just not up for visitors right now. We'll tell her you asked, though—maybe she'll feel up to it another day."

One of her more determined friends refused to take no for an answer and came by anyway, hovering outside Mom's room, trying to catch one of our eyes. Volunteering to be the bad guy, I jumped up and stepped to the doorway, blocking Mom from her curious gaze.

"I know you said no visitors," she said in a guilty whisper, smiling down at her feet like a naughty child, "but I was just driving by and thought I would take a chance."

"I'm so sorry—Mom just isn't up to visitors." Seeing her face fall, I could commiserate. How hard it must be to know your good friend is dying, and you can't say goodbye. But we have to trust Mom has her reasons, hard as it is to keep saying no to the people she's been friends with for so many years.

Stepping out into the corridor, I gave her a hug. "Want to go sit for a minute?" I offered, motioning to the sun room. She nodded, relief filling her eyes. I wasn't Mom, but I suppose I was the next best thing.

According to the hospice pamphlet we'd been given when we arrived—*What To Expect: Understanding The Last Months of Life*—it seems that one of the first signs death may be nearing is a 'withdrawal from people and activities,' something we had begun to notice with Mom in the months leading up to her fall. Maybe she had some kind of inner knowing that her life was nearing its end and was intuitively beginning to prepare for it. Perhaps her withdrawal from the people and things she enjoyed, like going to church, was her body's way of conserving its strength for the task ahead.

Because dying, we're learning, can take quite a bit of energy.

Okay, I think, glancing at my watch for the hundredth time as I've sat in the sun room waiting for the chaplain to come out, *forty-five minutes is long enough. What can they possibly be talking about for so long?* I gather up my things and head back to Mom's room, peeking around the door before going in. But Mom's alone, asleep again, with no sign of Rita.

I'm surprised and annoyed that the chaplain hadn't come to find me before she left—it would have been nice to know how she thinks Mom's doing. *I suppose it's how it should be, though,* I reason with myself. *I don't need to know everything, right?*

But still, as I settle back into the recliner to wait for Sal to come relieve me, I wish I knew just a little.

Day Thirteen

The morning before Mom's birthday, a howling wind wakes me up before dawn and, unable to fall back to sleep—high winds always put me on edge— I head over to hospice early. Leaving Sal a note on the kitchen counter, I slip out the apartment door, closing it carefully so as not to wake her.

There's something about being up before everyone else I've always loved. Padding around a shadowy house in the early morning hush, watching the sky lighten from dark gray to silver. Walking outside to get the newspaper, the bird calls sharp and distinct in the stillness. I especially love driving in the early morning on the empty roads, the houses dark and silent as I pass by. It's like having the world to myself.

But this morning, as I hurry through the empty lobby and out to the car, the world feels unsettled. The dark sky seems ominous, the bird calls like warnings. Tree branches are bending and rattling in the gusty wind, and I worry Libby will have trouble flying in later that afternoon.

The front door is locked when I get to hospice, and I'm not sure what to do—it's never been locked before. Should I knock? Call the front desk? Looking around for a sign with instructions, I notice an intercom box on the brick wall a few feet away. Pushing the button, I stand back, but nothing happens. Should I press it again?

Before I can decide, the intercom crackles. "Can I help you?" a distant voice inquires.

"Um, yes. I'm here to see my mom? Kay Ball? In room 102?" A big gust of wind pushes against my back and I have to brace my legs to keep from falling forward.

"Who?" asks the staticky voice. Whoever it is on the other end—a nurse I suppose, or maybe an aide—sounds harried, distracted.

"Kay Ball?" I repeat, a little louder. "In room 102? I'm her daughter."

"Please wait inside at the front desk," the voice instructs, and with a loud click the buzzer sounds. Hurrying to pull the heavy door open, I struggle with its weight even more than usual in the blustery wind.

Inside, I wait near the empty receptionist desk in the dimly lit front hall, a little put off by the nurse's brusque tone. In the week that Mom's been here I haven't encountered one person who's been anything but kind and patient. Well, except maybe that chaplain, and the two la-dies behind the counter in the cafeteria—they're often a bit grumpy, rarely smiling or engaging in small talk, though I try to be friendly. I suppose it's not much fun to be a cook in a hospice facility, where no one's too interested in food. But still.

A few minutes go by with no one coming to get me, and I start to get impatient. *Maybe it's been a hard night,* I reason with myself. *Maybe a lot of people died and they've been super busy.*

But as a few more minutes tick by and still no one appears, my impatience blooms into self-righteous in-dignation. *How can they make me wait like this?* I start to fume. *What if I had to get to work and this was the only time all day I had to visit?*

Irritation on behalf of my non-existent working self gets the better of me, and I head down the hall in a huff. Rounding the corner to the nurse's station, a smiling aide is hurrying toward me, raising her hand in a little half-wave when she recognizes me.

"Oh, it's *you!*" she exclaims, turning back to walk with me. "We couldn't hear very well through the inter-com, so weren't sure who we were letting in! Sorry to keep you waiting! It's been one of those nights!"

"That's okay, no worries." I return her smile, my indignant self instantly appeased by her warm greeting. "I figured you might all be busy. Do you know how Mom's night was?"

"Pretty quiet," she assures me. "She's such a gem, your mother. I have to tell you, we all really love her." The aide—Kelly? Sandy? Tracy? they're all starting to blur together—stops outside the nurses' station and plops herself down in front of the computer.

"Let me know if you need anything," she says, picking up a folder. "I'm here until seven".

I want to ask a few more questions—did Mom wake up at all during the night? Did she need any extra pain medication? But Kelly/Sandy/Tracy is already typing away, her attention intent on the screen.

I'm not sure what to do. It's never been my nature to be pushy, or expect someone to drop what they're doing because of me, but ever since Mom's been in hospice, it seems that's exactly what I do expect. If my mother's in pain, I want her to have pain medication, *now*. If she's hungry, I want her to get food *now*. And if I have questions, I want them answered, not later, but *now*. I don't want to wait. Not for anything. Like a petulant three-year-old, I want what I want when I want it.

But as much as I'd like to stomp my foot to get the aide's attention back on *me*, I can see she really is trying to get something done, so I decide to let it go. Turning away, albeit reluctantly, I head down to Mom's room.

Her door is slightly ajar and I push it open slowly, nervous to walk in and find her, well—dead. It's been an ever-present fear this past week, one that I have to tamp down whenever I walk into her room alone. Somehow, even though I want more than anything for her to slip away peacefully in her sleep, I don't want to be the one to find her. The week before, when I thought she had died in her recliner and had to check for a pulse, there had been a space between the not knowing and the knowing that I never want to experience again. If I can't be with Mom when she dies, I'd rather find out afterward, from someone else.

Pausing to let my eyes adjust to the dim light, I tiptoe over to the bed. Mom is sleeping, her eyes squeezed closed, her chest rising and falling under the blanket with each labored breath. Her head is turned toward the windows, as if maybe she'd been looking out when she'd drifted to sleep. My heart pinches to think of her staring into the dark sky, alone.

Except that, wait—she couldn't have been looking out because the window blinds are closed, *again*, despite our repeated requests to keep them open. It's not that we're trying to be difficult, but Mom loves having the blinds up, even at night, so she can see out. She always has. But no matter how many times we've asked, and we've asked *a lot*, the blinds are always closed when we arrive in the morning.

Making my way around the bed, I pull them up slowly, one at a time, so as not to wake Mom. The world outside is still in shadows, the pre-dawn light diffusing the room in a soft gray tinge. Even so, this is what we want Mom to be able to see, whenever she wants to look. It may just be trees and sky from her vantage point, and at times, like right now, they may be shrouded in darkness, but that doesn't matter. What *does* matter is Mom feeling like she's still part of something bigger than the four walls of this hospice room.

It's amazing to me how our world starts out so tiny when we're born, then gets bigger and bigger as we grow, until, if we live long enough, it shrinks again.

I remember watching this happen with one of our dogs as he aged. When Rip was young, we took him on long walks in the woods behind our house, never able to tire him out no matter how far we went. As the years passed, the walks became shorter and shorter, until one day he couldn't make it down the hill to the woods anymore, so we walked him around our yard, until he couldn't do that either. Then it was half the yard. Then just around the house. Smaller and smaller Rip's world got, until the day he couldn't even make it off his bed, and we had to put him to sleep.

The same thing has happened to Mom. First, she gave up traveling to other countries, something she enjoyed doing with Dad when he was alive, and later with a group of friends. She'd been all over the globe—England, Africa, China, Turkey, Chile, Egypt, Israel—her world ever expanding until the effort became too much. Next, she gave up driving herself to Maine, and with it the independence of coming and going on her own schedule. Then she gave up driving, period. Not long after that she moved into the small apartment in Sunrise Crest, and now here she is, in a world the size of a hospital bed and a twenty-foot square hospice room.

So if we have to ask a hundred times a day that Mom's window blinds be kept open, we'll do that for her. Because it's hard to watch the world of someone you love grow smaller and smaller, spiraling in on itself until there's nowhere left for them to go.

∞

I'm settling into the recliner when Mom's eyes flutter open. She stares out the window for a moment before turning her head toward the clock on the opposite wall.

"Hey, Mom," I murmur, not wanting to startle her. Moving to the side of the bed, I give her a gentle kiss on her forehead.

"Is it morning?" she asks, her voice fuzzy and thick from sleep.

"It is. Still early though–just past six." Her nasal cannula is a little askew, so I reposition it on her nose, pulling the tubing from underneath the pillow to give it some slack. Smoothing her hair off her brow, I try to be careful not to disturb the staples still in her head.

"Thank you," she murmurs, her eyes drifting closed again. "I love you."

"I love you, too, Mom."

"I'm sorry it's taking me so long to die."

My breath catches, and for a second I'm not sure if I should laugh or cry. It's so typical Mom not to want to be a bother, I want to do both.

"Oh, Mom, no...don't say that!" I sit down on the edge of the bed and rub her arm. "It's just not time. Maybe you're not ready to go."

A small, wistful smile crosses her lips, though her eyes remain closed.

"Maybe," she murmurs. "But I don't think so."

Waiting a few breaths to see if she says anything more, I wonder if there's anything more *I* should say. But Mom stays quiet, her face relaxing back into sleep, so I stay quiet, too.

∾

As Mom sleeps, I sit by her side and watch the world out the window lighten with the rising sun. Tree branches are bowing low in the gusting wind, dead leaves whirling past the window in a frenzied dance, much like the thoughts in my head. I'm trying to think of something, anything, to make this easier for Mom. Easier for me.

But what more can we do? She's safe and comfortable—or as comfortable as round-the-clock nursing and morphine can make her. Mom had seemed so ready to let go in the hospital. She'd been so weak—in both body and spirit—it had seemed her death was imminent, any moment away.

But now here we are, a whole week later, and though she still seems to be ready, her heart isn't getting the cue, continuing to beat away despite what her head might be telling it.

Unless, and this makes my own heart skip a few beats, what if we misread the situation in the hospital? What if Sal, Lib, and I were so tired ourselves we gave up on Mom too soon, and the reason she isn't dying is because she really isn't ready? What if we should have tried harder to get her into skilled nursing somewhere? What if we were wrong and she shouldn't be in hospice at all?

Hold on, Peggy, I chide myself, reining in my spiraling worries. *Stop second guessing. Remember she* couldn't *go to skilled nursing because they couldn't manage her oxygen. And remember how tired she was in the hospital, and how ready she seemed to die. You did the right thing. She's in the right place.*

I look down at Mom's sleeping face, gaunt and pale. Her mouth hangs slightly open, lips chapped and peeling, her labored breath stale and musty. I reach for the tube of lip balm on the tray table next to the bed, and my eyes fall on the picture of Dad we'd brought from her apartment. His pale blue eyes stare out at me from behind the frame, and I remember the sign I'd seen on the way to the hospital the week before. *That was no coincidence,* I remind myself, relief flooding through me the same way it had when I'd seen the hospice ad flash on the billboard that morning. *That was real. That was Dad telling me we were making the right decision.*

I didn't expect it to be like this, though. And I'm pretty sure Mom didn't expect it to be like this, either. In fact, if I know my mother, she probably thought it would be like that of her close friend, Tibble, who passed away from ALS in this same facility the year before. Tibble had made the decision to move here, and a few days later she was gone. It was the same with her other friends Carol and Toni. No lengthy, drawn out deaths for any of them—once they made the decision to move to hospice, that was that.

Maybe that's why Mom feels like it's taking so long, I muse, smiling to myself that my rather competitive mother is worrying because she isn't dying as speedily as her friends had. *Oh, Mom.* I lean over and kiss the top of her head.

Everyone dies so differently, I think, standing up to stretch my legs. I try to decide if it would be better to go quickly, like my dad, without the chance to say goodbye, or more slowly, like Mom, with so much opportunity for closure.

When our dog Nitro got sick the first time, the vet was able to drain the fluid that had built up around his heart, but warned us that it would fill up again and there wouldn't be anything more he could do when it did. He gave Nitro about two months and sent us home.

It was the hardest and best two months ever. Nitro, who had been raised as a hunting dog and had never, *ever* been allowed up on a couch or a bed, suddenly had free reign to do just about anything. He'd sit on the couch and watch television with the kids, their arms wrapped around his ninety-five-pound body as tight as he would allow. Where we used to sneak him tidbits from the dinner table, we were tossing them to him openly, trying to make the time he had left joyful and happy. We showered him with attention, bracing ourselves for the end.

When he died a couple of months later, we were devastated, but knew deep down we'd done everything we could to make sure he knew how much we loved him.

When our dog, Cassie, died, though, it was quite a different situation. Fast as a bullet, and with energy to spare, she had a buoyant spirit that I found hard to resist. She was kind of a pain, but an enthusiastic pain. I loved her a lot.

One early summer evening, I let Cassie and Rip, our older lab, out into the yard one last time before heading to bed. As usual, Cassie shot out the front door like a rocket, Rip a little more sedately, and seconds later I heard a yelp.

"Cassie?" I called, walking into the yard trying to spot her black shape in the dusky twilight. A movement over to my left caught my eye and I saw a giant buck loping toward the field below our house. "Cassie? Ripper?" I called again, my heart starting to thud.

Rip trotted around from the other side of the house, so I walked out toward where I thought I'd heard the cry, and found Cassie lying on the grass, making a horrible choking sound, her eyes wide with panic. I yelled for Bill and Jack who were inside—John was out of town on business—and ran to get the car to take her to the emergency vet. By the time I got back to her, though, Cassie was dead.

We'll never know for sure, but we think when she flew out the door, Cassie surprised the buck—who was most likely eating apples under one of our apple trees— and he reared up, his hoof kicking Cassie in her throat, breaking her neck.

Cassie's death was sudden and shocking. No chance to say goodbye, no chance to tell her how much we loved her. She was there, and then she was gone. We were traumatized for weeks.

Staring down at Mom, I imagine most people, if given a choice, would want to die quickly, even if it's painful, rather than linger on for days, knowing the end is coming. The scared me—the me who, despite all my spiritual bravado, is still a little frightened of being sucked into a deep, dark nothing—would certainly want to go fast so I wouldn't have to face the reality of my own mortality day after day. That would be unnerving. But the brave me—the me who believes that death isn't an ending—might welcome the experience of knowing I was going to die. How better to test my faith? How better to put into perspective the things that really matter in life? To have the chance to tell my family I love them one more time? Or a thousand more times, if I'm anything like Mom. She can't tell us she loves us enough.

The reverberating whir of the medicine cart being unlocked outside Mom's door interrupts my thoughts. Like clockwork, the hum of its locked drawer being opened and closed echoes up and down the corridor as the nurses make their rounds every four hours—eight, twelve, four, eight, twelve—day and night. On Mom's good days, rally days, I hardly notice it, often surprised it's been four hours when the nurse comes through the door.

But on the not-so-good-days, the days when Mom is restless and agitated between her scheduled doses, when her pain, so elusive it is sometimes hard for her to pinpoint, will break through in the oddest places—shoulder, heel, elbow, back—I sit by her side and listen impatiently for the reassuring sound of the cart, jumping up every few minutes to stick my head out the door to see where it is.

The last couple of days, Mom has made it from one dose to the next without much issue which, under normal circumstances, we would be happy about. But it seems, according to the social worker who we'd met with soon after Mom was admitted, Medicare will only cover the full amount of her care if the doctors need to 'adjust' her medications on a regular basis to keep her comfortable.

"So if your Mom is stable," the pert, dark-haired social worker had explained, sitting across from my sisters and me in the sun room, "and no adjustments are made to her medications for a certain number of days, then Medicare would require that she go from Level 1 to Level 2 care."

"What's the difference between the levels?" Libby had asked as we'd all looked at each other in surprise. No one had mentioned this to us before. Of course, in their defense, I don't think anyone expected Mom would last another day, let alone another week.

"Well, in Level 1 the nurse-to-patient ratio is much smaller, and Medicare covers it all," the social worker explained. "In Level 2, the ratio is a bit higher, and though the hospice care is covered, the same way it would be if your mom was at home, room and board here would have to be paid for privately."

"And how much would that be?" Libby pressed, glancing over at Sal and me with a look of concern. As CFO of our little team, I could almost hear her internal calculator clicking away.

"It averages about $285 per day for the room and board," the social worker admitted. "But it's all very fluid," she went on to assure us. "If your Mom started to go downhill again, then she'd go back to Level 1 and Medicare would kick back in."

"How long do people usually stay at Level 2?" I wondered out loud, remembering an elderly woman I'd visited as a hospice volunteer who was stable, though unresponsive, for several months. Week after week I would go to her house on my appointed day and sit by her hospital bed in the middle of her dim, musty dining room, wondering what in the world was keeping her tethered to life. She had no family, as far as I could tell, and except for the caregiver who disappeared up the stairs as soon as I walked in the door, she was alone. It was so sad. So seemingly pointless.

Unless, of course, there was some purpose in her lingering death, some metaphysical reason she was being held hostage in a body no longer fully viable. Maybe her soul was trying to learn something? A final lesson it needed to understand before she could let go? Patience, perhaps? Surrender? Acceptance? Maybe, despite it *looking* like she was lying there alone and without purpose, underneath the surface something spiritually profound was unfolding.

And maybe that's true for Mom, too. Though her situation is very different, surrounded as she is by three caring daughters in a comfortable, light-filled hospice room, perhaps her soul is working something out, and that's what's keeping her here. And if that's the case, who's to say how long it might take? If Mom's anything like my hospice patient, it could be months, and then what? We can't stay in Ohio indefinitely–can we?

A swell of panic swept through me at the thought of such an uncertain future.

"Well, I'm sure you understand it's different for each patient," the social worker's voice pulled me back into the sun room, and I glanced over at Sal and Lib, wondering if they were imagining the same worst-case scenario I was, with mom languishing in Level 2 for months on end.

"Can you explain how this decision is made?" Sal asked, pulling out the small notebook she always keeps in her bag to jot down medical notes. "Will someone let us know if Mom's being moved to Level 2?"

"Yes, of course," the social worker nodded. "The team meets on Mondays to go over patients' charts, and they'll let you know of any changes in the level of care."

"Okay," Sal made a note, then looked back up. "But just to make sure we understand—how often does Mom's medicine need to be adjusted in order to stay at Level 1? A couple of times a day? Every other day?"

"Again, the needs of our patients are all different, so it's hard to say for sure," the social worker replied, skirting Sal's questions as she glanced at her watch. "I'm sorry, I have another meeting to get to." Gathering her papers, she stood up. "But try not to worry too much about this—a lot can happen in a week."

The three of us watched her leave in silence, waiting until she disappeared around the corner before saying anything.

"Jesus!" I looked at Sal and Lib, shaking my head in disbelief. "What the heck? No one said a thing about Level 2 at the hospital! I had no idea!" Having been the one that met with the hospice liaison and helped Mom sign all the papers, I was worried I'd missed something in the fine print.

"It wouldn't have changed anything," Lib reassured me, "but we will definitely have to re-think some things if Mom goes to Level 2—that could get expensive."

"I think we should take this one step at a time," Sal interjected. "It's only Thursday. Let's see how the next couple of days go."

We started to watch Mom more closely after that, marching out to the nurses' station if we saw even the slightest hint she might be in pain. It felt counterintuitive—wanting Mom *not* to be stable—but at the same time we didn't want her to have to move, so we tried to play the game as best we could despite not being quite sure of the rules. Sometimes we were successful in getting her dosage 'adjusted,' but not always. Sometimes the nurse or aide would simply reposition her, using pillows to prop up Mom's arms or legs, depending on where the pain was.

"Is that better now?" they would ask, patiently moving things around until Mom nodded her head.

"Yes, thank you," she would whisper through her oxygen mask, her head relaxing back on the pillow. "That's better."

We were always happy they made Mom more comfortable, whatever they did, but the closer we got to the Monday meeting, the more worried we were getting. And not just about the expense of Level 2. The thought of moving Mom to a different room, with a different routine and nursing staff, overwhelmed us, and we knew it would overwhelm her as well. We'd only just gotten used to where she was.

So Monday morning, as Sal and I waited to meet with the doctor—Lib on standby in California to be conferenced in—I did a little research to see if it would be possible to get Mom to Connecticut, figuring if she was stable enough to move to Level 2, maybe she'd be stable enough to move somewhere else. John and I had discussed Mom coming to live with us a few times the past couple of years, most recently after her visit at Christmas when we'd noticed a subtle shift in her stamina. Normally anxious to be a part of whatever was going on, she seemed more content spending her day in our living room, reading the newspaper or dozing.

During that stay, we realized we had a perfect set up for her as the living room, which we rarely used, connects to the little bedroom and bath off the kitchen where Mom sleeps when she's with us. If she moved in, we could set it up with some of her things so she'd have her own space, and we would have ours. Not that either of us really wanted my aging mother living in our home full-time, but neither did we want her alone in a nursing home at the end of her life.

The first thing I searched for was an oxygen concentrator that could handle her significant need, and much to my surprise, found one we could buy for less than two thousand dollars—not cheap, but not as expensive as I'd thought it would be. Feeling a boost of optimism, I turned my search to long-distance ambulance services and found one in the local area that could take Mom from Ohio to Connecticut—with oxygen, a nurse, and room for one of us to go with her—for around four thousand dollars. Again, not cheap, but in the big scheme of things, considerably less than a lengthy stay in Level 2. And though I knew it was probably just a pipe dream, I felt a rush of adrenaline at having found a feasible alternative—a Plan B we could fall back on, if need be.

As it turned out, though, we wouldn't need it. Later that afternoon the doctor informed us that they'd be keeping Mom at Level 1—welcome news, though I must admit to a certain disappointment that my Plan B wouldn't be necessary.

Because Plan B meant action. Plan B meant a change of scene. Plan B meant I could go home.

The door opens and the nurse glides into the room, so softly I wouldn't have known she was there if I didn't see her. Making her way over to Mom, still fast asleep, she spots me on the recliner in the corner and smiles. "I'll be quick," she whispers. "Kay?" Her voice is soft, but firm as she touches Mom gently on the shoulder. "Sorry to wake you, dear—it's time for your medicine."

I look up at the clock and sigh—just past 8:00 a.m. It's going to be another long day.

Day Fourteen

Mom's eighty-ninth birthday dawns sunny and bright, a welcome reprieve from the gray March weather of the past few days. Mom is also brighter—eating a good breakfast and chatting away, happy to have Libby back and all three of her daughters in one place again. She even allows the aide to give her a sponge bath and change her gown, something she's refused more often than not so far.

It's a bittersweet day, made more so by the one gift we have for her—a photo album we'd put together to celebrate the upcoming hundredth year anniversary of our camp in Maine. The photo album is filled with old photographs from when the camp was first built up through the past summer when all eighteen of us had been there. It captures, we hope, the history of the place we all love so much.

Sitting on the edge of the bed, I turn the pages slowly so Mom can follow along as I read the poem I'd written to accompany the pictures, my fervent attempt to keep safe the treasure trove of stories we'd grown up hearing over the years. But even as my heart fills seeing how happy this gift is making her, it's also breaking knowing she won't ever be there again. In all of my fifty-nine years, I'd never been in Maine without my mom, and it's taking everything I have to keep down the lump of unshed tears throbbing in my throat as I turn page after page of family memories and imagine her not there.

The first time it sank in that there would, in fact, be a last summer in Maine for Mom, had been around eight years before. She was just eighty, still healthy and able to be there on her own for extended periods, but not able to do all the things necessary to open the camp for the season by herself. As the daughter living closest to Maine at the time, I volunteered to go with her for the first couple of days, something I hadn't done since I was a teenager.

I'd forgotten how fun it was to be with my mother going down the bumpy, rutted driveway for the first time since the summer before. Mom's excitement was palpable as she sat forward on the passenger seat anticipating the first glimpse of the camp as we rounded the bend—the cluster of white-shingled buildings vivid against the blue and green backdrop of river and woods. Pulling into the parking area, we grinned at each other like little kids, sitting for a moment as the sound from the tires on the loose gravel driveway echoed away in the late afternoon summer day.

"We made it!" I exclaimed, relieved to have the long drive from Bangor behind us, and eagerly opened the door, stepping out of the car and stretching my arms wide as if embracing a long-lost friend. Inhaling deeply, I savored my first breath of Maine air, a sweet mixture of fresh cut grass, saltwater and pine. "God, I love that smell," I sighed, joining Mom on the other side of the car. She smiled but didn't say anything as we made our way over the newly mowed lawn toward the camp. She walked much like a general inspecting her troops—arms crossed behind her back, eyes appraising the outbuildings and gardens for any damage the harsh Maine winter may have incurred.

Reaching the wide, stone steps leading down to the camp, Mom paused to look out at the river before carefully making her way down the stairs, one at a time. She paused again just outside the front door and leaned over the wood railing.

"Hello river!" she whispered down to the water below. "I made it back!"

Her words hung in the air and I realized, with a start, that when Mom left the past summer, she didn't know if she'd be back. Standing next to her, I took in the familiar vista and tried to imagine myself at Mom's age, not knowing from one year to the next if I would ever look out at it again. It was already hard enough to say goodbye when I had to leave—standing on the porch looking out at the view for the last time, I'm always amazed it will continue to exist without me there to see it.

It must be even harder for her, I realized, glancing sideways at her pensive profile. *And she's never let on.*

But that's my mom—stoic to the end. I recalled a few years before when I had, for the first time ever, stayed an extra week after all the kids had left. For ten whole days we'd had the entire family there—fourteen of us buzzing around each other like so many bees in a hive—always someone to talk to, or do something with. I was so sad when the last car drove away, the kids' sudden absence like a vacuum sucking up any remaining energy left in their wake, and I felt physically ill, nauseous, in fact, when I'd pass by their empty rooms.

"I know exactly what you mean," Mom reassured me when I'd tried to describe how I was feeling, "and it's no fun. But I told myself from the beginning that if I couldn't handle being sad when everyone left, then I just shouldn't come. Luckily it doesn't last long—it'll be better in a couple of days."

And she was right. A day or two later my sadness had dissipated and the void the kids had left was filled with a softer, calmer energy—not better or worse, just different. The camp, I came to learn that summer, has an uncanny ability to expand and contract as the family comes and goes, never feeling too small when we're all there, or too big when we're all not.

Mom turned to go inside, so I stepped ahead to push open the old wooden front door, somehow always sticky no matter how often we've tried to fix it. Following her in, we stood for a minute as our eyes adjusted to the dim light, taking in the large room before us. Like the Maine air, the camp has a certain smell when you first walk in—a nostalgic combination of old wood and mildew, with a trace of something sweet, like molasses. Everything was the same—hardly a piece of furniture changed since I was a little girl—and as we walked further into the room, I could sense the generations that had come before us rippling quietly through the rafters, welcoming us back into their warm fold.

I close the album and hand it to Mom, who holds it up to her chest and smiles, "It's perfect," she murmurs, her voice still weak despite her brighter spirits. "Thank you."

A soft tap on the door interrupts us, and we all turn to see Dora, one of Mom's dearest friends, smiling in from the doorway.

"I wanted to drop these off," she says, holding out a box of cupcakes. "I don't have to come in."

"Oh, you're so sweet," Lib says, jumping up to greet her. "Mom, look…cupcakes from Dora! Can she come and give you a quick birthday hug?"

Mom nods, smiling under her oxygen mask, so Lib ushers Dora into the room. "Don't tell anyone!" I whisper in her ear, half-joking, half-not as I give her a quick squeeze. God help us if word gets around town that Dora got to see Mom—we'll never hear the end of it from her other friends. Happy and relieved, though, that Mom wants her to stay, Sal, Lib, and I head to the sun room to give them some time alone, waiting until we see Mom's lunch coming down the hall to file back in. Dora has stuck a candle in one of the cupcakes and we all circle around Mom's bed—aides and nurses, too—and sing "Happy Birthday," another bittersweet moment in a bittersweet day.

So many last moments—last birthday, last birthday wish, last goodbye—it's no wonder Mom falls asleep almost the second Dora walks out the door. I can't begin to imagine how exhausting living so many last moments must be.

At first, we assume she's worn out from all the birthday activity, so we aren't too alarmed when Mom sleeps all afternoon. We aren't even that worried when we try to wake her for dinner and she only stirs enough to shake her head when we ask if she's hungry. Even when she still doesn't wake up when we kiss her goodbye before slipping out for our own dinner, we aren't too concerned, joking as we walk to the car that we hope her birthday party didn't kill her.

It's not until I pop back in after dinner to see who the night nurse is that my antenna starts to go up—she's still sound asleep and, again, doesn't stir a muscle when I whisper in her ear that I'm there.

Has she been asleep this whole time? I look around the room to see if there are any signs that she might have been awake while we were gone—an empty water cup, a crumpled tissue—but nothing seems to have changed since we left. Has anyone even been in to check on her? Fretting that she's been alone all this time, I glance at the clock. It's close to nine—someone must have been in to give her medication at eight, right? Curious to know if she'd woken up enough to take it, I poke my head out the door to see if I can find someone to ask for an update.

The hallway is busier than usual for this time of night, with many unfamiliar faces milling around what looks to be an empty nurses' station. Some sit in chairs talking in low voices, while others are pacing up and down the hall, their pale faces pinched with worry. I guess there must have been a late admission and, knowing the nurses and aides will be busy getting the new patient settled, I step back into the room, deciding to stay until someone comes in.

Settling myself in the recliner, I pull out my phone to text Sal and Lib:

"Mom resting peacefully," I report. *"Didn't wake again when I gave her a kiss. Very busy here tonight so I'm going to stay for a while. xoxox"*

Pushing the seat back as far as it will go, I wrap myself up in a spare blanket and try to get comfortable, figuring I should get some sleep while I can. But no sooner have I closed my eyes than I hear Mom groan, so I scramble out of the recliner and stumble to the bed in the dim light.

Mom is trying to sit up, her crooked fingers straining for the water cup, her eyes wide with panic. "Water," she croaks, her voice so scratchy and weak it's hard to understand. Grabbing the cup, I guide the straw between her dry lips.

"Okay, Mom, here you go." She sucks in feebly, then pauses to swallow, her throat muscle pulsing with effort. Taking another sip, this one a little stronger, she closes her eyes. "A little more?" I urge, wanting to be sure she's had enough. She nods and takes another little sip, then leans back against her pillow, the straw slipping out of her mouth, a thin string of saliva trailing in its wake. God, she would hate this. Setting the cup back on the table, I pluck a tissue from the box and wipe the drool away.

Pulling a chair up close to the bed, I watch her face relax back into sleep, though her fingers continue to grip the edge of the tray table. Scared to move back to the recliner in case she panics again, I consider crawling into bed next to her to try and get some rest, but worry it might be a little melodramatic. Although I've seen Libby do it a couple of times the past few days and it hasn't seemed weird, so I grab the blanket off the recliner and lay down next to her.

I can't remember ever lying in a bed next to Mom—she was not the kind of mother who liked to snuggle—anywhere. Public displays of affection were taboo in our family, whether out in the world or in our own home. A kiss on my cheek when I came down in the morning, a quick hug when I left for school, a cool hand on my forehead when I was sick—those are the ways I remember my mother's touch. She was a good mom, and always there for me, but I suppose, in hindsight, she was also a bit distant—there was a line between us back then I didn't dare cross. It wasn't until after I was married and had children of my own that I started to see Mom as someone I could talk to about things. Growing up she never seemed that available, or if I'm honest, that interested.

Although, now that I think of it, I was never a big snuggler with my children, either, so maybe it wasn't Mom who put distance between us back then, maybe it was me. Maybe I'm the one who doesn't like to get too close.

Mom stirs next to me and opens her eyes, staring straight into mine just inches away. "I have to stop," she says, her voice muffled and thick under the oxygen mask.

"What? Stop what, Mom?"

"I want to stop," she says, her eyes pleading. "It's time to stop."

"Okay, Mom…it's okay." My mind is racing to understand what she means—is she telling me she wants to stop living? Rubbing her shoulder, I try to think what to do, how to calm her. I've read that it can be helpful to tell a dying loved one it's okay to let go, that sometimes giving them permission is what they most need. Is that what I should do? Should I tell her it's okay to die? What if I'm wrong? What if she means something else?

"I have to stop," Mom's voice quavers, her eyes imploring, willing me to understand what she's saying.

"It's okay, Mom—you can. You can stop. We'll be okay." I try to give her a reassuring smile. "It'll be okay, Mom." I murmur again in her ear. "Everything's okay."

She closes her eyes, and I stare at the ceiling, scared to move, but scared not to move, too. If Mom's going to die right now then I don't want to be lying next to her when she does. Or do I? The scared me and the brave me are both unsure.

The aide pushes through the semi-closed door and I slip off the bed, grateful to have the decision made for me, though a little self-conscious to be found in bed with my mother.

"She's been a little agitated," I whisper in explanation as she lifts the covers to check Mom's brief. "Do you think it would be okay for me to spend the night?"

"Of course!" she replies, nodding for emphasis. "Families are always welcome to stay over if they want. I'll bring in a cot and get you all set up."

She disappears out the door and minutes later is rolling in a folded made-up cot, with extra blankets and pillows stacked on top. Unfolding it, she pushes it up against the wall opposite Mom's bed.

"Wow!" I exclaim. "That looks so comfy!"

"Well, some people say they prefer the recliner," she admits. "But at least you have a choice."

Smiling my thanks, I leave her to finish tending to Mom and go out into the hall to call Sal and Lib.

Lib picks up on the first ring. "Is everything okay?" she asks without preamble. Too late, I realize how scared she must have been to see my number on the caller ID this time of night and I blink back tears.

"I'm not sure—something's definitely changed, though, so I'm going to spend the night."

"Should we come back?"

"I don't know—she keeps talking about wanting to stop and it makes me scared to leave her alone." I pause, not sure what they should do. What if I tell them not to come, and then Mom dies? But then what if they do come, and she doesn't? God, this is so hard! "I don't think it makes sense for all of us to be here so late," I finally say. "Why don't we leave it that no news is good news for now?"

Lib murmurs something to Sal in the background. "Okay," she agrees, "but call if you need reinforcement."

Promising to let them know if anything changes for the worse, I hang up, staring out the dark window until the aide taps me on the shoulder, murmuring softly that it's okay to go back in.

It's a long night. The cot is terrible—the sheets scratchy and stiff, the mattress so thin the metal springs poke my back and shoulders whenever I move. And I move a lot. Mom's thirst is unquenchable and no sooner do I give her a drink and lie back down than I hear the rustle of her legs and then another low, raspy groan for water. Up and down I go, her clear distress the only thing keeping my growing impatience at bay.

I'm reminded of the sleepless nights with my newborn babies, their demanding cries piercing through my groggy consciousness seconds—or what felt like seconds—after I'd just fed them. *Not again!* I would groan, waiting a minute or two to see if they'd go back to sleep before guilt got the better of me and I'd stumble my way back to their room.

The first night we brought Bill home from the hospital he didn't sleep one second. I mean, literally, not one second. Thinking something must be wrong with him, I called Mom the next morning to ask her if I should be worried.

"Mom!" I cried when she answered the phone. "Billy was up all night! I didn't sleep at all! Do you think something's wrong? Should I call the doctor?"

"Oh, Peg," she chuckled, "you're not doing anything wrong! That's how it is with babies. It'll take a couple of months, but he'll sleep through the night. Don't worry."

"But Mom," I whined, "Why didn't you warn me? I had no idea it would be like this!"

"It'll be okay," she promised. "Try to sleep when he sleeps—that's all you can do. There'll be light at the end of the tunnel, you'll see!"

I laugh now at my ignorance, but back then I couldn't believe my mother hadn't prepared me better for the sleepless reality of a newborn baby—I felt annoyed with her for months.

Unlike with a newborn, though, when you know in the back of your sleep-deprived brain there is a light at the end of the tunnel, the only light at the end of what Mom is going through right now will be, well—the light at the end. Her end. And I can't bear the thought of it, even though I know it's coming, so up and down I go, grateful to be there, but wishing I was anywhere else at the same time.

Hearing another muffled moan, I hold my breath, waiting a moment in the silence that follows to see if this time she won't wake all the way up. But she does, so with a sigh I roll off the cot to her side and, picking up the water cup, hold the straw to her parched lips.

"There you go, Mom," I whisper, kissing her furrowed brow. She sucks greedily, closing her eyes in relief, then lets her head fall back on the pillow. Exhausted, I decide to abandon the cot in favor of the recliner, pulling it up next to the bed so I only have to lean over when she wakes up again. Sinking into its soft cushions, I close my eyes, praying she'll sleep long enough for me to get a little sleep, too. A minute later, though—or maybe an hour, I have no idea—an aide comes in.

"I need to reposition her," she whispers when she sees me peering at her from the shadows. I get up and push the recliner back into the corner, out of her way, when suddenly Mom starts to retch, vomiting all over herself and the bedclothes with a force so strong I'm sure it will kill her. Paralyzed, not sure what to do, I watch the aide grab a plastic tub off the nightstand and position it under Mom's chin, while at the same time pressing the intercom to call for help.

The nurse comes hurrying in seconds later, and the two of them systematically and oh-so-carefully-it-makes-me-want-to-cry clean Mom up, murmuring softly as they change her gown and sheets. The dark bay window reflects the scene in a ghost-like way, and I find a certain welcome detachment in watching the reflection rather than the real thing. I want to help, but there's nothing for me to do, my presence seeming as unnecessary as if I wasn't there at all.

I read in a spiritual self-help book once that when we find ourselves in a difficult situation, we should try to be curious about what good may eventually come of it. That if we shift our perspective from something that's happening *to* us, to something that's happening *for* us, we can open ourselves to a better outcome. Intrigued by the idea, I'd broached the subject one evening over drinks to a spiritually like-minded friend who'd lost her husband to cancer several years before, leaving her with two teen-age children to raise on her own.

"Do you ever wonder if what you went through was somehow for your soul's growth?" I asked cautiously, after explaining the premise of the book. "That maybe you had that experience in order for your soul to reach some higher level?"

She paused a moment, gazing at me over her glass of wine before shaking her head. "There is no way in hell anything good could possibly come out of what we went through," she said with certainty.

My first impulse was to push her to at least consider the idea—that by looking at her tragic experience from a more metaphysical perspective it might help her heal more quickly. But then I noticed a sadness in her eyes that hadn't been there moments before, and my face flushed with embarrassment at my thoughtless arrogance for thinking I might have some sort of spiritual insight that could help this poor woman make sense of her incredible loss. Who did I think I was?

Nodding my head that I understood, we moved on to other topics, but I promised myself right then and there to keep my quest for spiritual clarity to my own personal experiences, not someone else's.

Now, here in the middle of my own tragic experience, I understand how my friend felt. There is no way I want to be curious about how watching my mother die is going to somehow benefit my soul someday. I don't want to shift my f...ing perspective to see how this might be happening *for* me and not *to* me, even if it is for my soul's higher good. In fact, I'm beginning to question if there is any spiritual truth, or spiritual lesson, or spiritual anything that could make sense of this seemingly senseless pain.

What will get me through, I realize, holding the straw up to Mom's lips for what seems like the millionth time, is the same thing that got me through all the long, sleepless nights with my newborns. Love. Something I first learned about, not from a book, but from my mother.

Day Sixteen

After my terrible night with Mom, Sal, Lib, and I find ourselves swimming in an even deeper sea of angst and uncertainty than we'd been in before. And because we all have return flights scheduled over the next couple of days, we have the immediate concern of deciding who should stay and who should go.

Sitting in the sunroom so as not to disturb Mom, we try to come up with a plan.

"So, do we all want to stay indefinitely?" I wonder out loud. "Or maybe one of us should stay and the other two go home for a few days?" My mind is spinning with alternatives of what might be the best thing to do. "Or maybe two of us should stay so we have some moral support, and one of us goes home?"

"It's just she could be really close to the end now after the past couple days," Lib interjects. "Not sure I would want to be the one to leave right now."

Sal is staring down at the floor pensively then, giving a quick nod to no one in particular, looks up. "I think it's important" she begins, with such earnest I can't help but roll my eyes a little at Lib, "that we each make our decisions about staying or going based on our own needs, and not worry about what anyone else decides to do."

Her words make sense, but I'm annoyed nonetheless. It's usually not what my older sister says that gets my back up, but the tone she says it in—an exasperating combination of bossy big sister and dismissive know-it-all boss.

Obviously we have to make our own decisions, I grumble inwardly, staring out the sunroom window to give myself a minute to wallow in my irritation. *But shouldn't we be thinking about each other, too? Maybe I need some help deciding what to do,* my inner-child whines. *I'm the one who's been here the longest.*

The truth is, I've been starting to feel a little sorry for myself. Earlier that morning I'd woken up in the narrow, getting-more-uncomfortable-by-the-day twin bed in Mom's guest room, already exhausted by the prospect of the day ahead. Glancing over to see if Libby was awake to commiserate with, I was surprised to see her bed still neatly made, and it took my sleepy brain a minute to remember that it had been her turn to stay overnight with Mom. After the scary experience I'd had a couple of nights before, we'd agreed to take turns sleeping at hospice, just so one of us would always be there in case she took a final turn for the worse.

As I lay in bed trying to drum up the strength to start the day, I watched the gray sky lighten through the semi-open blinds, and my mind wandered back to the day Mom had fallen, over two weeks before.

God I've been here a long time, I lament, thinking about all that had happened since I'd been there. Images flashed through my mind; Mom in the hospital after she fell, her white hair tinged pink with blood, her head swathed in gauze; Mom writhing in pain on her recliner hours after we'd just gotten her home and my panicked 911 call; the enormous paramedics taking her *back* to the hospital; the kind emergency room nurse who so painstakingly cleaned the matted blood out of her hair; Sal and Lib walking into her hospital room for the first time, together; Mom on the ambulance gurney whispering 'I love you' over and over and over as they transferred her to hospice.

But then the images started to get less clear, a blurry thread of days melding together with no distinction, so

I let my mind flash forward, but that was even blurrier, the unknown future lying ahead feeling suffocating and ominous. It was like being caught in some nightmarish time warp with no beginning or end, where all I could see, whether I looked forward or back, was my mother dying, but not dying.

Even worse, when I started to think about home, and John, and all the day-to-day things that I normally took care of that he'd been doing without me for so long—feeding the dog, going to the grocery store, cooking dinner—the panic was compounded by the enormous guilt I was starting to feel for being gone so long. For not doing my job. For being a bad wife.

Okay, Peg! Hold everything! Sitting up in bed, I swung my legs over the side and took a few slow breaths. *There's no need to look backward or forward,* I reminded myself. *You just have to be where you are. Try putting up the stop signs.*

I had learned the stop sign trick a few years earlier after a tumor was discovered on one of my ovaries during a routine check-up. Not sure right away if it was malignant or benign, the two weeks leading up to the surgery were fraught with worry and fear, my mind taking me to such horrible places that I died of ovarian cancer at least a hundred times a day.

Luckily, I stumbled upon a book that offered different ways, both practical and spiritual, to prepare for surgery. I'm sure there were all sorts of other good tips in its pages, but the one that stuck, the one that got me through those two terrifying weeks, was the one to suggest that whenever I caught myself heading down the path to the worst-case scenario, I was to imagine a giant stop sign popping up and blocking my way.

It was hard at first to catch myself and I was often well on my way to the worst-case scenario—me bald and emaciated, lying on my deathbed—when I remembered what I was supposed to do. It took a couple of days, but soon I became more adept at recognizing the dark, scary thoughts before they led me astray, and up the stop sign would go, reminding me to make a different choice, to go down a better path. It was like having my own virtual crossing guard in the middle of my brain, stopping the negative thoughts in their tracks so the positive thoughts could pass safely through. The tumor was benign.

So sitting on my bed, breathing deeply, I imagined two stop signs; one to keep me from going back to where I'd been, and one to keep me from going too far in the future. And it worked. It felt restful in the space between them, and safe. I just had to find a way to keep myself there.

Now, after a few minutes staring out the sunroom window, I manage to get my whining, inner-child under control, and turn back toward my sisters.

"Okay, well, I just can't see myself leaving with Mom the way she is, so as long as John is okay with it, I'm going to stay," I declare, albeit a little tentatively. It feels scary to commit to staying longer, but even scarier not to.

"Me too," Lib agrees, without a moment's hesitation. "I already talked to Kit and he wants me to stay as long as I need to."

"Then it looks like we're all staying!" Sal smiles as she grabs her phone and heads out to the hall to call her airline. "We're the K-team after all, right?"

Pulling out my own phone to call John, I smile to myself as I watch her leave. My sisters—especially Sal—can push my buttons and irritate me faster than anyone else in the world. But there is also no one else in the world I'd rather have on my team.

Day Nineteen

"I want to stop the medicine." Mom's eyes are boring into mine as I lean in to give her a kiss good morning, her voice so clear I look at her in surprise. She hasn't spoken a complete sentence like this in days.

"What medicine, Mom? Your heart pills?" She nods, her gaze weary but resolute. Is this what she was talking about the other night? I wonder, glancing over at Lib to see if she's listening to this. But she's asleep in the recliner—having been there all night as the daughter-on-call she must be exhausted.

"Are you sure?" I press, wanting to make sure Mom's saying what I think she's saying.

She nods again, her eyes drifting closed as I sit by her side, staring at her face. It's so familiar, despite how pale and haggard it's become the past few weeks. *She wants this to be over*, I realize, my heart beating a little faster at the enormity of such a decision. *How scary it must be to know there's no way out of this.*

My thoughts take me back to the morning I was scheduled for the surgery to remove the what-turned-out-to-be benign ovarian tumor. I'd just woken up and was lying in bed, so scared about what the day ahead would bring I didn't want to get up. Suddenly, out of nowhere, a phrase from a children's book I'd read to my kids when they were little called *We're Going On A Bear Hunt*, popped into my head.

"Can't go over it! Can't go under it! Oh no! I've got to go through it!"

Over and over, like a song set on repeat, the words kept looping through my mind, somehow managing to give me enough courage to make myself get out of bed and face the uncertainty of the day ahead. There was no way to get around what was going to happen no matter how scared I was, so the only thing to do was get on with it.

Of course, facing surgery and facing death are hardly comparable, but looking at Mom so frail and sick, I think I understand her decision. That even though she doesn't want to die, it's happening, like it or not. Scary as it is, there is no way around it. She has to go through it.

And Mom being Mom, a woman with a strong propensity for action when she wants something done, she has probably figured out that stopping her heart medication is the one thing still in her control that might speed things up. That will get her through what she has to go through, faster.

Growing up, I didn't appreciate Mom's just-get-it-done nature, rolling my eyes and inwardly groaning whenever she made me help her do whatever it was she wanted done. Mom could be fairly insistent when she'd made up her mind about something, and rarely took no for an answer—from anyone.

Take our summer place in Maine, for example. My grandparents, who owned the riverfront camp along with the farmhouse across the street, had decided to sell both as they were getting older, and it was too hard to make the long trip from their home on Long Island. Mom, who had spent every summer of her life going to Maine, convinced them to let her keep the camp, despite the fact that it was falling down from age and neglect.

"I think you're crazy," my grandfather reportedly told her when she broached the idea. "But if you want it you can have it. Don't come crying to me, though, when it falls into the river!"

But Mom had a big vision for the aging camp, so the following summer piled three daughters, aged thirteen, eight and six, along with a twelve-year old niece and a crotchety old Welsh Corgi named Friar Tuck, into our family's dark blue Buick station wagon. Waving goodbye to Dad, who would join us in a couple of weeks, our very determined mother drove us over a thousand miles, by herself, to spend the month of August in Maine.

Looking back, I don't know how she did it. After driving two and a half days with four young children and a dog, Mom then had to open up the run-down camp that had been boarded up and empty for years. Mildew covered everything, the musty smell still sharp in my memory from the hours she had us scrubbing it off all the furniture in those first few days.

There was no plumbing, so we took turns filling buckets of water from a hose, then carrying them up the crooked stone steps to the kitchen where Mom, like a general at a command post, would issue more orders, sending us off to bring in firewood, or sweep the floor, or scrub more mildew.

And though I'm sure we helped a little, it was Mom whose sheer willpower and hard work brought her vision into focus that summer. She cooked our meals on a single burner Coleman stove. She boiled an endless supply of water to cook with and do the dishes. She filled and emptied the chemical toilet—basically a bucket with some sort of solution to keep it from smelling too bad—that we used instead of an outhouse. She cleaned and organized, cooked and shopped, all the while taking care of us and Friar Tuck as she transformed the mildewy old camp into a warm and welcoming summer haven where our family would gather for the next fifty years.

Of course, Mom's single-mindedness when she wanted something done could be annoying, especially as she got older and wasn't able to do things for herself anymore. She could be a real nudge, often making repeated requests for the same thing if she didn't think whoever was helping her was moving fast enough.

One night up in Maine the previous summer, as Mom was kissing us all goodnight before heading to bed, she mentioned to Paul that there was a branch on a tree outside her room that was blocking her view.

"Would you like me to prune it off?" he asked her. "I'd be happy to do that."

"Well, if it's not too much trouble," Mom replied. "Yes, that would be nice."

"I'll do it tomorrow," Paul promised.

But it seemed that 'tomorrow' wasn't quite fast enough, because when Paul came in for breakfast early the next morning, Mom was a bit put out that he hadn't taken care of it yet.

"I'll get to it, Kay," Paul reassured her with a patient chuckle, no stranger to his mother-in-law's tenacious tactics. "Mind if I have a little breakfast first?"

Overhearing the conversation, I had to smile. Judging from Mom's tight-lipped nod in response, I was fairly certain that she did, in fact, mind quite a bit.

∞

"Okay," I kiss the top of Mom's head, and stand up from the edge of the bed where I've been perched. "But I think you need to tell this to a nurse yourself so they'll know it's your decision, not mine. Don't want anyone to think I'm trying to kill you off faster!"

My weak attempt at humor brings a small smile to Mom's face. "I wouldn't blame you," she counters. "This is no fun."

"What are you guys talking about?" At the sound of Lib's voice, Mom and I turn our heads in her direction, watching as she pulls herself out of the recliner.

"Mom says she wants to stop her heart medicine," I tell her, and Lib glances at Mom with a surprised frown.

"Okayyyy…" she says, raising an eyebrow at me, then sitting down next to Mom and taking her hand. "Maybe we need to ask someone, though?"

"I was just going to get the nurse so Mom can tell her. I'll be right back."

Making my way down the corridor, I can't decide if I'm feeling trepidation that Mom wants to stop her medicine, or anticipation for what might happen next if she does. Questions whirl through my head as I march toward the nurse's station to report this latest development: *Will stopping the medicine make Mom uncomfortable? Will she die faster without it? How fast? Days? Hours? Is this finally it?*

My heart tightens as I contemplate the reality of Mom's decision, of losing her for real. Not that it hasn't been real up to this point, but somehow Mom wanting to stop the medication—the same medication she's been so conscientious about taking since her stroke six years before—seems so final. There will be no turning back once she stops it, no miraculous bounce back, no surprise happy ending.

Jenny, Mom's nurse for the day, looks up from her clipboard as I approach the desk.

"Mom told me she wants to stop her heart medicine," I tell her, feeling a rush of adrenaline at being the bearer of such news. "I thought maybe you or the doctor would want to hear it directly from her?"

"Yes, of course," Jenny says, her voice so calm it's as if she's been expecting this news all along. "I'll be down in a minute."

I'm a little surprised by her placid response, but I suppose I shouldn't be—Jenny never seems to get ruffled, her soothing demeanor steadying our jangled nerves time and time again since we've been there. It's why she's our favorite nurse. Small in stature, with short hair, glasses, and pleasant features, she's like a sturdy lifeboat in a stormy sea, making us feel safe no matter how choppy the waves around us might be getting.

And though I may not yet understand the implications of Mom's decision, as I walk back to her room there's no doubt in my mind the waves are about to get choppier. In fact, I can already feel them starting to swell, making me grateful, once again, for Jenny's steadying presence on our slowly sinking ship.

∽

Despite the excitement of the morning, the rest of the day creeps along like any other, with Mom sleeping and

Sal, Lib, and I, sometimes together and sometimes alone, keeping vigil by her side.

Often our vigil is a passive thing—we'll read, or nap, or surf the internet as we try to distract ourselves from the tediousness. But then there are other times, somehow equally tedious, when Mom is quite needy, requiring our full attention as we try to make her more comfortable in between nurses' visits.

We dab ointment on her cracked lips, taking special care not to disturb the peeling pieces because, tempting as it is to pull them off, we've learned the hard way that doing so only makes matters worse. We sit by her side, gently rubbing her arm, or leg, or shoulder, or wherever her elusive pain might be at that particular moment, and try to soothe her agitation. We offer her countless sips of water in an effort to quench her seemingly unquenchable thirst—between the morphine and the oxygen, Mom's mouth is always parched, making her desperate for relief.

The past couple of days, though, she hasn't been swallowing the water. She'll take a sip, swish it around in her mouth for a second, and then spit it out into another cup. Sip-swish-spit, sip-swish-spit, over and over and over.

"I wonder if she *can't* swallow?" I whisper to Sal and Lib now, holding up the *What To Expect* pamphlet I'd been leafing through to pass the time. "It says here that 'difficulty swallowing' is something that happens in the last few days or hours."

"Hmmm…" Sal murmurs, looking up from her book. "What else does it say?"

Glancing through the rest of the list I hold back a bemused snort because, based on what I was reading, Mom should already be dead. For almost three full weeks she's been experiencing many, if not all, of the signs that supposedly presage death in the final days and hours:

- *Sleeping most of the time.* Check.
- *Surge of energy.* Check.
- *Restlessness.* Check.
- *Not eating.* Check.
- *Eyelids no longer able to close completely.* Check.

"Whoever wrote this obviously never met our mother," I joke, wanting to laugh and cry at the same time. "Maybe when this is all over we should offer to rewrite it for them. We could call it *What To Expect When Your Loved One is Dying* —EXCEPT *If You're Like Kay Ball.*"

Looking for signs of my mother's imminent death has, in truth, become a bit of an obsession with me. Maybe I'm hoping for a heads up so I'll have a chance to be with Mom in her final moments. Or maybe I want more proof that there *is* a higher power at work and I'm connected to something bigger than myself, bigger than this sad physical reality I'm in the middle of. Maybe, though, what I really want is to feel more connected to my mom—that our souls are so intertwined that I'll know intuitively before everyone else when she's ready to let go.

In any case, not only do I watch her deteriorating body like a hawk, but I also find myself analyzing every dream I have, every bird that crosses my path, every song I hear on the radio. I pay attention to *everything*—scared I'll miss the sign and she'll die without me, but equally scared to see it, and know what's coming.

A few days earlier I'd been talking to a good friend whose father had recently died in hospice care, and she asked me if Mom's feet were 'mottling' yet.

"I'm not sure," I told her. "What's mottling?"

"It's when the feet start looking like purple marble," Annie explained. "Kind of spotted and cool to the touch. It means the heart isn't pumping hard enough to get blood all the way down to them—Dad's nurse showed me his feet the night he died and it's quite noticeable."

"That must be why the nurses are always checking Mom's!" I exclaimed, having wondered what they were looking for but felt too intimidated to ask.

Somehow, though, despite now knowing what to look for and wanting to check all the time, I'm scared to. What if a nurse or aide walks in and catches me in such a grim act? Checking my mother's feet feels intrusive and predatory, like a vulture circling its dying prey. Even worse, what if Mom should wake up and ask what I'm doing? What would I say? *Oh, don't worry, Mom…I'm just checking to see if your feet are mottling so we'll know if you're going to die today. No big deal! Go back to sleep!*

It's a strange dance we're in with our mother, trying to find a rhythm that allows us to be honest and straightforward with her, but at the same time not get mired down in the doom and gloom of what's happening. My instinct, sometimes for better and sometimes for worse, is to push back the scary shadow hovering around us by trying to bring some levity to the situation with a joke or a little laugh.

When I was six, my grandfather, my dad's dad, died suddenly of a heart attack at the age of sixty-six. I recall meeting Dad on the stairway of my childhood home—he's on his way up as I'm about to go down—our long-ago selves caught in a moment that has stuck with me all these years.

"I have some sad news, Peg," Dad told me, his voice strained and weary even to my own young ears. "Granddad Ball died this morning."

His words hung between us for a second as I tried to make sense of what he was saying. I'm not sure at age six I knew people I loved could die. But rather than starting to cry, which you would expect a child to do when she heard such news, I did something I've never been able to forget. I smiled.

Confused, I remember trying to stop it, because even my six-year-old self knew that smiling when someone died was wrong. I loved my granddad! But I couldn't pull it back—it was as though some outside force had control of my mouth. Was Dad shocked? Did he reprimand me? But the memory of that moment stops with that smile, and I can't remember another word spoken, a tear shed, a hug given.

I wonder now, though, if maybe I had understood on some unconscious soul level that death wasn't an ending, and I smiled at the news my grandfather had died because, deep down, I knew he was okay. That I didn't need to *be* sad.

Of course, it wasn't too much later that my intense fear of death took root, and the big, dark nothing that would terrify me for years to come planted itself firmly into my consciousness, erasing any vestige of spiritual understanding that long ago me may or may not have had.

Sal and Lib leave to get some lunch, and standing up to stretch, I glance over at Mom still asleep. Do I risk it? Stepping over to the end of the bed I hesitate for a moment, before oh-so-carefully-so-I-don't-wake-her-up pull out a corner of the bed cover to expose her dry, aged feet. Like everything else about my mother, her feet are so familiar, and it makes my heart ache to see them lying there so impotently. But they are still pinkish and warm to the touch, so I tuck the blanket back into place.

Not today, I guess.

Day Twenty

The next afternoon, I'm doing some errands in town when I get a text from Lib:

"Mom's just woken up and said she'd like some lunch! Jenny is going to bring her some broth and some ice cream."

Standing in the middle of the store, I have to choke back a laugh, or maybe it's a groan. Only our mother can go from death's door one minute to eating ice cream the next. Is this normal? Do other dying people have this many ups and downs? On my drive back to hospice, angst begins to bubble up as I consider the implications of another 'rally.' There doesn't seem to be any rhyme or reason to Mom's dying process—she just stopped her heart medication for heaven's sake and should be going downhill, not up.

I've been away from home for almost three weeks, and I'm starting to worry about a few things falling through the cracks, the main one being getting the taxes organized and to the accountant on time. It seems ludicrous to be concerned about such a thing right now, but it's already the middle of March and the Capricorn in me can't bear being so unorganized. Pulling into the hospice parking lot I wonder—assuming Mom *is* having another rally—whether I can risk going home for a few days. *I'll give it until tomorrow,* I decide, not for the first time. *If she's still eating then, maybe I'll go.*

Lost in thought, I make my way down the corridor, surprised when I see Sal and Lib sitting in the vestibule outside Mom's room.

"What's going on?" I ask, my heart speeding up. "Is everything okay?"

"Everything's fine," Lib says. "Mom's asleep, so we're waiting to talk to the doctor out here." She glances over my shoulder. "Here she comes now."

We all watch Dr. B, a tall, lanky woman with an upbeat, matter-of-fact manner, coming toward us, a sympathetic smile crossing her face as she approaches our little huddle.

"I hear someone's decided to eat again," she says, pulling open Mom's file. "She's a fighter, that one."

"We're kind of struggling with what to do now," Sal admits, and Lib and I nod in agreement. "It feels impractical at this point for all of us to still be here, but we can't decide if it's okay to leave."

"I totally understand," Dr. B. commiserates. "It's hard enough knowing what to do when you live nearby, let alone being from so far away. But here's the thing," she pauses, glancing up from her notes. "Your Mom's path right now is much like a leaf that's floating to the ground—one minute it's falling fast, but then it gets caught in a breeze and drifts sideways, or even spirals back up for a moment or two. Eventually, though," she pauses again, looking at each of us in turn, "it's going to land—but because its path is so unpredictable, it's impossible to say when."

Sal, Lib, and I are quiet, absorbing the doctor's words. An unexpected wave of calm washes through my tense body imagining Mom as a gently falling leaf, dipping and swirling her way to the ground. It's such a peaceful image, and the angst I felt only moments before is lifted a little. At least for a minute.

Because as calming as it might be to watch a leaf make its unpredictable way to the ground, it can also be frustrating if you are waiting to see it land. Turn away for an instant, it might take a sudden dive and, just like that, its dance is over.

So even though this latest rally of Mom's gives us all a little boost of confidence that it might be okay to slip home for a few days, making the decision to go is one of the hardest things I've ever done. It seems impossible that I would leave, to willingly sacrifice even one second of my time left with her, but it also seems impossible to stay, because every day the pull from home is getting stronger. I miss John. I miss our dog. I miss the ordinariness of my life before Mom fell.

But having no idea how long Mom's rally will last, Sal, Lib, and I finally agree that, as much as we want to be here together, it doesn't make sense anymore.

So we come up with a plan. Lib has already gone home for a few days, so she offers to stay first while Sal and I fly home to regroup. Then, because Sal and Paul are about to pick up a new puppy, I'll come back early the following week, crossing over with Lib for a night before taking over as the sister-in-charge. Then Sal will come back a week or so after that and take over from me.

And so it will go, week to week, as long as is necessary—Lib, Peg, Sal; Lib, Peg, Sal—each of us taking our turn watching our tiny, frail, ever-so-loved leaf swirl and dip her way to the ground.

Day Twenty-One

I suppose it's not the worst thing that we're going to start a sister rotation—after two weeks of all three of us here together, a little break from each other might be a good idea. Not that we've been arguing, at least not outwardly. At times I've found myself frustrated with Sal's bossy big sister tone, or Libby's I'm-sadder-than-you-because-I'm-the-youngest woeful expressions, but I've tried hard to shrug off my annoyance. Mom's dying, after all—I need my sisters more than ever.

And I know they're both trying hard, too, because, well, there *hasn't* been a blow up. At least not a big one—Sal and Lib have sparred a little, but that's typical. Not that I'm an angel, but most of our arguments over the years have tended to start between Sal and Lib. I'm not sure why. It could be that, unlike me, they both inherited the 'like to argue' gene from our parents. They tend to embrace conflict while I avoid it at all costs.

I know my sisters get frustrated with my overly sensitive nature, my tendency to run away rather than confront a disagreement. But in my defense, as the middle child and therefore, according to many birth order experts, the 'family peacekeeper,' I feel a certain responsibility not to rock the boat, and if the boat is rocking, to try and steady it as best I can. When Lib and Sal butt heads, my instinct is to straddle the middle and hold my breath, hoping that whatever the issue is will blow over and I won't have to get involved. Many times, though, I have an opinion, too, which ends up tipping the balance to one side or the other.

And so it is the last day we're all together before Sal and I leave to go home. It starts out like any other morning with the three of us filing into Mom's room, hanging our coats one by one on the hooks inside the door, then fanning out to claim our seat for the day, rotating by unspoken rule whose turn it is to get the recliner, the most comfortable spot. Mom's asleep, so we take turns whispering a soft hello in her ear, so she'll know, *maybe*, that we're here.

"Hey look you guys," Lib points to the oxygen flowmeter on the wall over Mom's bed. "It's down to eight! Do you think that's a good sign?"

"I'm guessing it's probably down because she's not moving that much," I reply, not wanting Lib to get her hopes up—of the three of us I know she still questions whether we gave up on Mom too soon. "I'm sure if she tried to stand up, or even sit up, it would have to be put back up to ten."

"But it might be worth asking the doctor, right? I mean if she's not needing as much oxygen now maybe there's still a chance she could try skilled nursing?" Lib looks from me to Sal, the want in her eyes so intense it hurts me to see it.

Sal glances over at me before saying, in a tone that is maybe a tiny bit big-sisterish, "I think Peg's right, Lib—it's not like her lungs are miraculously getting better."

"Well, I don't see how it can hurt to ask," Lib retorts. "We should give Mom a chance if there is one!"

I look down at my hands to hide the flash of irritation Lib's seeming denial triggers in me. *What does she think?* my indignant-self grouses. *That we don't want to give Mom a chance? That she loves Mom more than we do?*

But because it's unusual for me and Lib to be on opposite sides of the boat—she and I are typically united in our younger sister's annoyance at something Sal has said or done—a different, calmer voice is cautioning me to let it be, so I bite back my reply.

Just then, the doctor appears in the doorway and, not wanting to disturb Mom, we file back out into the hall to get her update.

"For now your mom's condition is stable," Dr. B. tells us. "She didn't have any breakthrough pain last night, so no changes to her medications today. We'll see how the weekend goes."

"Is there a reason her oxygen level is lower?" Lib asks, staring fixedly at the doctor, avoiding Sal's and my eyes. But before Dr. B can respond, Sal is waving the question away like a pesky fly, dismissing it out of hand. "Will this latest rally affect Mom's level of care?" she asks instead.

Uh oh. My eyes dart over to Lib to gauge her reaction—we both hate it when Sallie brushes us aside like this—and just as I expect, her jaw has set, her green eyes now staring stonily out the window at the gray, March day. She's turned inward, shutting out Sal, me, and even the doctor, as definitively as if she's closed a door in our faces.

Dr. B assures us that Mom will stay at Level 1 through the weekend, then leaves us to continue on her rounds. Lib disappears down the hall without a word, her anger leaving a trail of tension that wraps around my heart, squeezing it tight.

Slipping back into Mom's room, Sal and I tip-toe around the bed to our respective seats, both lost in thought. The hiss of the oxygen and the tick, tick, tick of the wall clock seem louder in Lib's absence, the room somehow unbalanced without her in it. I can't bear that she's so upset, that our last day together is now edged with friction. I think about going after her to try and smooth things out, but know that if I do it could just make things worse. I'm not the one who needs to go.

Suddenly, though, as if reading my mind, Sal stands up and walks toward the door, grabbing her coat from the hook. "I'm going to find her," she whispers over her shoulder, leaving me in surprised silence. Watching her go, I breathe out a sigh of relief. Sometimes all it takes to steady our rocking boat is a simple shift in position, and I'm grateful Sal decided to shift hers first.

Day Twenty-Two

"I won't be gone long," I promise, leaning over to kiss Mom goodbye the next morning. "I'll see you in a few days."

"I love you," she whispers, her cloudy blue eyes focused on mine, her gnarled hand squeezing my own. How many times over the past three weeks has my mother told me she loves me? A hundred? Five hundred? She says it when she wakes up and when I kiss her goodnight. She says it after I give her a sip of water or dab ointment on her lips. She'll whisper it when I rub her arm or straighten her sheets or untangle her oxygen tubing. Again and again and again. She can't seem to say it enough.

Squeezing her hand back, my heart dips at the enormity of what is happening.

Breathe, Peggy, I hear my stoic-self urging. *You can do this. Be brave. It's going to be okay.*

No it's not! my panicked-self snaps. *It's never going to be okay again!*

Time stands still for a moment as I stare down at my mother, her face still so beautiful though creased and sagging with age. Could it be possible I might never see it again, this face I've known longer than my own? I feel like I'm standing at the edge of a steep cliff, and by saying goodbye I'll be stepping off on purpose, plunging myself into the unknown emptiness of a world without Mom in it. I'm terrified.

Somehow, though, my brave self takes over, tamping down the rising panic.

"I love you too, Mom," I smile back, my voice surprisingly calm even to my own ears. "And Lib will be here—you won't be alone."

"You girls are too good to me," she murmurs. "I don't know how I got so lucky."

"We love you, that's how." Gently kissing her pale cheek, I force myself to stand up from the edge of the bed, letting go of her hand with reluctance and smoothing the bedcovers one final time.

"I'll call when I get home," I promise, more from reflex than anything else. Growing up Mom had always been a 'no news is good news' kind of parent, but in her later years she'd begun to worry when any of us were traveling, so we made a point to call when we were home safe and sound.

But her eyes are closed and I'm not sure she heard me. I guess it doesn't really matter anymore, I realize, a fresh wave of grief threatening to spill out. Swallowing hard, I force back the sob pulsing in my throat. Am I really going to leave?

"Ready?" Lib pokes her head in the door, and I nod numbly, hoisting my bag over my shoulder as I follow her out of the room, stepping off the cliff to whatever is going to happen next.

Day Twenty-Eight

My time at home flies by in a blur, and in what seems like a blink, I am back in Ohio, falling back into the numbing hospice routine as if I never left.

Sitting outside the cafeteria with Lib my first day back, we're waiting for our lunch order when Rita, the hospice chaplain, stops in front of us.

"I was hoping I'd run into you," she says, peering down over her wire-rimmed glasses. "I've been thinking about my conversation with your mom," she continues, before either of us has a chance to even say hello, "and after talking it over with the rest of her team just now, well, I believe she may be having a spiritual crisis."

Lib and I stare at her, speechless.

"What exactly do you mean?" Libby finally asks, breaking our stunned silence.

"I think your mom is trying to work through something that she's finding difficult to process. It's not necessarily a bad thing," she explains quickly as Lib and

I glance at each other in alarm, "but something I thought you should be aware of. I was actually on my way to see if she might be up to talk a little with me now." She pauses, looking from me to Lib before adding, almost as an afterthought, "If it's okay with the two of you, of course."

What *is* it about this chaplain I find so vexing? From the moment she stepped into Mom's room last week I'd felt an unsettling edge to her presence. If she had concerns about Mom's spiritual welfare after their conversation, why didn't she come and find me afterward? Why would she wait an entire week to let us know she thought our mother was having a spiritual crisis?

"I'm not sure today is the best day," Lib tells her, looking over at me as I nod in agreement. "Mom was a little confused this morning when we got here. She's asleep now."

I'd flown in late the night before so hadn't had a chance to get over to hospice until earlier this morning. I'd been anxious to see Mom again after being away, but when I bent down to kiss her hello, she hadn't been able to remember my name. Or Lib's. Or who we were married to.

I was reminded of the morning a few years earlier when I'd walked into the hospital the day after her stroke and, giving me a big smile of recognition, had said, "Oh Louise! I'm so glad you're here!'

Louise? Who the heck is Louise? I was terrified Mom didn't know my name, but not wanting to confuse her even more, I decided to play along. It wasn't easy, though, especially when she could remember everybody *else's* name in the family, including Elizabeth's new boyfriend, Sam, whom she'd never even *met*.

I tried to comfort myself by imagining that maybe Mom knew me as someone named Louise in a previous life, and even though she didn't recognize me as Peggy anymore, she still recognized my energy as someone she knew and loved because, thankfully, she was always happy to see me. And as the days went by and she continued to call me Louise, I realized that names aren't all that important in the end. I was sure Mom knew who I was in her heart, and for me that was all that mattered.

This time around Mom at least *knew* she was confused, but the more we tried to help her remember our names, the more frustrated she got.

"It's okay Mom," I reassured her, "Names are just names. You know who we are in here, right?" tapping on my chest.

Nodding her head, she gave me a relieved smile. "I should remember, though," she murmured.

Poor Mom. Yes, she was definitely a bit confused

this morning, and right now my instinct, and Libby's, is to protect her from anything that might upset or confuse her more.

Like this chaplain standing expectantly in front of us, waiting for an answer. What should we do? If Mom *is* having a spiritual crisis then we can't ignore it—she needs to talk about it with someone. But Rita? Not for the first time I wish we could call the minister at St. Tim's, but there's no way Mom's going to talk to him. And Reverend Johanssen lives too far away to ask him to come again.

"I guess you can see if she's awake," I concede. "But please come find us if you do talk to her—this is a little worrisome!"

Assuring us that she will, Rita hurries away down the hall leaving Lib and I staring at each in bewilderment.

"I can't believe this!" I scowl after the chaplain's receding figure, watching until she disappears around the corner. "Why would she wait so long to say something? What if we hadn't been sitting here just now?"

"I don't know." Lib frowns, shaking her head. "I can't bear thinking Mom is having a spiritual crisis! I'm not sure I know what that even means!"

I rack my brain to remember what I'd learned in hospice training about spiritual crises at the end of life, but it's been so long all that comes to mind are big issues like unresolved family problems, or doubts about the purpose of life. Maybe for some it's a struggle with forgiveness, or questioning their religious faith.

Could that be it? I wonder. Is Mom questioning her religious faith? There *had* been the recent breakup with her church that we'd all scratched our heads over, but Mom kept insisting it was because she didn't like the new minister. What if there was something more to it? What if we'd all been so worried about Mom's physical health we had overlooked her spiritual well-being? And now here she is, having a spiritual crisis on her frigging deathbed, and the only person to help her through it is a chaplain she doesn't even know, and we don't even like?

"Maybe the chaplain's wrong," Lib says suddenly. "I mean, it's not like Mom's been able to talk that clearly the last couple of weeks. Maybe the morphine's confused her, and whatever she said to the chaplain came out the wrong way."

"It *is* weird that Mom would open up so easily about something so personal," I agree, adding peevishly, "*especially* to someone she'd never even met before."

I can't remember Mom ever discussing things like God and heaven, though she took us to church with her every Sunday and listened to our prayers every night. And because God has always been a given for me, I've never questioned his existence, so it's never occurred to me that my mother would either. She and I *had* recently had that conversation about dying, but questioning her Episcopal faith hadn't come up at all.

So maybe Libby's onto something. Maybe the spiritual crisis the chaplain claims Mom is having doesn't have anything to do with Mom's religious beliefs after all.

But if not that, is there something else in her life that she may be questioning or anxious about? I can only imagine the kinds of worries and doubts that might fill someone's head when they're dying, especially if, like Mom, you're dying really, really slowly.

Another thought pops into my head. *Could it have something to do with Billy?* I wonder, thinking about the baby Mom and Dad had lost to SIDS when he was four months old. Billy had been their second child, born thirteen months after Sallie, but four years before me, so he'd always been a bit of an enigma in my life—a brother I knew of, but never knew.

And even though I can't remember Mom or Dad talking to me about what happened, I somehow seem to know the story. Maybe Sallie told me, or maybe I made it up from bits and pieces I picked up here and there. Or maybe Mom or Dad did tell me and I just can't recall.

In any case, the story I've had in my head all these years goes something like this:

Mom and Sallie are downstairs while Billy is taking a nap upstairs in his crib. Mom hears him crying but then he stops, so she doesn't go up right away hoping, as any mother would, that he's fallen back to sleep. When she finally does go up to check on him a little while later, she can't wake him up. He'd stopped breathing.

That's as far as the story I know goes—whatever happened next no one's ever talked about, and I've never been brave enough to ask. I'm hardly brave enough to even imagine it. The idea of Mom picking up Billy's limp body from the crib and realizing he's not breathing breaks my heart into so many pieces I can't bear it. And because I don't have to, I don't.

But Mom did. She *did* have to bear, and then survive, the most impossible moment any parent could ever have to face, and one that must have haunted her the whole rest of her life. It haunts mine and it wasn't even my moment.

Standing up to follow Lib into the cafeteria to pick up our lunch, I wish I'd had the courage to ask Mom to tell me about it, especially once I was a mother myself and could appreciate the inconceivable pain she must have gone through.

Maybe if I knew more of the story, I wouldn't feel so helpless now. Maybe I'd know better if Mom ever blamed herself for what happened. Maybe she's scared she somehow failed as a mother and God is going to judge her for it.

Maybe, maybe, maybe.

We're finishing our lunch a little while later when Rita strides into the sunroom, stopping in front of us like a stern schoolmarm getting ready to address her unruly students.

"Who's been talking to your Mom about energy?" she demands, peering over her glasses first at Lib, then at me.

Her words ricochet around my head like so many bullets, their force sending pulse waves of fear straight to my core. *Oh my god oh my god oh my god.* My face flushes hot, my mind racing to think of a way around having to admit, to Rita of all people, that *I'm* the one who's been talking to Mom about energy.

"*Don't say anything!*" a voice screams in my head. "*She doesn't need to know it was you! It's none of her business what you talk to Mom about!*"

"But you have to tell her!" another voice screams back. *"Don't be such a chicken! You didn't do anything wrong!"*

These voices aren't strangers to me—they've been around for years, arguing inside my head if I do something I perceive might get me into trouble. The scared voice is forever panicking, trying to find a way out of whatever it is I think I've done wrong, while the braver voice always pushes me to stand up for myself and do the right thing.

I was around fifteen the first time I remember hearing them, when Mom found a pack of cigarettes in my coat pocket. She'd just come back from taking the dog out and, walking into the den where I was watching TV, stood staring at me pensively. I was about to say "What the heck, Mom?" when I noticed the coat she was wearing.

Uh oh. Rather than the oversized down vest she usually wore to walk the dog, for some reason Mom had on my navy-blue blazer, the same one I'd worn to school that day. A shiver of alarm shot through me as I watched her reach into the front pocket and, without saying a word, pull out a half-empty pack of Tareyton cigarettes.

She held them out to me at arms' length, the crushed cellophane wrapper crinkling in her fingers.

"Are these yours?" she asked in her I-will-brook-no-nonsense tone of voice.

I sat there paralyzed, my mind scrambling to think of a reason why I would have cigarettes in my pocket if they weren't mine.

"*Tell her they're someone else's!*" the scared voice urged loudly in my head. "*Tell her you were just holding onto them for someone else and forgot to give them back!*"

"*No, no don't say that!*", the brave voice, equally loud, countered back. "*Then she'll want to know who, and you'll get someone else in trouble! Just tell her they're yours...be brave, Peggy!*"

"*But if you tell her they're yours then* you'll *get in trouble!*" the first voice warned frantically. "*She'll be so mad!*"

God, I wanted to lie so badly! I couldn't bear the thought of disappointing Mom, and then even worse, Dad, when he found out. But lying straight to my mother's face was the worst thing I could do, so scary as it was, I listened to my brave self, and confessed that yes, the cigarettes were mine.

"Well..." Mom paused, and I watched her nervously, unsure what would happen next. Would she ground me? Lecture me?

But much to my surprised relief, she did neither. Instead, she slipped the pack of cigarettes back in the pocket. "I'm glad you were honest," she said, turning to leave. "But I wish you wouldn't smoke. It's a terrible habit."

So yes, the two voices screaming in my head as I sit staring at the chaplain are quite familiar, though I'm not sure they've ever been as loud or insistent as they are being right now. I glance over at Lib, who's watching me closely, worried, I'm sure, that I'm doing exactly what I'm doing—blaming myself for our dying mother's spiritual crisis. She flashes me a supportive smile, giving me courage, so I sit up a little straighter and take a deep breath.

"Um, that would be me," my brave self confesses, forcing myself to look Rita in the eye. "I've talked to Mom about energy a lot."

She looks at me in surprise. "You don't believe in God?" she asks with a puzzled frown.

Wait, what? Her question catches me off guard and I'm confused. What does my believing in God have to do with talking to my mom about energy? In my mind God *is* energy.

"Yes, of course I believe in God," I tell her, trying not to sound defensive. Waving my hands vaguely around my head, I add, "But more like a source. Something bigger than myself but you know…still part of myself."

I wish I knew how to explain what I believe the same way I understand it in my head. I've always believed in God, and even as I learned about energy, quantum physics, life after death, angels and spirit guides, I never once questioned that belief. God may not be the big bearded figure sitting on a gilded throne up in heaven the way I'd pictured as a child, but more like an infinite point of source. *The* source. The source from which everything else emerges and has emerged. It doesn't matter what we call it—God, Allah, Buddha, the Universe—it's all the same thing. And we, as individual sparks of energy emerging from that source, allow it to grow and expand through our life experiences. For me it's as simple and as complicated as that.

But my rather nebulous answer to Rita's question doesn't elicit any reaction—not even a raised eyebrow. Instead, she leans toward me, her expression intent. "What you need to understand," she says, her tone serious, "is that your Mom has believed in God her whole life, and that when she dies, she'll be met by Jesus. She doesn't know how to connect that with the idea that everything is energy."

My heart freezes again. Those words—*everything is energy*—are exactly the same ones I used during our recent conversation about dying. On top of that, just about a month before Mom fell I'd started a memoir writing workshop with the ambiguous idea of writing my thoughts around death out in letters to her, hoping they might spark more conversations. My plan was to not only share them with my class, but to send them to Mom every week, too. I was nervous to share them, but Mom responded to all four letters I wrote—one for each week of the workshop—the last one sent just four days before she fell.

My poor mother! Had I confused her so much with my spiritual musings that now she's scared to die because she doesn't know where she's going? Who did I think I was trying to explain something I don't really understand myself? Why didn't I ever ask her more about what *she* believed?

Shifting uncomfortably, I'm not sure how to respond. Does Rita expect some sort of explanation from me? A prickle of anger pokes its way up through my guilt—what Mom and I talk about is between her and me and I don't need to explain it to anyone, especially this woman who doesn't even know us.

Standing up, I mumble that I'll be right back and leave Lib to finish the conversation, ducking into the bathroom next to the sun room. Pulling the heavy door shut behind me, I brace my hands on the sink for support, staring at myself in the mirror, tears blurring the reflection.

"Oh my god," I whisper to the pale face looking back. "What have I done?"

A knock on the door startles me, but it's just Lib making sure I'm alright. Wiping away my tears, I pull it open to let her in.

"Don't go there, Peggy," she says firmly, seeing my tear-streaked face. Putting her hands on my shoulders, she looks me square in the eye and repeats, "Do. Not. Go. There."

"But what if I did this to her?" I groan. "What if I'm the reason she's so confused?"

"It's not you, Peg. You've done nothing wrong! That chaplain is horrible. Don't listen to her."

Wanting to believe her so badly, I give her a tight hug, then dry my eyes with the back of my hands.

"I'll talk to Mom," I resolve as we walk down the hall to her room. "Maybe if I explain that I still believe in God she'll be less confused."

"Maybe," Lib replies, "but I'm not sure she's really that confused. Maybe it's the chaplain who's confused."

I smile at my younger sister's unwavering loyalty. What would I do without her?

∞

Mom seems a little brighter when we get back to her room and much less disoriented than earlier in the morning. She's semi-sitting up, and smiles when she sees us.

"You're back!" she exclaims. "I thought I'd lost you!"

"You can't ever lose us," Lib says, giving her a hug. "How was your visit with the chaplain?"

"Oh, it was fine. I think she likes to talk."

Rolling my eyes at Lib, I settle myself in the recliner for a little rest, letting the murmur of their voices soothe my rattled nerves. A few minutes later, though, I hear Lib sigh, and look over to see her staring out the window, her face creased with worry.

"What's wrong?" I whisper, seeing that Mom's dozed off again.

"I don't know what to do," Lib says, "I have to cancel my flight if I'm going to stay, but I've been here so long!"

At this point, Lib's been in Ohio for a full two weeks, and the plan was for her to go home once I came back. But the past couple of days she'd been noticing subtle changes in Mom's pattern, so had been considering staying a little longer, just in case.

"Staying doesn't feel right—Kit's been alone with Henry so long! But then I can't imagine leaving."

"It's definitely a tough one," I agree, sympathizing with her quandary, but knowing only she can make the decision. It's so hard, though—if she stays, Mom could linger for weeks and she'll have to keep making the decision over and over. But if she goes, Mom could die tomorrow and she might always regret she hadn't stayed a little longer to be here at the end.

Following Lib's gaze out the big bay window at the sunny, cold, March afternoon, I remember Sal telling me that Jenny had been a big help when she was making her own decision to go home the previous week.

"Maybe Jenny could help you decide what to do," I suggest, thankful she happens to be on duty today. "I think she helped Sal."

"I guess I could ask her," Lib replies, glancing at the clock. "I have to make up my mind pretty soon. I still have to pack if I'm going to leave!"

She stands up, smiling sadly at me over our sleeping mother. "This really sucks," she murmurs, turning to go.

"It really, really does," I agree, my heart breaking inside at the enormity of the decision she's having to make.

The room feels very still after she leaves, a harbinger perhaps of what the days ahead will be like if I'm there on my own. Part of me has been looking forward to being the lone sister in charge, the one on the front-line reporting back to Sal and Lib. It feels important, purposeful. And as someone who enjoys her alone time, the prospect of being on my own is not unappealing.

But as my eyes drift around the room, I keep noticing all the things we've brought over from Mom's apartment to make it feel less hospice-y, more like home. It had been such a team effort—the three of us putting our heads together to think of ways we could make Mom more comfortable, perhaps even coaxing a little smile to her face.

There's the blue glass vase of white hydrangea sitting on the windowsill, and the blown-up photograph of the view from Mom's room in Maine hanging on the wall opposite her bed, the one we'd rushed to have made the day she moved to hospice. On the recliner is the needlepoint heron pillow Lib had stitched for Mom after Dad died, and folded over the arm, one of the small, blue, perfect-for-a-nap comforters Mom had bought when she'd had all seven grandchildren visiting at once when they were little. Framed pictures of our family line the small table, and the soft, cream-colored cable knit blanket we'd given her for Christmas one year is spread over the more practical hospital bedding. On top of that is the small, square, dusty rose floral quilt handmade by hospice volunteers and given to Mom the day after she arrived, adding a touch of color to the otherwise monochrome room.

Everything has a story behind it, and Mom, Sal, Lib, and I know them all. The four of us have shared so many stories in the years since Dad died, forging a bond between us that I, for one, glean great strength from. And great comfort. So even though part of me knows I can handle things on my own, another part is sad that I have to. That our little team of four will never be together in this room, or any other room, again.

Looking over at Mom, I wonder what will happen to us after she's gone. Not that I doubt the strength of my relationship with my sisters—we are the three Ball girls after all, and will always share that tie to each other. But as Mom has aged, her needs and desires have been like an invisible force pulling us together again and again. What will happen when that force isn't tugging at us anymore? What will pull us together when we don't have Mom?

We have Maine, of course, which I know will always be a constant in our lives, but I can't imagine only see-ing Sal and Lib in the summer. What about the rest of the year? Mom has always been the drive that's propelled us into making plans to get together, whether for her birthday, or a holiday, or a trip south in the winter. Without her, I'm not sure what that drive will be.

Mom's eyes flutter open, so I move from my seat in the recliner to the edge of her bed.

"Hey sleepyhead," I murmur softly, glancing at the clock to see if it's time for her medicine. "Are you feeling okay?"

She nods, offering me a tenuous smile, but then closes her eyes again. Relieved that she doesn't seem to be in pain—there are still two hours left before her scheduled medication—I sit quietly next to her, watching her sleep.

A few minutes later, Lib pokes her head around the door, and seeing me sitting next to Mom, motions for me to come out into the hall. Pulling the door a little way closed, she says, "So I talked to Jenny and you were right— she was a huge help. I'm going to leave."

"Oh wow, okay. What did she say that helped?" I ask curiously, not sure if I'm relieved or sad that she's made the decision to go and leave me here alone.

"She told me she was going to ask me two questions, and if I could answer yes to both of them, then it was okay for me to leave."

"What were the questions?" I prod when she pauses, intrigued but not too surprised that Jenny, with her soft, soothing presence, would have the perfect solution to Lib's dilemma.

"Well, first she asked, '*Do you believe your mom knows you love her?*' and I told her yes, I know she does. And then she asked, '*Do you know your mom loves you?*'" Tears well up in Lib's eyes, and she brushes them away. "And I told her yes, I absolutely know that." Her voice is shaky, and I can see how hard she's trying to keep it together.

"It's gonna be okay," I say, giving her a quick, tight hug. "You're doing the right thing. And you know it's what Mom would want, right? She'd want you to go home to Kit and Henry."

"I know." Lib pulls a wadded-up ball of tissue from her pocket and dabs at her tears. "But it doesn't make it any easier."

No, I think, following her back into the room. *There is just nothing easy about this at all.*

∞

Mom is unusually wakeful that afternoon, so while Lib is back at the apartment packing, I take the opportunity to reassure her, as I'd promised myself I would after the scene with the chaplain earlier, that despite all my talk about energy and such, I have never stopped believing in God.

"You know, Mom," I begin hesitantly, not sure where to start. "Whatever else I may have ever said, I want you to know I've always believed in God. And Jesus. I just know he'll be there waiting for you. With Dad, and Billy...Uncle Bob..." I let my voice trail off, nervous to say too much and confuse her more than it seems I already have.

Mom is quiet, and for a minute I'm not sure she heard, her eyes focused on something, or maybe nothing, outside the window. But then she turns her gaze toward me and, with the tiniest hint of a smile, whispers, "I hope so."

Smoothing a few stray wisps of white hair off her forehead, I pull the bed covers up over her shoulders, then lean in to kiss her pallid cheek. "I *know* so," I murmur close to her ear, "they'll all be so happy to see you."

She drifts off then and as I watch her sleep, I hope more than anything that I'm right. That Dad and Billy, Uncle Bob, Grandmom and Granddad and, yes, even Jesus, will all be there waiting on the other side, enveloping her back into what I can only imagine is an enormous, ever-expanding bubble filled with all the love they'd shared with her when they were alive.

Because honestly, how could all those people Mom had loved and who had loved her have just disappeared when they died? They had to be somewhere, right? What would be the point if all their energy, all their *love*, simply vanished into nothing?

I'm reminded of a dream I had years before where I was in a crowded room of people waiting in line to get somewhere, I wasn't sure where. There were two men in front of me talking, and I overheard the man closest to me say to the man in front of him how lucky he was to be further along in the line because he'd be finding out sooner what happens when we die. I tapped the man nearest me on the shoulder and told him, quite loudly so he could hear me over the crowd, that we don't really die, because why would God bother creating us if we were just going to disappear? Over and over, I kept telling him that it just didn't make sense. That God wouldn't go to all that trouble if we were just going to die and turn into nothing.

Now, so many years later, sitting in my mother's quiet hospice room watching her sleep, I decide there's a reason that dream has stuck with me for so long. Perhaps my long-ago dream self had been preparing me for this exact experience when I would be bearing witness to my mother's steady retreat from life, watching her energy slip away right before my eyes, and terrified of the moment when it will disappear for good.

Maybe my dream-self was right, though, and Mom's energy isn't, in fact, disappearing. Maybe, instead, the beautiful, feisty, sometimes stubborn but incredibly loving energy that is my mother is simply in the process of transforming as, it turns out, energy can only do.

Of course, watching Mom's painfully slow transformation process firsthand is about the hardest thing I've ever done, her once strong body and mind fading into mere shadows of what they'd been. So, it helps to imagine that once she is through it, once the transformation is complete, that Dad, Billy, Uncle Bob—all the people she's loved who have gone before her—will be there waiting, in the ever-expanding bubble of love on the other side.

Lost as I am in my musings, I don't hear Lib come back into the room, her sudden presence next to me startling me out of my thoughts.

"How's she doing?" she whispers, seeing Mom is asleep again.

"Okay," I whisper back. "She was somewhat alert until just a bit ago. Hope I didn't wear her out for you."

Standing up, I grab my phone and purse from the table, then lean down to kiss the top of Mom's head. "I'll be back," I promise, even though I know she probably can't hear me. But they say hearing is the last sense to go, so I always tell her I'm leaving, just in case.

Shooting Lib what I hope is a reassuring smile, I head out to the hall, leaving her alone with Mom to say her own impossible goodbye.

The corridor is empty, so rather than waiting in the sun room where I would normally go, I settle myself in the little desk alcove across from Mom's room so I can keep my eye on the closed door, unsure what to expect when Lib emerges from behind it.

Because, really, how strong is she going to have to be to walk out of that room a final time? It's hard for me to imagine, and I worry that once she comes out, she might crumble into a thousand pieces at my feet.

Then what? I wonder, watching the door nervously. Will I have the strength to pick her back up, or will I crumble, too, under the weight of our shared grief? The big sister in me hopes I'll stay strong. That I'll find a way to put my own sadness aside and let Lib be sadder than me, at least until I get her to the airport.

Growing up, I'm afraid I wasn't the best big sister in the world, the two and a half years between us just enough to make Lib feel more like a pesky nuisance than a comrade in arms. She and Sal, despite their seven-year age difference, were closer back then, often leaving me on the outskirts with their whispered giggles and code names. I can't remember now what they called each other, but whenever I overheard their secret sister banter I felt left out, separate from the whole.

I don't know, maybe I was *overly sensitive,* as Sal and Lib were (are) always quick to point out. Or maybe I suffered from what psychologists refer to as Middle Child Syndrome. Maybe I still do. Because even now, so many years later, I can still feel the angst of my younger middle-sister-self that Sal and Lib, for whatever reason, might share things with each other that they don't share with me.

The dynamic changed a little when Sal was fifteen and headed off to boarding school in Connecticut, leaving me and Lib to navigate the next few rocky years of early adolescence without her. But because my experience was far less rocky than Lib's, I was often heedless, if not outright oblivious, to what my younger sister was going through.

For instance, while my biggest adolescent worries were a flat chest and an occasional pimple, Lib had full blown, painful acne and a tendency toward pudginess. Where I had a close-knit group of friends all the way through high school, Lib got ousted from her friend group in the fifth grade, in the worst mean girl kind of way. I wasn't unsympathetic—I'd had my own 'war' with my best friend in fifth grade, making all our other friends choose sides—so I think I figured Lib's troubles would blow over the way mine had, and subsequently didn't offer too much in the way of sisterly support.

Then, just as I was getting to the age when I might have started to see Lib as more friend than foe, I left for boarding school, too, and lost track of both my sisters' lives for the next few years, caught up as I was in my own. We'd see each other on vacations and such—Mom and Dad were great about getting us together as much as they could—but for many years Sal, Lib, and I were like three planets spinning around the same solar system, each on our own separate axis so our paths rarely aligned.

But then we grew up. One by one we got married and started families of our own, and our paths, once so separate and apart, began to converge more and more in our mutual desire for our children to know each other. And through that shared experience of parenthood, I got to know my sisters in a new way, realizing we had way more in common than I'd thought.

Then, when we were all in our thirties, Dad died, and the three of us found ourselves together on a difficult and unfamiliar path. Certainly not a path we would ever have chosen, and certainly not one we wanted to be on, but nevertheless there we were, stumbling along beside each other the best we could.

My sisters' presence in my life then, weighted with so many shared memories of our father, was what got me down that painful path in one piece. Sal and Lib were the only people in the world who understood my overwhelming grief, and they became more important to me than I ever would have imagined when we were growing up.

And now here we are again, stumbling together down another painful path, this one even more difficult because we know where we're headed—and there's no way to turn around and go somewhere else.

The door opens and Lib slips out, the look on her face at once shell-shocked and resolute. Standing up, I wrap my arms around her, swaying back and forth in the middle of the hall as I hug her to me, my big sister-self trying hard to be strong. An aide walks by and, catching my eye, offers me a soft smile as she puts a hand to her heart in silent sympathy.

Oh god. I squeeze my eyes shut, the aide's kind gesture more than I can bear. My throat is so tight I can hardly swallow. But then, thankfully, because I could never have pulled away first, Lib takes a step back and gives me a small, watery smile.

"I'm okay," she says, taking a shaky breath. "Let's just go."

We walk out to the parking lot, the cool March air refreshing after my long day inside, and I follow Lib as she threads her way through the maze of cars to where she'd parked a little while before. Reaching out to open the passenger door to get in, Lib suddenly doubles over, like the wind's been knocked out of her.

"This can't be happening," she moans under her breath. The fear in her voice is so palpable I feel it like my own, and for a moment I can't breathe. The deep, dark nothing I so feared as a child has found me again, right in the middle of the hospice parking lot, and is threatening to swallow me into its frightening void.

"Don't go there, Peggy," I hear a voice in my head warn. *"Remember who you are. It's going to be okay."*

I'm not sure whose voice it is—my big sister-self, my higher self, God—but it somehow gives me the courage to take a step back from the dark edge I'm teetering on and help my little sister get into the car.

It feels strange pulling back into hospice by myself a couple hours later, an odd combination of dread and anticipation at being there on my own. It's like I've been promoted to a bigger, more important job and though I'm looking forward to being the one in charge, there's also a certain amount of anxiety at having so much responsibility without anyone there for support.

Like my sisters—the one home in Maine with her new puppy, and the one on her way back to California, who I've just said goodbye to.

Dropping Lib off at the airport had not been uneventful. We'd gotten there early thinking we could grab a drink together before she had to board, but it turned out that Toledo's small, regional airport only had one bar, and it was on the other side of security.

"I think I saw a restaurant on our way in," Lib suggested, climbing back into the car after having gone inside to check out our options. "Let's go try that."

She was right, and a few minutes later we were walking into a nondescript Mexican restaurant, its parking lot surprisingly full though it wasn't even five pm.

"Pretty popular spot in the middle of nowhere!" I laughed, following Lib through the door into an open, bustling dining room. At first glance we weren't sure there even was a bar, but weaving our way through the crowded tables we spotted a small counter at the back with a couple of empty stools.

"What can I get you?" the bartender asked in a heavy accent, polite but distracted as he filled a pitcher with beer from the nearby tap.

"Umm, do you have any chardonnay?" I asked, glancing around hopefully for some kind of wine list.

"Si, we have white wine. Dos?" he looked at Lib, who nodded, though I could tell by her face she wasn't so sure.

Moments later he deposited two single serving bottles of white wine in front of us, like the ones you get on an airplane, though maybe even smaller, along with two equally small wine glasses. Lib and I, both self-confessed chardonnay snobs, grimaced sideways at each other as we looked at the bottles doubtfully.

"Well, how bad can it be?" I whispered, unscrewing the top and giving the wine a little sniff before pouring it into the glass. Lib followed suit.

Clinking our tiny glasses, I took a sip, braced for the worst.

"Oh, thank god," I laughed under my breath, "I don't know if I'm desperate, but this doesn't taste so bad!"

"I think maybe we're desperate," Lib smiled back, then took a sip herself. "But you're right! It could be worse!"

Sitting at that bar, I felt, for a few blissful moments, like we were two normal sisters sharing a drink and a few laughs. The boisterous energy of the people enjoying an early weeknight dinner reminded me that life isn't always so hard, that mothers aren't always dying.

Our little moment of respite didn't last long, though, and soon we were two sad sisters again, hugging each other goodbye in front of the terminal. I watched from the car as Lib made her way through the revolving door, waiting to see if she'd turn back for one last wave before disappearing inside. She did, and I blew a kiss back, hoping she could see.

Trying not to cry, I pulled away from the curb and headed toward the airport exit, realizing as I did that I wasn't sure how to get back to hospice. Lib had been in charge of directions on the way over, and I hadn't paid any attention to where we were going, just turning when she told me to turn.

Stopped at a red light, I grabbed my phone to pull up some directions, only to discover the battery was dead. Crap. Knowing there wasn't a charger in the car because I'd left mine back in Connecticut, I stared at the sign for the Ohio Turnpike across the road and wondered which way to go—east or west?

Trying to picture the map of Toledo in my head, when the light turned green, I made a snap decision to head west, figuring if I was wrong, I'd notice something and could turn around. At first the landscape seemed familiar so I relaxed, letting my thoughts drift as I followed the highway, a road so straight I barely had to hold the steering wheel. Of course, everything in northwest Ohio looks the same—miles and miles of flat, rural countryside interspersed here and there with aging farms and giant billboards—so I shouldn't have let my guard down so soon.

But it was so peaceful driving along, my thoughts taking me back to when I was a teenager and, needing space from some family drama, real or imagined, would take one of my parents' cars and go for a drive. The roads around Perrysburg, like the highway I was on, all ran straight as far as the eye could see, and I would drive and drive, singing along to the radio, relishing the solitude and freedom as the miles flew by.

And, incredibly, there I was, so many years later, driving alone in a parent's car across the familiar Ohio landscape, feeling a similar sense of solitude and freedom as my long-ago teenage self. I couldn't sing along to the radio—it had suddenly stopped working, along with the clock, a year or so before and Mom hadn't cared about getting either fixed. So, to keep myself company I sang old Peter, Paul, and Mary songs that I'd sung to my children when they were little, the words as soothing as they were nostalgic.

Between the songs and the landscape, I was lost in a happy time capsule of memory, until I saw a sign for Archbold, a town where my friend, Becky, had grown up. Archbold? That couldn't be right! Archbold was nowhere near Perrysburg! Alarm bells started ringing in my head, and I sat up a little straighter, my hands tightening on the steering wheel as the realization sank in that I had just driven a really long way in the completely wrong direction!

Jesus, how long had I been driving? Without a clock or a phone I had no way to tell, and chastised myself for not paying more attention, for being so absorbed in my thoughts that I'd lost all track of time. I got a little panicky, realizing that not only was I miles away from my dying mother, but if something had happened to her while I was gone, I'd be the last to know because my phone was dead! No one could even reach me!

Pressing my foot down on the accelerator, I sped up as much as the old Honda would allow, getting off at the next exit so I could turn around and go back the way I'd just come. Such a waste of time!

But then again, maybe it wasn't. Maybe, like drinking cheap wine with my sister in a random Mexican bar, driving by myself through the flat landscape of my youth had offered me another little respite from my stark reality, and for a few tranquil minutes, I'd been able to forget.

But now I'm back. The early evening light is casting deep shadows around the remaining cars scattered in the parking lot, and I sit for a long moment staring at the low, brick building in front of me. I dread going back in, part of me wishing I could be anywhere else. But anxious as I am to make sure Mom's okay, another, bigger part knows there's nowhere else I would rather be so, grabbing my purse, I open the car door and head in.

Day Twenty-Nine

The next morning Mom is awake and agitated, trying to sit up while at the same time pushing the call button she has gripped like a vice in her hand.

"Mom, what's wrong?" Dropping my purse and coffee on the table I hurry over to the bed. "What's going on? Are you in pain?"

"I forgot to fill out the form!" she cries, her eyes darting around the room like a trapped animal.

"What form?" I ask, taking her hand, trying to calm her.

"The one for the church!" Her words are slurred and thick, making them hard to understand. "I was supposed to hand it in but I don't think I did!"

"I'm sure it's okay, Mom, we'll figure it out." I rub her shoulder with gentle pressure, trying to keep her from getting out of the bed. But she's too anxious, lost in whatever fragment of memory her morphine-hazed mind has taken her, and she won't lie back, her frail body trembling with the effort to sit up. Wrapping my arms around her,

I'm wondering what to do next when an aide bustles into the room.

Without acknowledging me, she steps to the side of the bed, forcing me to unravel myself from Mom to give her some room.

"Sit back now, Kay," she demands, prying the call button out of Mom's deathlike grip with one hand while keeping her on the bed with her other. I'm surprised by her gruffness—the nurses and aides are always so patient—and am about to say something when she catches my eye.

"Sorry—it's just she's been pushing the button all morning."

"Oh dear," I murmur, not sure how to respond. I feel like the parent of a difficult child, and wonder if I should apologize for Mom's behavior, knowing how busy they all are. But one look at my mother's tired, anxious face, and I squash the thought. Whether real or imagined, Mom is clearly worried, and the fact that she's been pushing the call button all morning breaks my heart.

"Could she be in pain?" I wonder out loud, glancing at the clock. It's nine-thirty, not even two hours since her last dose, but still more than two hours until the next one. In the past few days, Mom's been experiencing more and more breakthrough pain, requiring extra morphine to help her get through between doses. But because she can't seem to vocalize her discomfort with words, I often have to rely on her non-verbal signs. She'll start to become restless, for instance, perhaps shifting her legs beneath the covers, or clearing her throat over and over. Sometimes she'll settle back down on her own, but other times the restlessness intensifies, and so I'll try to get her to articulate.

"Mom, do you hurt somewhere?" I'll prod.

She'll stare at me, her eyes cloudy with confusion. "I don't think so," she'll murmur, but then shift to another position. And then another. Of course, Mom's threshold for pain is unusually high—she lived with a fully torn rotator cuff for almost two months before going to get it checked.

"Are you sure?" I'll ask again.

She'll think for a moment, then admit that yes, maybe her elbow hurts. Or her toe, or her shoulder, or her finger. Mom's pain is pernicious, sneaking around her body like a snake, then biting her in the most random of places. More often than not, though, she can't pinpoint where it hurts, leaving me trying to guess if she's even in pain at all.

Like now. Mom's agitation over the imaginary form could be from too much morphine, but it could also be that the morphine is wearing off, and she *is* in pain.

"The nurse is aware of the situation," the aide replies in a clipped tone, even as she gently repositions the pillows behind Mom's head. "How's that, Kay? Better?"

Mom nods and lays her head back with a weary sigh, her agitation lessening as her eyes flutter closed. The aide, softening a little now that she has things under control, looks over at me with a sympathetic smile.

"Will you be okay here?"

"We're good," I tell her, settling myself in the recliner. "But could you make sure the nurse knows I'm here?"

"She'll be in soon," she assures me, taking one last look over at Mom before turning to leave.

"Try to get some rest," she adds, "you look a little tired."

Jerking hard on the lever to raise the footrest, I force myself to take some deep breaths as I watch her go out the door. Really? Me tired? I'm so beyond tired it's not even funny. Tired is how you feel after a long day working or hiking or gardening. Tired is when you haven't had a good night's sleep, or your children are running you ragged. Tired is normal.

But when you're in a hospice room day after day, watching your mother dying right before your eyes, deciding again and again if she should get more morphine so she's comfortable, or less because you know more will make her die faster, all the while trying to stay upbeat and positive for your family and friends even though all you want to do is cry every second, and at the same time trying to remember to eat and sleep so you can do it all again the next day, well, that's not just normal tired—it's soul-crushing tired.

Mom stirs, then opens her eyes, looking a bit panicky for a moment, like she doesn't know where she is. Watching from the recliner, I see her gaze fall on the picture of Dad on the tray table. She stares at it for a moment and then, much to my surprised relief, closes her eyes again. I guess Matthew, Mom's nurse last night, knew what he was doing when he moved all the pictures closer to her. "This way," he'd explained, "she won't feel so alone if she wakes up scared."

And just now it seemed she *had* woken up scared. And she *had* seen Dad's picture. And it *had* calmed her down, almost as if she could hear him saying, "It's going to be alright, Kaysie. Don't be afraid. Go back to sleep."

Maybe Dad *is* here. Maybe he's right by her bed, biding his time, waiting patiently for Mom to let go. And maybe, the closer she's getting to letting go, the more she can sense his presence, and it's bringing her comfort.

Maybe, maybe, maybe.

Day Thirty

It's been a long day. Mom had a couple of breakthrough episodes in the morning requiring extra doses of medication, and when it came time for her regular dose in the afternoon, she couldn't be woken up enough to safely swallow it, which was a first. Looking at me with sympathy, the nurse suggested it may be time for subcutaneous 'butterfly' injections, allowing them to give Mom her medicine without disturbing her.

"I guess so," I agreed hesitantly, a part of me scared that such a decision meant Mom might never wake up again. Although maybe that would be a blessing—I know she's ready, even if I'm not.

Now it's evening, and I'm waiting for the night nurse who hasn't been in yet, though it's way past the 8:00 p.m. shift change. Deciding to stay, I turn the lights down so only the bedside lamp is on, and curl up with a blanket in the recliner. Moments later—I swear she somehow knows when my focus has strayed—Mom calls out for water, and sighing, I lumber over the footrest back to her side.

She takes a little sip when I hold the straw to her lips, but then lays back, so I lean over to give her a quick kiss, resting my hand on her arm. Suddenly, her eyes flash open, and peering past me, she says, as clear as day, "Bill, is that *you*?"

I freeze, my hand rooted in place on her arm, scared to move. Is this really happening? Holding my breath, I watch Mom's face, her eyes fixed on something only she can see. And then, glancing slightly to her right, she whispers, "And Bobs?"

Oh my god. I follow Mom's gaze toward the empty space at the end of the bed. Are Dad and Uncle Bob really here? The shadows are deep in the dimly lit room, the quiet so still it *feels* like maybe they could be. I wait, hoping she might say something more, but Mom stays silent, and after a few more moments, closes her eyes.

Making my way back to the recliner, I feel almost giddy, like I've been given a surprise gift I've been hoping for as long as I can remember. I *knew* it! I knew Dad hadn't disappeared into nothing when he died! And now I have proof because not only did Mom see him *and* Uncle Bob, she spoke to them, too—with me bearing witness no less.

And though I can't see them, I know without a sliver of doubt they are here in this room, making sure Mom knows she isn't alone, and making sure I know she isn't alone, too.

Day Thirty-Three

The morning of the fifth day on my own, I wake up earlier than usual and, rather than rushing over to hospice as I've been doing, decide to take my time. Padding into the kitchen, I make myself a cup of coffee and grab my laptop, crawling back into bed to enjoy a few minutes for myself. There's an email from Lib, telling Sal and me that when she'd called for an update last night, the nurse had reported that Mom had told her, "she just wanted to get to Maine".

"Maybe she's holding on to get there?" Lib wonders in her note. *"Crazy I know, but maybe there's a way to talk to her and let her know we would do anything in the world to get her there if she wants???"*

Though it's a little hard to believe Mom said such a thing—she's hardly spoken at all in the last few days—a part of me can't help wondering if maybe she did. She loves our place in Maine so much it makes sense she would want to get back one more time, even if it is to die. One of the hardest things my sisters and I have to face in losing her is that she won't ever be there again. It seems inconceivable we'll never see her puttering around the kitchen, fretting that there are too many leftovers in the tired, old fridge, or standing at the porch rail watching her grandchildren swim in the river below. Never see her catching that last bit of afternoon sun on the bench outside the front door, or walking across the gravel driveway to the bathhouse in her sneakers, with only a towel wrapped around the rest of her.

No, Maine without Mom seems impossible, and now, hearing that maybe she's still wishing she could go despite how sick she is, the idea of Mom without Maine feels equally unimaginable. We have to do something.

"I'm going to call and find out how much it would cost to get her there." I write back. *"I guess we could just as easily sit in an ambulance on our way to Maine as in her room at hospice talking about it."*

So I do. Having looked into the logistics of moving Mom to Connecticut a few weeks earlier, I already have the name of an ambulance transport service I can call, and a few minutes later have their quote in hand: $6500 to get her from Perrysburg to Robbinston, with an RN and oxygen included, plus room for me in the ambulance to go with her.

Not too bad, I think, feeling a tingle of adrenaline at the possibility we might be able to pull this off. Sixty-five hundred is a lot but, I reason, if Mom's in Maine then we won't need her apartment here anymore, so we'll be *saving* money by moving her.

I call Sal next because it's only March and since the camp isn't winterized, Mom would have to stay with her and Paul in their farmhouse across the street, at least until the weather warms up. But having spent her childhood summers in that same farmhouse, I know Mom will be as happy there as at the camp—kind of like coming full circle back to where she started.

"What do you think?" I ask Sal, after explaining my idea. "Am I crazy to think we can do this?"

"I don't think there's anything any of us want more than for Mom to be here, looking out at her river, when she dies," Sal agrees. "So no, you're not crazy. I'll talk to Paul and start figuring things out on this end, but you probably need to talk to the doctor and see if they'll even let us take her."

Propelled by the possibility of imminent action, of doing something to disrupt the lonely monotony of the past few days, I jump out of bed and throw on my clothes. Rushing around the apartment, I grab all the things I'll need for the day—computer, phone, chargers, book, needle-point—stuffing them into my tote, before pulling on my coat and snatching up the car keys from the little pewter bowl Mom always keeps them in. *She'll be so happy!* I think, adrenaline zipping up my belly again as I imagine telling her the news.

But she's asleep when I get there so, checking the white board on the wall and seeing that Jenny is the nurse today—thank god—I drop my things and head back out to find her. Just as I get to the door, though, the aide walks in.

Breathlessly, I tell her our plan, my enthusiasm building with every word.

"It sounds like a wonderful idea," she replies, with a genuine smile. "But let me go find Jenny. She'll know better than me."

A few minutes later Jenny walks in, and though she's smiling, she's shaking her head slowly side to side.

"No way?" I venture, as we stand facing each other in the middle of the room.

"No way," Jenny tells me, though not unkindly.

"Even with a nurse on board to give her medications? And oxygen?" I press. "I think Mom would rather die in an ambulance if it means there's a chance she could get to Maine."

"I know she would," Jenny agrees, "but I'm afraid she would never make it. Not now. And the way things are," she adds gently, "if your mom were to pass somewhere between here and there—say the middle of Pennsylvania—the logistics get very complicated between medical examiners, and funeral homes…" her voice trails off as she reaches out to touch my hand. "I'm sorry. You girls are so sweet to want this for your mom. I wish it were different."

"Me too," I agree, glancing over at Mom. "I'd give anything to have it be different."

Feeling deflated, I try to be grateful that at least I hadn't gotten Mom's hopes up only to dash them moments later. Watching her sleep, the naivete of our plan is foolishly obvious. She's so old and sick—her mouth slightly agape, her loose, pallid skin grayish in the early morning light, her breathing shallow and uneven. She never would have made it. What were we thinking?

Gazing out the window at the overcast March day, contemplating the empty hours lying ahead, I'm not sure who I feel sorrier for—Mom because she won't get to see Maine again, or me, because I won't be able to take her. The flurry of activity this morning only emphasized the tedium of the past few days, and I would have welcomed the disruption that a cross country ambulance ride would have brought to my lonely vigil.

Mom stirs, shifting ever so slightly beneath the bed covers as her eyes, squinting open, stare out the window for a brief moment before slowly closing again. *She's sad,* I think, wondering what it must feel like to wake up to yet another day waiting to die. She stirs again, this time reaching her gnarled hands toward the tray table in front of her. I jump up and move to the side of the bed, pulling a chair up so I can sit down close to her.

"Thirsty, Mom?" I swish the pink sponge swab around in the plastic cup to absorb some water then hold it over her mouth until her lips open, like a baby bird looking to be fed. I roll the sponge over the inside of her cheeks until the stringy threads of white saliva coating her teeth and gums begin to disappear. When it seems she's had enough, I leave the swab in the water cup and dab some lip ointment on her cracked lips.

"Thank you," Mom murmurs with a faint smile, "that feels better."

I lean over and kiss the top of her head, careful to avoid the long, pink scar traversing her scalp. Its healing presence taunts me—proof that some of Mom's cells are still working, though the rest of her body is shutting down.

The aide pokes her head in the door. "Sorry your plan isn't going to work out," she says when she sees me.

"Thanks, I know. It was worth a try, right?"

"Definitely. Are you guys okay here? Need anything?"

Assuring her we're fine, I watch her disappear back into the hall, as Mom, with her eyes still closed, murmurs "What plan?"

Smiling to myself that Mom still doesn't miss a trick, I tell her what we were hoping to do.

"But I guess there's just no way," I finish with a sigh. "We'd do anything to get you to Maine if we could. You know that, right?"

She nods. "I know," she whispers. "You're wonderful to try."

A pang of regret shoots through me. *Did I try hard enough?* I wonder, worried that maybe I gave up too easily. Maybe I should have asked to speak to the doctor, or called the ambulance company back to find out what would happen *if* Mom died on the way. Maybe if I'd been a little less quick to accept the 'no way' verdict, we might have been able to figure it out.

Maybe, maybe, maybe.

"Hey, Mom?" I touch her shoulder and she opens her eyes to look at me. "I know we can't get to Maine in real life, but how about we try going in our imaginations? Let's pretend I've picked you up at the airport, and we're about to get on Route 9. Close your eyes, and I'll tell you what I see, okay?"

With a small smile, Mom does as I ask, closing her eyes as I begin to describe everything I can remember about the two hour drive from Bangor to Robbinston, a trip we've both made countless times over the years. At first, I'm a little tentative, not sure Mom's memories will be the same as mine, but soon the familiar landmarks are flashing by in my mind as though we really are together in a car, driving to Maine.

I take her past the motel with the billboard 'Sleepy People Wanted,' a rundown looking place that has been looking for sleepy people as long as I can remember. We drive through the town where American flags fly from every telephone pole, and the RV campground on the lake, the one I thought looked like so much fun with all the boats and campers when I was little. We pass by the Eagle's Nest restaurant whose parking lot is always full, no matter what time of day we're driving by, and then the long stretch of miles with nothing but Maine woods as far as the eye can see.

"Halfway there," I tell her, going by the Wilderness Lodge, an outpost of some unknown (at least to me) purpose that somehow, no matter how fast or slow I'm driving, is always *exactly* halfway between the airport and the camp. Then comes the old fire lookout station and the life size Smokey the Bear with his fire danger level sign, long gone now but still there in my memory. There's the ice cream place where we sometimes stop, though usually not when I'm driving because by that point I've been in the car for close to eight hours and I just want to get there. Then comes the rest area we had to pull into once when my cousin got carsick, with the picturesque stream where Mom cleaned him up. And finally, the Lord's Well Drilling truck hoisted high up on a tall, metal shaft so it looks like it's hanging in mid-air, always a welcome sight because it means we're nearing the end of Route 9.

"Getting closer!" I say, turning onto Route 1. I take us past the old Baring airport—a rusting, battered hangar with a grass-rutted landing strip—where we once anxiously waited for Dad, flying in from Bangor on a tiny charter plane. We pass through the Moosehorn Preserve, looking to see if there are any osprey sitting on their nests, then around the rotary to the turnoff for the shortcut, taking us past Walmart (that we hate because it took business away from all the small shops in town) and Shop & Save (that we love because it's managed to survive despite Walmart opening next to it) before spilling us back onto Route 1.

The closer we get to the camp, the more excited I'm getting, the same as in real life. Passing by the little cemetery where Dad's buried next to generations of Mom's family, my heart speeds up with anticipation as we round the big curve in the road and get our first real glimpse of the St. Croix. Even in my imagination, seeing the river is like seeing an old friend I haven't seen all winter, and I let out a happy sigh.

"Okay, we're turning down the driveway now! Look how tall that little pine tree's grown!" I exclaim, gratified to see a tiny smile pass over Mom's face. She loves that pine. "Going around the bend now—there's the boathouse, and the camp! We made it Mom! We're in Maine!"

And so for the next couple of days, whenever Mom is at least a little bit awake, I take her to Maine again. We do all the things she loves to do—from walking down to the camp for breakfast to sitting outside her bedroom with a small glass of cranberry juice in the late morning sun. We have cocktails on the porch and watch the osprey fishing, and sit out on the knoll having a sandwich watching the tide come in. We go for a boat ride on the river to look for seals, and walk through the woods to the Bluff, where we sit looking upriver at the clouds skirting over the horizon. We even go to Shop & Save and over to Canada for a little lunch at the Kingsbrae Gardens, one of her favorite places.

And when I run out of ideas, I reach out to the grandchildren for some help, reading Mom their emails as they come in, one after another, holding back tears as I share their memories, so intertwined with my own:

The salty taste of the river after a boat ride

The smell of the camp when you walk in for the first time every summer

The parade of people and hugs whenever someone new arrives

The sound of someone dialing the rotary phone

Grandmom working in the garden by the camp with the bumble bees buzzing in the clover

Eating the massive blueberries off the bush by the bath house

Always checking the weather stick, even if no one really knows if it works

Lounging around in front of the fireplace on that big, round rug like a family of lions

Jumping off the roof deliberately in front of Grandmom

Mom's eyelashes flutter at the last one from Bill, another ghost of a smile flickering on her lips. She hates it when the kids jump off the roof, and Bill is always the first one to do it.

What a gift she's given us, I think, not for the first time, standing up to stretch after reading the last email. It occurs to me that maybe the reason Maine without Mom feels so impossible is because her spirit is imbued in all of our memories of it. For our family, Maine *is* Mom and I don't know how it will ever not be.

Day Thirty-Four

Mom's slow, unpredictable decline continues, and as her moments of awareness become fewer and more far between, I can feel my own energy—already precipitously low—slipping away along with her. The fatigue in my body keeps getting heavier, the weight of it like a thick cloak impeding my every move. Nothing feels easy, and as the days slide by, one into the next, their sameness is an onerous burden I carry around with me, making everything I do feel that much harder.

Like waking up in the early morning after a fitful night's sleep waiting for the phone to ring, only to realize it hadn't rung, again. Then dragging myself out of bed and back over to hospice, walking down the long corridor to Mom's room, sharing sad smiles with the nurses and aides because, well, there I am, walking down the hall, again. Mustering up the energy to go to the cafeteria for lunch because I have to eat and ordering the same grilled cheese, potato chips, and iced tea day after day, because it's too exhausting to think of anything else I might want to try. Then, hours later, after double checking with the night nurse that she knows how to reach me, wearily making my way back down the corridor, out to the car, and home to Mom's apartment, where maybe I'll scramble an egg for dinner as I suck down a glass of chardonnay before crawling into bed for another fitful night's sleep, waiting for the phone to ring, again.

This morning's been particularly difficult, and as I sit staring out the window next to my now always sleeping mother, feeling depressed and tired, and, most of all, guilty to be wallowing in such self-pity, Rita, the chaplain, pokes her head in the door.

"Just checking in," she says when she sees me, then glances over at Mom. "Oh, she's asleep...I'll try to come back later."

"Okay," I reply, shrugging. I'm beyond caring what Rita does or doesn't do at this point, even if she is being a little less abrasive than usual. "Mom's not awake much these days, though."

She pauses, then walks further into the room toward me. "How are *you* doing?" she asks. "It must be hard without your sisters here."

Willing back tears, I look down at my hands, not wanting to admit, especially to her, how hard it's been. But

I'm so tired, the words fall out of my mouth of their own accord.

"It has been hard," I confess. "It's been a long five weeks."

"Yes," she agrees. "And a long time to be away from home."

The tears I've been holding back begin seeping out the corner of my eyes at this unexpected acknowledgement of what is the root of my guilt—that in trying to be a good daughter, I'm being a bad wife. I've been away from home for such a long time, and though John has never complained, there's a deep-seated angst churning inside me that by choosing to stay here with Mom, I am, at the same time, choosing not to be with him.

"How horrible am I to want Mom to die faster so I can go home?" I whisper, tears now streaming down my face. "What kind of daughter could ever want that?"

"A daughter who loves her Mom," she assures me, perching herself on the arm of a nearby chair. "Believe me, how you're feeling is more normal than you think. Try not to be so hard on yourself—it isn't easy what you're going through."

She pauses, her gaze falling on Mom, still sleeping soundly, despite our conversation. "This is actually a special time for you and your mother," she says, turning back to me. "How often do you get to be just a daughter?"

I look up in surprise and manage a watery smile. "Not that often," I admit, not sure if I've ever been just a daughter without being a sister, wife, and mother at the same time. In fact, I'm not sure it's ever occurred to me that I *could* be just one or the other, intertwined as they are in my perception of who I am. But Rita is right. Being in this hospice room, alone with my mom day after day, I don't have to be anything *but* a daughter. And with that subtle shift in perspective a certain lightness begins to diffuse the heaviness inside me, allowing me to breathe a little easier.

"Thank you," I say, standing up to give her a quick hug. "I can't tell you how much hearing this helps."

"Sometimes it's hard to see things when you're so close," she replies, turning to leave. Pausing at the foot of Mom's bed, she lightly touches the quilt covering her frail body before heading out of the room.

I sit back down, trying to digest how I can feel grateful to this woman who has irritated and upset me since the moment we met. Perhaps she and I have some sort of karmic tie we're trying to resolve, or some sort of spiritual contract that's playing out in my mother's hospice room. But unlike my other encounters with her that have left me

angry and uncertain, this one has me feeling more hopeful. More sure that my feelings, as mixed up as they are,
don't make me a bad daughter or a bad wife.

This time alone with Mom *is* a gift, I realize, bittersweet as it may be. Because what's true—and what I
imagine Rita was gently trying to remind me—is that once
Mom's gone, I'll never be just a daughter again.

Day Thirty-Six

"Sorry again we went dark on you yesterday. I promise to be better about keeping you in the loop." Hitting the send button on my email to Lib, I hope when she gets it later that morning in California it will help diffuse the tension that's sprouted up between us since Sal got back to Ohio the day before. Not that we'd done anything intentional to cause the friction, but when neither Sal or I replied to Lib's texts last night when we were out having some dinner, she'd gotten frustrated with our lack of communication. I suppose I can't blame her—I'd have been upset too if I was looking for updates on Mom and both my sisters ignored me. But still, it wasn't deliberate.

After such a long week alone, I was pretty happy to have Sal back, and being out at a restaurant, away from hospice and its permeating specter of death, my tired soul just wanted to revel in a few minutes of normalcy without interruption from the outside world. Even if that outside world included my younger sister.

The restaurant, Stella's, a favorite of Mom's and brimming with memories of the many times we'd eaten there with her, was bustling when we walked in, so Sal and I decided to sit at the bar rather than wait for a table. Grabbing the last two stools at the end of the long, wooden counter, we stuffed our coats and bags underneath us and tried to catch the bartender's eye. It was noisy—the hum of conversations and clatter of dishes and silverware reverberating around us—and I could see why Mom always insisted on sitting at a table in the back. It was hard to carry on a conversation over the din of the crowded bar, and Sal and I had trouble hearing each other, let alone an incoming text.

So it wasn't until we were back in the car afterward that I thought to check my phone. "Shoot," I said, when I saw the missed messages. "Lib's wondering where we are." I started to text her back, but since Sal and I were together, decided it might be better to call instead. She picked up on the first ring, and as soon as I heard her voice I knew we were in trouble.

"Where did you guys go?" Lib demanded, her tone somewhere between a whine and a rebuke. "I was worried!"

"We went out to grab some dinner," I told her, annoyed to feel so defensive. "You must know we'd call you if there was any big change."

"You guys can't leave me hanging here like that. It's not fair. You have to keep me in the loop!"

"I know, you're right. And we will, I promise. But we were just having some dinner! There was no loop to be in!"

"You could have at least texted me that's where you were! For all I knew something bad was happening with Mom."

Sighing, I apologized again, knowing she had a point, but still annoyed. I mean, of course we would call her if something bad was happening with Mom! No news had always meant good news in our family, hadn't it? But keeping the three of us on an even keel was more important to me than being right so, swallowing my irritation, I promised we wouldn't disappear on her again.

Now, finishing my coffee and thinking about getting dressed, Sal comes into the living room and sits down across from me, her brow furrowed, her mouth set in a serious line.

"What's up?" I ask, bracing myself. I know that look.

"I've scheduled a meeting with Daniel at Carranor to talk about a memorial service," she announces, her tone brisk. "I know you and Lib don't think we need to do one here, but I do, so I'm going to move forward with a plan with or without your help. It's at 10:30 if you want to come."

Bristling—nothing like having your older sister proclaim what is or isn't going to happen—I mumble that I'll think about it and retreat to my bedroom on the pretext of getting dressed. Needing some moral support, though, I call John instead.

"Sal's being so bossy about having a service in Perrysburg," I complain, pacing around the small room. "And now she says she's going to have it even if Lib and I don't want to."

"Of course you have to have a service in Perrysburg!" John exclaims, surprising me with his vehemence. "Why wouldn't you?"

"Because we're having one in Maine this summer," I remind him. "It feels like a lot to ask the family to do both." I stare out the window at the courtyard below, wondering absently if Mom ever went down there. It doesn't look too inviting on this late March day, but maybe when it's warmer it might be a nice place to sit and get some air on the benches scattered around.

"Peg," John's voice pulls me back into the room. "The family will do what they'll do, you can't worry about that. But this is your mom. She's lived in Perrysburg for sixty years. You have to let her friends say goodbye. You have to say goodbye to them."

John's certainty cuts through my resistance in a way that Sal's hadn't been able to—though she's been equally as certain with the exact same reasons. Maybe the younger sister in me didn't want to give her the satisfaction of being right—Sal can be so patronizing sometimes. After talking to John, though, I get it—it would be selfish of us not to have some sort of formal farewell. We might never have a reason to come back to Perrysburg after Mom's gone, so in a way we'll be losing it, too.

Sal is gathering up her things when I go back out to the living room.

"Okay, so John agrees we have to do something here for Mom, so I'll go with you to Carranor," I tell her, humbled when I see the visible relief on her face. It hadn't occurred to me how hard it might be to plan this without Lib's and my support, and I feel bad for having been so unbending—in hindsight it feels very petty.

"I'm so glad," she says, giving me a hug. "Thank you."

"Not sure Lib is going to budge, though," I say over my shoulder, heading back to my room, making a mental note to call and tell her my change of heart. I hope she'll understand.

∽

Walking into Carranor is like walking into the affectionate embrace of a dear friend I've known forever—the comforting smells and familiar trappings wrapping me in a warm, hazy glow of nostalgia. The labyrinth of rooms inside the unpretentious, gambrel colonial—set on the corner of two residential streets half a block from the house I grew up in—are as familiar to me as my own, their understated charm reminiscent of a beloved grandparent's home rather than a staid tennis club. Swarming with memories from years of tennis lessons, dancing school and field day races as children, to Thursday night buffets, Thanksgiving dinners and Christmas caroling as we grew up, Carranor was, and is, a centerpiece in my family's life.

And like any old friend, we've always been able to count on Carranor to be there when we need it. Like now. Having never planned a memorial service before, Sal and I let Daniel, the club manager, guide us along as we try to make as many decisions as we can so we don't have to make them later. What time of day? How many tables? What kind of food? Daniel isn't hesitant to chime in when Sal and I aren't sure, and I find myself smiling that he knows Mom's tastes so well. Of course, I'm not surprised—she's never been one to keep her likes and dislikes to herself, especially as she's gotten older.

But planning a memorial service for your mother while she's still alive is pretty morbid, so I'm grateful when Daniel closes his notebook and pushes back his chair.

"We'll make sure everything is just the way your mom would like it," he promises, as Sal and I put on our coats. "She's going to be missed."

Blinking back tears, I look around the big dining room, memories spilling out of every corner. John and Sal were so right—it would have been a huge mistake not to let Perrysburg say goodbye to Mom, and for us not to say goodbye to it.

∾

Later that evening, back in Mom's apartment after another tiring, but uneventful day, Lib calls.

"How's it going?" she asks when I answer.

"We're doing okay," I tell her. "Mom's the same. Had a good meeting with Daniel at Carranor this morning."

She's silent on the other end and too late, I realize I'd forgotten to call her. Shoot.

"About a memorial service?" she finally asks, breaking the awkward silence. "I thought you and I agreed we didn't want to have one."

"John made me see it differently," I explain, kicking myself for forgetting. "He reminded me it's not just about us, which I have to admit is true." Glancing over at Sal who's pouring herself a cocktail in Mom's small kitchen, I catch her eye, pointing at myself and nodding to please pour me one, too.

"Believe me," I add, when Lib doesn't respond, "I'm so tired—the idea of planning a memorial service on top of everything else is the last thing I want to worry about. But I think Sal and John are right—we really have to."

"Well, you guys do whatever you want," Lib says testily. "You're there and I'm not. But I can't see bringing Henry so far for such a short time, and I don't know if Nick can make it, so it'll just be me I guess."

At the mention of Henry, a familiar pang of guilt flashes through me and I waver, the pull of my younger sister's needs momentarily stronger than my own. But then a rare frustration with the ever-present Henry card pokes its way through the guilt, and I find myself wanting to push back.

Which is strange, because Libby doesn't use Henry as an excuse very often. As his parents, both she and Kit work hard to make his life as normal as possible, even if it might make their own lives more difficult. In fact, it's often *me* telling Lib she should pull out the special needs card, especially when she's dealing with the airlines or trying to get seats for a show or movie. "Just tell them about Henry," I'll urge. "Everyone else does it! It'll make things so much easier!"

"It's too exhausting to explain to someone," she always replies. "It's easier not to."

Under normal circumstances I'm sympathetic when Lib's overwhelmed by her life, but not tonight. Tonight, I'm overwhelmed by life, too, and I don't want to think about Libby and what her family will or won't do. Sallie's, either, for that matter. I hardly want to think about my own. My brain hurts from all the worries crowding inside it—from Mom, to memorial services, to being away from home for so long—each one's like a tiny shard of glass pricking my consciousness, making me feel ragged and edgy.

"I guess we'll all do what we have to do," I murmur, rolling my eyes at Sal as she hands me a glass of wine.

"I guess so, too," Lib says, her voice sullen. "But now I feel like the bad guy—it'll be really hard if my family's the only one not there."

Biting my tongue so I won't say what I want to say— that if it's going to be so hard then they should all simply come—I take a sip of wine.

"We don't know when this will even be," I remind her, "and we're all tired. Maybe we should talk more tomorrow?"

"Okay," Lib agrees with an audible sigh.

"Okay, then," I echo, hesitant to end the call with the tension still high, but not sure what else I can say to make it better. "Love you."

"Love you, too."

With that uneasy truce between us, we hang up and I look at Sal, shrugging my shoulders.

"I don't know—I guess she's feeling a little sorry for herself. Can't say I blame her. It would be hard to be the only one not here."

"Well, then she should come back," Sal says, shaking her head. "Sometimes Lib is her own worst enemy."

Not wanting to get into a 'what Libby should or shouldn't do' debate—an easy trap I sometimes fall into with Sal—I stand up.

"I think I left my charger in the car. I'll be right back."

A few minutes later, rummaging around Mom's car trying to find my missing charger, a piercing shriek slices through the dark night, freezing me in place. Another shriek and then a cacophony of high-pitched chattering seems to be coming from the edge of trees just beyond the parking area. A little nervous, but curious what can be making such a racket, I climb out of the car, leaving the door open behind me in case I have to make a quick dash to safety.

Turning on my phone's flashlight, I point it up into the nearest tree where the angry noise is coming from and see three racoons, two of them together at the very top, hissing and screeching at a third one a few branches below, who then hisses and screeches back.

"Wow, you guys scared me!" At the sound of my voice, the chattering stops and all three turn and peer down at me through the bare tree limbs, like three mischievous children caught by their mother doing something naughty.

"You should be nicer to each other," I admonish, laughing at the irony. What are the chances I should witness such a spectacle while in the midst of my own squabbling threesome? I have no doubt these raccoons are trying to tell me something—I'm just not exactly sure what.

Finding my charger, I make my way back across the parking lot, pondering what the symbolic meaning of the screeching raccoons might be. Is their quarreling presence a physical reflection of the tension between my sisters and me? Back in the apartment, I do a quick internet search on raccoon symbolism and have to smile when I read that they are very protective animals and are often a sign that it's time to put family first. Not only that, but an encounter with one could mean it's time to let go of a situation.

Well, it can't get clearer than that, I think, closing up my laptop. I promise myself I'll take heed of the raccoons' perspicuous message and find a way to smooth things over with Libby as soon as I can.

But she beats me to it, sending Sal and me an email that we wake up to the next morning.

"If I've caused you both more angst than we're already dealing with, I'm so sorry. I'm so grateful you're there with Mom and I know I could get on a plane and be there too. I want to believe I'm okay with not doing that, but maybe my uncertainty is coming out in ways that make it harder for both of you. Please know that is not my intention."

Reading Lib's note, the word 'angst' pops out at me, and though I know its general meaning, it feels like it's the perfect word to describe how I'm feeling, so I look it up to find its exact definition.

Angst: A feeling of deep anxiety or dread, typically an unfocused one about the human condition.

Oh my god, yes! Angst *is* the perfect word to describe my current 'human condition', and lately it's been all encompassing. Every thought I have, or word I utter, feels fraught with it—even in my dreams.

"*Yes, the angst is overwhelming,*" I write back, "*and I know we're all feeling it. So please know, if I don't say the right thing, or worse, say the wrong thing, it's not from lack of love or compassion for how you're feeling—it's only that I'm in the same angst-filled boat and trying my hardest to stay afloat.*"

Sal chimes in, too, reiterating the intention she had set when we were helping Mom move out of her house, only a year and a half before:

"*I made a promise that I would love you both more at the end of moving Mom than at the beginning. This promise still holds now more than ever, no matter what swamps each of us fall into!*"

And that's all it takes. Three heartfelt emails between sisters and the tension dissolves, allowing us to all breathe a sigh of relief. Because even though we might hiss and screech at each other as loudly as any raccoon, there's no one else I would rather have in my horrible, angst-filled boat than my two sisters.

Day Thirty-Seven

I wonder if people remember the last thing someone they love says to them. The last time that person looks at them and knows who they are and says their name. Watching Mom die has been like watching the tide go out in Maine, her energy seeping away in such tiny increments it's impossible to measure moment to moment. And like an ebbing tide, her voice has disappeared by such imperceptible degrees I don't notice its absence until it's gone.

In a similar way, her breathing pattern is changing in small ways, too, becoming more irregular and uneven day to day, her mouth always hanging open now as if trying to tempt in the air. I'm scheduled to fly home on Sunday, as it's Sal's turn to be the sister-in-charge, but when the nurse reports Saturday morning that Mom experienced several episodes of apnea the night before, I decide to stay, canceling my flight and keeping my return home open-ended.

Apnea, in my experience, is not a good thing. When Elizabeth was born four weeks early, she was just under six pounds and though otherwise healthy and well, they kept her in the nursery the first night to keep an eye on her. The next morning when I went to see her, she wasn't there—they'd moved her to the newborn intensive care unit because she'd stopped breathing and they'd had to give her chest a tap to wake her lungs back up.

"Try not to worry," the nurse reassured me as fear bubbled up inside my own chest. "Apnea is very common in newborns, especially when they're premature. Elizabeth only had the one episode, so I'm sure she'll be fine. Come with me. I'll take you to her."

I'd never heard the word 'apnea' before, and as I followed the nurse down the hospital corridor, I repeated it over and over in my head, like a mantra, so I'd remember it when I talked to John. "Apnea, apnea, apnea. Elizabeth had an apnea."

The nurse was right and there were no more episodes, but to be extra cautious, because of our family history with SIDS, they put Elizabeth on a home apnea monitor to measure her breathing twenty-four hours a day. John and I were trained in how to use it, and how to do infant CPR if the alarm ever went off and she had stopped breathing. What I don't remember being trained for were the many 'false' alarms—the times when the ear shattering alert would go off, not because Elizabeth wasn't breathing, but because one of the electrodes on her chest had become loose or detached.

One night we were both in the deep, exhausted sleep only parents of an eighteen-month-old and newborn baby could know, when the blaring alarm jarred us awake. Before my mind could make sense of what was happening, John had jumped out of bed and raced to the door, which he didn't realize was closed, so hit full on, the impact stopping him up short.

"Oh my god, are you okay?" I struggled out of bed to get over to him, but he had already yanked the door open and was running down the hall to Elizabeth's room. Following in a bleary fog, I found him leaning over the crib with two fingers on her chest, his head bent low trying to determine in the dark room if she was breathing. I pushed the button on the monitor to silence the alarm, the sudden quiet almost as deafening as the blaring sound had been.

"She's fine," John whispered, his shoulders sagging over the crib rail with relief. "Oh my god—that was terrifying!" I rubbed his back in commiseration, my own heart still pounding as we both stared down at our sleeping baby.

Over the next few months, we would experience several more false alarms, each one triggering the same blinding panic, the same heart-pounding fear that Elizabeth had stopped breathing, and it was up to us to save her. It was up to us to get her to breathe again.

With Mom, though, it's the opposite. Well, almost the opposite. While there are no apnea monitors or shifting electrodes to worry about—and no lifesaving interventions to prepare for when she does stop breathing—there are equally as many, if not more, false alarms. Paralyzing moments when the pause between her exhale and inhale is so long I'm certain it has carried her away, and I hold my own breath, waiting to see.

Since Sal got back, we've been taking turns sitting with Mom, partially to give each other time alone with her, but perhaps more importantly, to give each other time away. Not from Mom—it's hard to leave her for any reason—but from Mom's increasing absence. At times being in her room is like being in a vacuum where some unknown force is sucking her away, leaving behind a palpable emptiness.

There are other times, though, when a profound sense of peace will come over me as I sit alone with her, like I'm feeling now. She's sleeping comfortably, so I curl up on the recliner and try to rest, my own sleep having become increasingly elusive the past few nights. The swooshing and gurgling of the oxygen concentrator muffles the sounds coming from the hall, and the weight of its familiar rhythm allows my thoughts to settle, my body to relax.

Dozing in and out of wakefulness, I hear the housekeeper come in, her movements as she maneuvers the dust mop around the room so measured and smooth, I hardly know she's there. Her soft presence adds to the peaceful weight I'm under and I don't want to move, not even to say thank you when I hear the door open as she slips out of the room.

Somewhere in the back of my mind I become aware of Mom's breathing, or lack of breathing. I sit up and peer over at her sleeping form, trying to see if there's any movement coming from her chest. *I'll count to ten*, I think, forcing myself to stay put, to not jump up and shake the missing breath back into her. "*One, two, three, four...*" I glance at the big wall clock, watching the second hand tick away as I count silently in my head, "*five, six, sev...*" and Mom breathes in, loud and jarring. I close my eyes in relief.

And so it will go the next couple of days, counting the seconds in the pauses between Mom's shallow breaths, fearing and hoping with each one it will be her last. The spiritual me, the one who trusts that death is merely a transition, not an ending, hopes Mom will let go, wanting her to be at peace, her struggle over. *"Please, please, please,"* I pray as I count the seconds in my head. But at the same time, the physical me—the flesh and blood me sitting in the recliner anxiously watching the secondhand on the wall clock tick away the seconds—is terrified of the moment when Mom *will* let go, the lengthening pauses like spiraling black holes threatening to suck in her last breath while I sit there counting. *"Thank God,"* I sigh when Mom finally breathes back in.

The truth is, the physical me and the spiritual me have been in a constant state of conflict since we brought Mom to hospice, their battle inside me an exhausting tug of war between acceptance and resistance, trust and fear. I don't want my mom to die but I do.

Day Thirty-Nine

It's been said that people often die in the manner they live, so I guess it shouldn't be surprising our tenacious mother has been as unyielding in her dying as she'd been in her living. Over the weekend, though, Mom's body has finally begun to show increasing signs that perhaps death is, at last, drawing nearer—a thready pulse, mottling in the feet, restlessness. Sunday afternoon, I get back to her room after lunch and find her moving restlessly under the covers, like she can't get comfortable. She seems to be in a different place than earlier in the day—her eyes are open, but not seeing; she's making sounds that, though unintelligible, seem quite anxious. Worried, I track down the nurse to see about getting her a breakthrough dose of morphine, in case she's in pain.

"It might not necessarily be pain that's making her so restless," Nan explains as she gives Mom some extra morphine and a dose of Ativan for her anxiety. "Your mom's had a long journey—she might be working through some anxious events in her life in order to finally let go."

My accepting, spiritual-self nods sagely at Nan's explanation, trusting that Mom's soul knows what it needs in order to make its transition to the other side, even as my physical heart sinks like a stone. The idea that Mom is still working through some unknowable, anxious event in her life—this time completely on her own because she can't talk to anyone about it—is beyond distressing, especially because there's nothing I can do to help her through it. Helping my mom get through things is what I *do*.

But as I watch the drugs work their magic and Mom settles back down, I realize she's entered a stage on this seemingly endless hospice journey that doesn't include me. She's on her own, navigating her way along some mysterious spiritual path I will never know, and hard as it is to sit by and watch her, it's the only thing left for me to do.

Day Forty-One

Lib and I are walking along the beach in Maine when her cell phone rings. It's Sal, calling to tell us Mom died. I'm sad but thankful I'm with Libby, and that Sal was with Mom when she passed. Looking up to the sky I see what appears to be a platypus flying over us, so close I can see its underbelly. Then there are more platypuses circling around, and one of them turns into a big white polar bear. I hold my breath, scared to move when it comes close to us, my heart pounding as it starts to nuzzle my neck. But then I realize it's not trying to hurt me—it just wants to be with us. So I relax, feeling safe with Libby and this bear, when suddenly it turns into a brown bear and I get scared all over again. But it doesn't seem like this bear wants to hurt us either, though it's staring straight at me, its big snout so close to my face I can barely breathe.

I wake up with a start, my heart racing as I look around the dimly lit room, trying to remember where I am. Oh, right. I'm in my mom's room, in her apartment.

I squint over at the clock on the bedside table to check the time, the red numbers glowing eerily bright in the gray, dawn light. Not even six. Tired from tossing and turning in the narrow twin bed, I close my eyes to try and go back to sleep, but the dream is so vivid I can't stop thinking about it. Replaying it over in my mind, I try to make sense of the disjointed scenes, as absurd as they are unsettling, and decide I should maybe write it down so I don't forget.

Stepping out to the kitchen, I turn on the coffee maker and sit down at the small counter, opening my laptop to jot down all the details I can remember. I wonder if there might be some significance to such random animals showing up in my subconscious and do a quick search on each one's symbolism, surprised, but not surprised, at what I find.

Platypus: *Draws our attention to the grit of experience, not allowing us to look away from unpleasant details.*

Polar Bear: *A spiritual animal who helps guide souls to the other side when a person dies.*

Brown Bear: *Stay grounded, no matter what.*

A shiver tingles down my spine and I stand up to pour myself a cup of coffee, marveling at the power of my subconscious to know things my conscious mind has no idea about. Like animal spirit symbolism. Walking over to the living room window, I peek through the wood blind to check the weather. There's a spattering of raindrops on the glass, the early morning sky a heavy, leaden gray—another dreary, Ohio day. I'm so tired of the weather, of not sleeping, of Mom dying. My eyelids feel like they're lined with sandpaper, scratchy and abrasive every time I blink. There's a constant low hum buzzing in my ears, and my brain feels coated in a thin layer of fuzz that makes it hard to think clearly. Even the dream, so vivid a few minutes before, is starting to fade, the edges of it blurring in my weary mind, and I'm not sure it matters if it was a harbinger of my mother's impending death, or simply a crazy concoction of meaningless jumble made up by my overtired mind. What does matter, I decide, turning away from the window and heading back to Mom's room to finish my coffee in bed, is figuring out a way to get something to help me sleep.

The day after Dad died, my sisters and I arrived in Perrysburg en masse with our six children, ranging in age from four weeks old to six years. None of us had gotten any sleep the night before, especially Mom, and after getting all the kids to bed, the four of us sat around the dining room table, picking at the casserole the next-door neighbor had dropped off earlier that day. A knock on the back door startled us, but before anyone had a chance to even stand up, Dr. Jim, our family's physician for as long as I could remember, and a dear friend of Mom's and Dad's, came striding into the dining room, his tall, lanky frame so familiar my eyes welled up at the sight of him.

"Don't mean to barge in," he apologized in his deep, gravelly voice, rounding the table to give us each a long-armed hug, "But I'm guessing no one's had much sleep around here."

Nodding our heads mutely, we watched as he plunked his well-worn doctor bag on the table, pulling out a small vial and twisting off the lid. He shook a tiny white pill out next to Mom's placemat, then rounding the table again, repeated the process at each of our places.

"This is Xanax," he explained, leaving the vial next to Mom, then zipping his bag back up. "It's not going to knock you out, but it will help you relax, maybe take some of the edge off."

And wow, was he right. It *did* take the edge off. Lying in bed later that night, the tension melted off my bones in steady ripples, relaxing me enough to drift away—if not into a deep sleep, into a restful sleep. It was magical.

Of course, Dr. Jim and house calls are both long gone and, not sure where else to turn, I wait until eight o'clock to call my doctor in Connecticut, hoping she might be able to send over a prescription to Mom's pharmacy in Perrysburg.

"I don't need a lot," I tell the receptionist, trying not to sound like a crazy drug addict. "I only need enough so I can sleep for a couple of nights. My mom's been dying for a really long time and I'm just so tired!"

"I'm sure we can figure something out," the receptionist assures me kindly, promising to call back once she's spoken with the doctor.

Sal pokes her head through the door. "I'm heading over now," she says, "I'll text you when I see how she's doing. Did you sleep?"

"Hardly a wink, crazy dreams. How about you?"

"Terrible."

"I called my doctor just now. Hopefully she'll come through with something. I promise I'll share it if she does!"

Sal blows me a kiss and disappears out the door. I look at the clock again. Eight fifteen. The day ahead stretches before me like an infinity line and, not wanting to face it quite yet, I let my head drop back on the pillow and give myself a few more minutes to rest.

∾

About an hour later, as I'm puttering around the apartment, tidying up the kitchen, watering the plants and debating between taking a shower or doing a quick load of laundry, I hear my cell phone ping.

"Mom had a restful night with no breakthroughs," Sal reports. *"She seemed uncomfortable when I arrived, so they're adding a dose of Ativan this morning. Her heart rate remains high. Her lungs are congested. Matthew says her color is different, too. Lots of changes."*

Reading Sal's message, I'm relieved that Matthew, one of our other favorite nurses, is on duty, but I can't decide if there's cause for immediate concern. *Should I go over sooner?* I wonder, staring down at the phone as if it might tell me what to do. Not wanting to overreact, and figuring Sal will call if things get more serious, I decide to take a quick shower in case I don't have another chance for a while. I'm drying my hair when my phone lights up and my heart dips when I see that it's Sal.

"Hello?" I answer cautiously.

"Hey, Peg," Sal says, her voice quiet, almost hesitant. "I don't know for sure, but Matthew is seeing a lot of changes this morning. You probably should head over sooner than later."

"Oh, wow, okay! I wasn't sure from your text. I'll be there as soon as I can. Tell her I love her!"

Hanging up, I stand motionless for a long moment staring at myself in the mirror. *Is this it?* I wonder. *Is Mom going to die today?* It feels possible and impossible all at the same time, and though my mind is screaming at me to *hurry,* that I have to *get* there, I find myself moving around the apartment in slow motion, as if I have all the time in the world. I brush my teeth, I make my bed, I gather up all my things—computer, chargers, needlepoint—like it will be just another day at hospice, all the while wondering *why* I'm moving so slowly. It makes no sense, and I *know* it makes no sense, even as I'm doing it. But I can't seem to make myself move any faster. Am I scared? Am I somehow trying to put off the inevitable? That if I act like it's just another day, it will *be* just another day?

Finally, about twenty minutes later, when I can't find anything left to do, I'm shrugging into my coat when my phone rings again. It's Sal.

"Hey," I answer, "I'm literally walking out the door."

"Peg, wait," she says. "Mom just died."

Her words—the ones I've been expecting and dreading for so long—hit me like a punch in the stomach, and a heaving sob erupts from the depth of my belly with such force it's as though it's been waiting in there all along, gathering intensity, for this exact moment. There's a whooshing in my head and I have to sit down, sinking into the loveseat in Mom's living room like a deflated balloon. Despite the weeks and weeks of preparing for this, at times even longing for it, the shock is visceral, and I can't speak. Bent over, I cradle my forehead in one trembling hand, gripping the phone to my ear with the other, tears streaming down my face. Sal lets me cry, her quiet presence on the other end at once comforting and grounding.

Finally, with a tremulous inhale, I force myself to sit up, wiping at my wet cheeks with the sleeve of my sweater. "Okay, wow. Sorry. Does Lib know yet?"

"No, not yet. I'll call her now."

"Okay—I'll be there as fast as I can." Pushing myself up from the couch, I'm shaky but numb, my mind trying to make sense of what needs to happen next. Mom is dead. She died, and I'm here, not there. I need to go.

"Peg," Sal's voice is low and serious, and I force myself to focus on what she's saying. "Please drive really, really carefully. I mean it. Please."

"I will, I promise. Don't worry."

We hang up, and I try to call John, my body buzzing with adrenaline as I listen to it ring. No answer. I hit redial, but again, no answer. Where *is* he? How can he not be answering? I try our home phone, thinking maybe if he sees it's me on the caller ID he'll pick it up, though he rarely ever does. But still, no answer.

Frustrated, wanting to talk to *somebody*, I call Lib, figuring if she's still on the phone with Sal at least she'll know I tried, but she picks up on the first ring. "I'm okay," she reassures me when she answers, her voice so soft I can barely hear her. "Are you there yet?"

"No, not yet. I'm heading over now. I just—I don't know. I can't believe it. It doesn't seem real."

"I know," she agrees, "I wish I was there."

"Oh god, me too."

Promising to call again once I'm with Sal, I hang up and try John one more time, a panicky impatience bubbling up in my chest when, again, he doesn't answer. The urgency to get over to hospice that eluded me earlier is now coursing through my veins unimpeded, so I grab my purse and hurry out of the apartment, the door closing heavily behind me.

It's funny how the mind works when it's been dealt a shock, even if that shock is completely expected. I'm desperate to let John and the kids know Mom has died, but somehow it's in my head that I have to call them in a certain order—John, Bill, Elizabeth, Jack. I can't see any way around it, and even when I can't reach John, it doesn't occur to me to skip ahead and call the kids before I talk to him. So, I keep pushing redial, getting more and more frustrated with each unanswered call.

Then, about halfway to hospice, I have the anxious thought that one of Sal's daughters might reach out to my kids before I have a chance to tell them myself. The cousins are all very close, and it would be the most natural thing in the world for them to want to share their grief with each other. But again, in my overwrought mind, I can't see past my rule that John has to be told first, so rather than simply calling my kids and putting my mind at ease, I frantically call Sal to ask her to intervene.

"I can't reach John," I choke out when she answers, "and I can't tell my kids before I tell him and I want them to hear it from me and not Kate and Claire so can you tell them not to say anything?" My voice sounds unhinged, even to my own ears, but I can't slow down, my mind imagining all kinds of scenarios where my family hears about Mom from everyone but me. Then, remembering a horrible story my friend Annie told me about how some of her family found out a favorite uncle had died by scrolling through their social media feed, I start to worry *that* might happen, too. "And we should have a rule that no one posts anything online until we've had a chance to tell people in person. Okay?"

To Sal's credit, she listens to my semi-hysterical rant without interrupting, then murmurs her assurance that she'll talk to Kate and Claire.

"But, Peg, please get here in one piece, okay?" she begs. "Pull over if you have to. There's no rush now."

Promising her again that I'll be careful, I hang up and put my phone down in my lap, forcing myself to concentrate on the road in front of me, so familiar I could almost drive it blindfolded and still get there in one piece. I pass by the Five Guys where Mom and I had lunch just a few months before. I can see her so clearly, sitting at the picnic table in front, head tilted back toward the sun as she waited for me to bring out the food. Grief grips my throat, the silence in the car suddenly so loud I can't bear it one more second, and I grab up my phone to try John again.

This time he answers, his steady, familiar voice at once calming and centering.

"Hey, Peg," he says, sounding a little rushed. "Everything okay? I'm about to jump on a conference call."

"Mom just died," I tell him, swallowing back the sob lodged in my chest. And even though I know keeping track of missed calls and texts is not one of his greatest strengths, I can't stop myself from adding, "I've been trying to call you. Where have you been?"

"Oh my god, I'm so sorry, Peg! I was walking Bo and left my phone. Where are you? Are you okay?"

"I'm fine...a little numb, to be honest. It doesn't feel real."

And it doesn't. It's as though I'm playing the part of a daughter whose mother has just died so I feel a certain detachment, like I'm one step removed from the me talking on the phone to my husband. But I suppose that's why I'm able to assure him—and then Bill, Elizabeth and Jack when I call to tell them—that I'm *fine*. It's a *blessing*. Mom is finally *at peace* and that's all that matters, *right*?

Pausing outside the closed door to Mom's room, I stare at the little rose card that's been placed next to her nameplate, the discreet hospice code for 'deceased patient.' I'd thought it was such a sweet, subtle way of letting people know someone had died, but seeing it here brings me up short. My mom is really dead. They've put the rose card next to her name. I have to force myself to push open the door and go in.

At first, nothing seems different and, like every other morning for the past six weeks, I go straight to Mom's side and give her forehead—oddly still warm—a soft kiss. The room feels stuffy, and I'm reminded of when my friend Wendy was dying from cancer years before, and her Jamaican nurse had opened the window, explaining that it would help her soul get to heaven faster. I loved the idea of Wendy's soul flying free out of that sterile hospital room, and I guess the memory has stayed with me, though I don't remember consciously thinking about it since—until now.

Feeling a sudden anxiousness that Mom's soul is stuck in this stuffy room with no way out, I stride over to the bank of windows and push one open a crack. Sal watches from her seat on the other side of the bed, but stays quiet—from confusion or curiosity I'm not sure—and I'm grateful, again, for her steadying silence. My mind is in overdrive with thoughts going every which way—it seems like I should be doing something, but I'm not sure what that something is, and it's putting me on edge.

Matthew pokes his head through the door. "We'd like to get your mom ready now, if that's alright?"

"Of course," Sal says, glancing at me as she stands up. "Is that okay for you, Peg?"

I nod, grateful to be given some sort of direction. But once in the sun room, I still can't settle down, my footsteps loud and echoey on the flagstone floor as I pace from one side to another. I don't want to think about what's going on in Mom's room—her lifeless body being lifted and turned in order to get her 'ready.' Ready for what? The body bag? The funeral home? It seems unnecessary, like busy work for Matthew and the aide. Mom had looked fine to me—I wish they could have let her be.

Trying to distract myself, I sit down next to Sal. "Was it peaceful at the end?" I ask her.

"I wasn't actually in there," she confesses, surprising me. "Matthew was with her. I stepped out for a second to make a quick call."

A ripple of relief sweeps through me. Selfishly, if all three of us couldn't be there at the end, I'm grateful none of us were. If Sal had been with Mom the last few moments of her life, and Lib and I hadn't, well, in my mind, the scale would have been forever tipped in her favor. It would have felt like Mom loved Sal more.

And whether it was chance, or some higher power orchestrating from above, I'm grateful Mom found the perfect moment to let go—when none of us were with her.

We sit quietly, both lost in our own thoughts, until Matthew sticks his head around the corner. "We're all set," he says. "Take as much time as you need—all day if you want. There's no rush at all, really. Come find me when you're ready."

Trailing behind Sal down the hall, I wonder how we'll know when we're ready. What if we never are?

Back in Mom's room, the first thing I notice is what *isn't* here. Gone is the gentle hiss of the oxygen concentrator, and the long snaking tube of the nasal cannula into Mom's nose. Gone is the tray table in front of her with its familiar clutter of family photos, lip ointment tubes, plastic water cups, and sponge swabs. Gone is the angst-filled sound of her ragged breathing. The silence is startling.

Mom's body lies prone on the bed, covered half way up by a clean, white sheet folded down neatly. She's wearing her pale pink and white striped flannel nightgown, the one she liked best because it covers the dark brown age spots on her chest, especially the big one above her collarbone. We'd considered something more dignified for her to be cremated in, like her nice black pants and a favorite sweater. But which one? She had so many none of us could choose. Then there would be the matter of shoes—her black leather dress pair would make the most sense, but it felt cruel putting her feet in something so restricting when she hadn't had shoes on in weeks. Her sneakers were the most comfortable, but Mom would never wear them with her good pants, so they wouldn't do.

When Libby suggested one of her nightgowns, I balked at first—what would the funeral home people think? But then again, did I really care? We finally agreed on the pink nighty, and though my mind freezes whenever it imagines my mother being loaded into the crematorium oven, it helps to think of her tiny, worn out body covered up in the cozy, familiar flannel.

Her hands are crossed below the belly, her crooked fingers clenched in loose fists. A pale white, artificial hydrangea blossom rests between them, its presence giving me pause. A part of me is grateful to Matthew for the kind gesture—Mom clearly loved hydrangeas as there's been a vase full of them on her windowsill for weeks—so it's nice he noticed. But if I know my mother, she would *hate* it. She'd consider it cheesy—nice for someone else, perhaps, but not for her, thank you very much—so another part of me wants to grab it off and throw it away.

And then there's her face. Oh god, her face. Mom's head is lying flat on the single, white pillow, her jaw jutting forward, her mouth open, as if death caught her trying to take in that one last breath of air. Her eyes are closed, her skin pale and waxy, though still pinkish, not the gray I've always imagined a corpse would be. If it weren't for the absolute stillness of her body—no throbbing pulse in her neck, no rise and fall of her chest, no erratic breathing— she could just be in a deep sleep. But the stillness is profound, as though the air around her has stopped moving, too. It's peaceful and unsettling at the same time.

"Do you want to spend some time alone with her?" Sal asks.

"I guess so," I respond, not sure if I really do, but it seems like I should. Pulling a chair up close to the bed, I stare down at Mom's lifeless face. I'm surprised to feel the same awkwardness I'd felt years before with Nitro after he'd died—I guess I'd assumed it would be different with Mom, that there would be more, well, *something*. But there isn't. Mom's soul may be hovering around somewhere nearby, but she is definitely not in this motionless body lying on the bed next to me.

Pushing the chair back to stand up, I lean over to kiss her forehead one last time, letting my hand rest for a moment on top of her head. Her skin is dry and cool, her white hair still soft under my touch.

"Love you, Mom," I whisper, the words sounding as empty as the space around her. Is it possible for someone to know how much you love them? I hope so, but in this moment, after a million I love you's have been said between us, especially in the past few weeks, I wish I'd said it a million times more.

Sal is waiting in the little alcove across the corridor when I open the door. "Okay?" she asks when she sees me, and I nod.

"I guess I'll go tell Matthew we're ready," I offer, adding as an afterthought, "unless you want more time?"

"No, no—I'm good." Sal smiles wistfully. "We've had lots of time already, I think."

Things start to move quickly then, and it seems that the funeral home people arrive impossibly fast, like they've been lurking outside in the driveway waiting for the call. The two attendants dip their heads solemnly toward Sal and me as they roll the gurney past us into Mom's room, the door closing behind them with a soft click. Moments later—at least it feels like moments—they roll it back out, their movements slow and exact as they maneuver it through the door and into the hall. Wrapped now in a stiff, black bag, Mom's already tiny body seems even more diminished, like it's disappearing of its own accord now that she no longer needs it. It's hard to imagine it's my mother in that bag. My *mother*—how can that be? I take a step closer to Sal as they wheel the stretcher past.

Not sure if we should follow them, Sal and I stand motionless watching the procession disappear down the corridor. It feels a little careless letting them take Mom away without us—kind of like sending a child off with someone you've only just met, trusting it'll be okay. At the same time, it's clear Mom is in the hands of professionals, and Sal's and my presence in their methodical process seems as intrusive as it does unnecessary.

We walk back into the room and, without a word, begin to gather up all the things we'd amassed over the past few weeks—quilts and blankets, pillows and photos, vases and cards. We'd brought it in so gradually I'm surprised by how much there is. And though Matthew has assured us we can take our time, Sal and I, by unspoken agreement, work quickly, each making a couple of trips to our cars to get it all cleared out as fast as we can. I'm reminded of moving my children out of their dorms at the end of the school year—back and forth down the hall, arms laden with boxes and bags until nothing is left but the furniture, the room empty and impersonal again, ready for whoever moves in next.

And then, it's over. As long as it took for Mom to die, she's gone in what feels like a heartbeat. I feel untethered, like a kite that's been cut loose, adrift on a breeze with nothing to keep me from floating away into the sky's vast emptiness. I wish there was a way to slow things down, to put off the inevitableness of walking out into the world without my mom in it.

But there's not—life continues to press forward around me and there's nothing to do but move forward with it. Sal and I take turns hugging Matthew and the aides goodbye, thanking them one by one for all they did to take care of Mom. But even as they murmur their condolences, I can sense their focus being pulled in other directions, away from us. As it should be, of course, but still. It's hard to leave center stage, even when you know the show is over and there's no one left watching.

"We should go," I murmur to Sal, and she nods, picking up her bag. Turning to leave, I stare down the long corridor, the same one I've walked up and down countless times the past six weeks, dreading and longing for this very moment. And now it's here. Taking a deep breath, I give a little wave to Matthew over my shoulder and follow Sal out of hospice for the last time.

Two Weeks Later

"Ready?" I glance over at the passenger seat as I put Mom's car into reverse, and a little face with two enormous ears looks back at me nervously. I try to give her a reassuring smile, but inside my heart is racing. What in the world have I done? It's been said to never make any big decisions for at least a year after a loved one dies, but I didn't even wait a week before deciding to adopt this tiny, one-year-old Papillon sitting next to me.

In my defense, I'd been thinking about finding a small dog to adopt because Mr. Bojangles, our four-year-old labrador, is really more John's than mine. Bo tolerates me, and certainly doesn't *dis*like me, but recently I'd started to wish I had a dog that looks at me the way Bo looks at John. Just a pipe dream, of course, and nothing I'd ever given any serious thought to—at least not until the night after Mom died.

Sal and I were having dinner at my friend Dean's house—a welcome distraction from the past twenty-four hours of phone calls and funeral arrangements—when Winnie, one of Dean and his late wife Becky's two Papillons, climbed into my lap. Her warm, quiet presence was beyond soothing, like the comforting weight of a heated blanket, and every so often she would reach her tiny face up and lick my cheek. It was as if she knew how sad I was and was trying to make me feel better.

"Well, if Winnie is missing next week, you'll know I've kidnapped her to Connecticut!" I joked. "I'm not sure I can live without her after this."

Everyone laughed, but honestly, I'm not sure I was really joking. I was pretty smitten.

The next morning I awoke to a cryptic email from Dean with nothing but the contact info of their breeder over in Cleveland, an hour and a half away. I stared at it for a long minute. Do I dare? Am I crazy? Taking a deep breath, I typed out a quick inquiry and pushed send, shaking my head at my impulsiveness. This was so not like me!

The breeder responded within the hour, explaining that she wouldn't have any new litters for at least three months, but she did have a very small female—too small to breed—that she was looking to find a home for. Would I be interested in her?

Looking around Mom's living room, scattered now with moving boxes, sheaths of packing paper and tape dispensers, I wondered. *Am* I interested? Or am I just trying to fill up the hole Mom's death left in my heart, the one that's growing undeniably deeper with every box packed, every cabinet cleaned out.

In the few days since Mom died, Sal and I had been steadily making our way through her things, trying to get as much cleared out as we could before the movers came the following week. For the most part, it wasn't too hard—Sal, Lib, and I had already decided who would get what of the important things—so it was mostly a matter of emptying all the closets, drawers and cabinets. But still, every so often something would bring me up short—like when I had to box up all Mom's shoes for Goodwill and I cried inconsolably for an hour. Or when I found her dental bridge in the medicine cabinet and had to consult with Sal whether it was okay to throw it away. We decided it was, only to have it inexplicably reappear on the kitchen floor a couple days later. Crying and laughing at the same time— was Mom trying to tell us she still needed it?—we decided to take it over to the funeral home and have it cremated with her, just in case.

So maybe I wasn't thinking completely clearly when I replied to the breeder that yes, I might be interested in the small, unbreedable Papillon.

"Does she have a name?" I asked, making a silent deal with myself that if I didn't like what she was called, it would be my sign I shouldn't get her.

"Harriet," was the quick reply, and well, just like that, I was getting a dog. Mom's all-time favorite Perrysburg store was a small ladies boutique called Harriet's—a mainstay in our family for Christmas and birthday gifts, and always a destination stop whenever I was home visiting. How could I possibly turn down a dog named Harriet? It would be like taking a little piece of Mom and Perrysburg home with me.

So a few days later, Dean drove me to Cleveland to meet her. Walking into the breeder's kitchen, we were met by not one, but two excited Papillons corralled in a giant playpen. Dean and the breeder mysteriously left me to go look at something in another room, and I found myself staring at the two dogs trying to decide, from the one picture I'd seen, which was Harriet. Both were small and female, with the same butterfly winged ears, so it wasn't an obvious choice. Nervous, sensing it might be some kind of test, I decided the one on the left was maybe a tiny bit smaller than the other, so I leaned in and picked her up.

"Hello," I whispered, cradling her so I could look in her eyes. "Are you Harriet?" She blinked up at me, and stretched out for a tummy rub, so trusting my heart immediately melted. God, I hoped it was her!

Dean and the breeder swooped back in, exchanging knowing smiles when they saw who I was holding.

"Glad to see you two already bonding," the breeder rasped before sitting down to go over the details. Harriet lay curled on my lap as if she'd always belonged there, and as we made arrangements for me to swing by on my way back to Connecticut in a couple of days to pick her up, my nervousness over what I was doing drained away. Even though I hadn't even told John what I was up to, it just felt so right—Harriet had come into my life on purpose.

Halfway back to Perrysburg, John called, and I answered with a bit of trepidation, wondering if he had some inner knowing what I'd just agreed to. But he was only looking to go over the travel logistics for his trip out to Ohio the next day for the memorial service, so I filled him in on what he needed to know, glancing over at Dean every few seconds, trying not to laugh. John and Dean are like twin spirits—they wear the same clothes, drive the same cars, drink the same drinks—and the fact that Dean was at the root of this craziness would be a story to tell for years to come.

"So, what are you up to?" John finally asked, and unable to keep it in any longer, I let out a gust of a laugh.

"You're not going to believe it," I told him, "but I just bought a Papillon."

Bless his heart, John didn't miss a beat, listening calmly as I recounted what had transpired the last few days, accepting it as if it was the most natural thing in the world that his grieving wife went out and bought a dog—a tiny five-pound Papillon no less—seemingly out of the blue.

"That's quite something, Peg," he said, blowing out a soft whistle. "Harriet, huh?"

And now here we are, me and my Papillon, side by side in my mother's old Honda Civic, both of us about to leave worlds behind we'd known our whole lives.

"It's going to be okay," I whisper, whether for Harriet's benefit or my own, I'm not sure. Patting her on the head, I turn to back down the driveway and start the long drive to Connecticut. And though it feels somehow bittersweet to be leaving Ohio for what may be the last time, I'm excited to, finally, be going home.

Three Months Later

It's a perfect Maine day. Blue sky so clear and pure it feels like I could see right up to heaven if I look long enough. *Are you there, Mom?* I whisper in my head, but she doesn't answer. It seems she never does.

My mother's absence is like a deep, dark void that even Harriet hasn't been able to fill. I was so sure when I got to Maine, to this place she loved beyond all measure, she'd find a way through to me. But though I sense her presence everywhere—on the beach, in the woods, on the porch, in the camp—she's just fleeting glimpses of memory, making the empty spaces she once filled feel even emptier. I miss her so much—her voice, her laugh, her smile. I even miss her perturbed frown, and her annoying nudging. Most of all, though, I miss her beingness in my life. I want her back.

White clouds sail across the horizon, their shadows chasing each other across the river in the afternoon light. The tide is almost full as my sisters and I paddle away from the beach, the bright blue and orange of our kayaks vibrant against the darker blue of the water surrounding us. Our families stand gathered on the porch that hangs out over the river—husbands and children, spouses and significant others, lined shoulder to shoulder along the painted white railing above us—watching as Sal, Lib, and I maneuver our boats around each other and stow our paddles out of the way. The soft sounds of guitar and banjo waft over and around us in the gentle but steady late day breeze.

Lifting the lid off the linen covered box in my lap—the one I'd found on Amazon after the funeral home director told us we didn't need to spend a lot of money on an urn if we didn't want to—I pull out the two plastic bags we'd stored carefully inside, handing one to Sal and the other to Lib.

"Ready?" I ask, offering an encouraging smile, grateful to be an observer rather than an active participant in the task at hand. They both nod, then open their bags and empty the contents gently into the river. I watch, mesmerized, as my parents' ashes billow and swirl below the dark surface, merging together in a milky white cloud.

I take my peony blossom, the coral pink one I'd picked from the bucket of colorful blooms a neighbor dropped off earlier that morning, and lay it over the dispersing cloud. Sal and Lib follow suit, and I notice they both brought two flowers—one for each parent, I suppose. *Oops*, I think, sending a silent apology to my father that I'm more focused on saying goodbye to Mom today, even though, technically, we're saying goodbye to him again, too—albeit twenty-five years later.

A week ago, we had Dad's ashes exhumed in order to scatter him and Mom together in the river, something it seems he had told Mom he wanted, but she chose *not* to do after he died. According to her own confession, she wanted to know exactly where he was, and at the last minute decided to bury his ashes in the small family plot up the road. After Mom died, Sal, Lib, and I decided we couldn't very well honor her wishes and not Dad's, so arranged with the cemetery people to have his ashes dug up—a rather morbid undertaking, but it seemed the only thing to do.

The five blossoms float together between the kayaks and as I watch, two of them begin to drift away from the others, bobbing for a moment side by side before moving apart in opposite directions, circling around the three that remain in a tight cluster between them. I'm transfixed by their movement—it's like they're telling me a story. Our story. I glance at Sal and Lib to see if they're watching, but they're both staring upriver, lost in their own thoughts.

When I look back, the flowers are drifting away, caught in the current of the incoming tide, though the cluster of three remains intact, bound to each other by some invisible force.

Ever since Mom died, I've been waiting for a sign from her because she and I (well, mostly me) had made a deal that when she got to heaven, she'd send me one. In fact, I'd even reminded her about it in the last letter I wrote in my writing class—the one I sent to her right before her fall:

"...So I think the reason I'm sharing this with you is because I want you to remember the deal we made the last time we talked about all this. That when you die, and you realize I was right—that you are still very much around us and aware of us, and haven't disappeared into a deep, dark nothing—you will send me a sign. I promise I'll know it when I see it. Love, Peg"

I'm not sure what kind of sign I expected—maybe a kingfisher, her favorite bird, landing on the porch rail as I sipped my coffee one morning—and, in hindsight, I wish we'd agreed on what it would be ahead of time. But in my spiritual cockiness, or maybe my spiritual naivete, it never occurred to me that would be necessary. I was just so *sure*—not only that Mom would send me a sign, but that I would recognize it without a sliver of doubt. Since she died, though, her silence has been deafening, making me feel sad and disconnected.

Until now. Though very subtle, I have to believe the flowers are the sign I've been waiting for—there's no way they could move the way they did by mere chance. It had to be Mom, and maybe Dad, too, choreographing their movement to reassure me they are still around us, even in death.

Sal, Lib, and I let our kayaks drift along as our family, each in turn, toss their peonies over the rail into the cloud of ashes below. A ripple of soft laughter floats above me in the air, and I smile at the sound, the love emanating from the porch spilling down around me like a warm mist. Over the breeze, I can just make out the words of the song John and Elizabeth are singing:

> *"Lay down my dear sister, lay down and take*
> *your rest*
> *I want to lay your head upon your savior's breast*
> *I love you, but Jesus loves you the best*
> *So I bid you goodnight, goodnight, goodnight..."*

Letting my gaze drift out over the river, I breathe in the view, so familiar it's like looking into the face of someone I've known my whole life and, for a moment, the dark void of my mother's absence seems lighter, less empty.

Surrounded by the river and woods, family and camp that Mom so treasured, a wave of peace washes up through me, filling me with a bittersweet solace. My mother's at rest—in the place she loved, surrounded by the people she loved—and for now, at least, I know where she is, so I can stop looking.

Epilogue

As it turned out, the solace I found in Maine that day was short lived. Summer ended, and as I watched the rest of the world pick up their lives, the void Mom had left spiraled bigger, like a giant black hole in my heart, draining my energy as I floundered to keep from getting sucked down into it. I didn't know what to do with myself—taking care of my mother had filled my time in so many ways that without her around to do things for, I felt useless, unnecessary.

It was a little like when Jack, our youngest, left for boarding school, and I found myself at loose ends with all my free time. The afternoons were especially hard—for so many years my day had revolved around the three o'clock arrival of kids home from school, and it was disorienting to be so unfettered. I think Jack may have felt it, too, because he'd often call to check in around that time, at least in the beginning, helping us both recalibrate the cadence of our days.

With Mom, it was empty-nest syndrome of a different sort, though equally disorienting. She was gone, and with her all the health problems, appointments, travel arrangements and decisions I'd spent so much of my time planning and worrying about. I didn't know how to *be* without her, and I found myself lost in my own life.

But at some point you have to move forward. Grief, I've learned, has no timeline, and I'm not sure the void Mom left in my life will ever fill all the way up. I'm not sure I want it to. So, on the days when the void feels deeper than usual, I try to remind myself of a long-ago March afternoon, sitting with my sisters in her hospice room. A soft, steady snow had begun to fall outside the window, blanketing us in a quiet stillness. Libby was painting, her movements slow and mindful as she tried to capture a vase of hydrangeas on her watercolor paper. Sal was writing in her journal, her concentration intent on the pages before her. Mom was sleeping.

Like Sal, I was also attempting to put my feelings down in writing, but although I've kept a journal on and off since I was in seventh grade, sometimes I find it easier to express myself through a few good lyrical verses than through any number of pages of prose. That particular day I'd woken up with a certain phrase running through my mind—usually a precursor to a poem trying to come through.

I'd been working on it all morning, the words flowing out of me effortlessly, until suddenly they dried up, and I was stuck.

How do I explain, I wondered, staring at the computer screen, *that even though I'm scared of losing Mom, I also have complete faith that a part of her will always be with me, even though her physical self will be gone?*

Flummoxed, I looked out the window at the falling snow. *How do I explain something I can barely explain to myself?*

My gaze had wandered away from the window and fallen on the array of framed family pictures spread out on the tray table in front of Mom. There was my dad, his blue eyes twinkling out at me the same way they had when he was alive. There were the grandchildren, all seven caught in a moment of time, sitting on the steps in Maine. And there was Mom, with Sal, Lib, and me—happier, younger versions of ourselves—on one of our many trips together to New York City.

Looking over at my sisters—Sal still intent on her writing, Lib staring pensively down at her painting—it came to me what I was trying to say. Yes, Mom was going to die. And yes, I was terrified of losing her. But what I realized in that moment, cocooned in that hospice room on a cold, snowy Ohio afternoon, was that Mom wasn't going to disappear into nothing. How could she? There were sparks of her energy all around me—in my sisters' smiles, in her grandchildren's eyes, in my memories, in me. Little pieces of herself she'd be leaving behind for me to find, and as long as I remembered to look in the right places, I could never really lose her.

Over the years since then, I've found that some days are easier than others to find those pieces—in the eyes of my newborn grandchildren, for instance, when I meet them for the first time, or visiting Sal and Lib and seeing her things scattered around their homes. And, of course, when I'm in Maine I can find her just about anywhere I look. She's hanging tea towels on the clothesline and watering the hanging basket of bright begonias by the front door. She's sitting at the dining room table writing a note to a friend and at the kitchen counter arranging pine boughs in the old copper kettle to put on the mantle. She's in the sparkle of sunlight on the river and the rustle of poplar leaves on the river's edge. Mom is everywhere and nowhere, all at the same time.

I don't know. This physical world is just so real, so solid, it's hard to remember, or maybe hard to trust, that something is there even if I can't see it. But when I remember to shift my focus from everywhere Mom *isn't*, to everywhere she *is*, the energy of her love is so strong it's as if she's standing right next to me, and it feels like I never lost her at all.

Author's Note

About a year after Mom died, Sallie shared an article with me and Lib called "Getting Grief Right," written by Patrick O'Malley, a PhD who specializes in grief counseling. It is his premise that grieving people just want to tell someone the story of their loss—that by sharing the painful details of how their loved one died, they're reminded that there's a reason for their grief, that it makes sense. *Of course I'm sad,* they can say to themselves after telling someone what happened. *Look what I've been through. Look what I've lost.*

At the time, the grief I was experiencing after my mother's loss was so deep, I almost couldn't feel it. I mean, I knew it was there, but I couldn't get to it. I couldn't touch it. When my father died, I'd sobbed with abandon for weeks on end, my grief so raw and painful it was like a deep cut that wouldn't stop bleeding no matter how many bandages I put on. It was horrible, but it was tangible, my tears a physical release of the anguish I felt inside.

With Mom I barely cried, my unshed tears so heavy inside me I often couldn't move under their weight. I thought maybe a bereavement group might help and signed up for one at our local hospice. But it didn't. The stories I heard, each one so much sadder than my own, only added to the weight of my grief, and I left feeling heavier than when I arrived.

After reading the article Sal sent, it occurred to me that maybe, instead of *telling* someone the story of how I lost my mom, I could *write* about it instead. As an English major in college, I've always loved to write—poems, letters, I even had a blog for a while—the written word always providing an outlet for the niggling thoughts in my head that won't leave me alone.

So I decided to give it a try. First, to jog my memory, I made a list of everything I could remember during our time at hospice—the big things and the little. I transcribed the text trail between Sal, Lib, and me, and printed out all the emails from family and friends we exchanged during that period. I signed up for another memoir writing workshop to keep me accountable, and then well, I just started.

Writing the story of losing my mom was as cathartic as it was challenging, as frustrating as it was enlightening. It took way longer than I ever would have imagined, but I think that was because it was keeping Mom close to me. As I recounted the last six weeks of her life, so many memories surfaced—some happy, some sad, some surprising—reminding me over and over how lucky I was to have her as my mother. I was reluctant to end it; it would be like losing her all over again.

But I couldn't keep writing forever. The story had to come to an end, the way it had in real life. And as I wrote the last few words, it occurred to me that by writing *Losing Mom*, I had given myself a way to always find her.

Everyone, if we live long enough, has, or will have, a story to tell about losing their mom. This is mine. Thank you for reading it.

Peggy Ottman

Pieces of My Mom

3/13/17

Time is such a fragile thing and hard at times to grasp
Flashing by so quickly when I most want it to last
Then slowing down to nothing during times I wish would pass
But spiraling ever forward whether going slow or fast

A moment lasts forever if it's etched in memory
Or disappears without a trace into eternity
I sit and wait and hope that these moments here with her
Will be the kind that always last, though now they're all a blur

Her spark of light is dimming and it's hard to watch it fade
It's been a guiding force for me, and always shown the way
It flickers in the shadows and I watch it carefully
Scared to take my eyes away should she decide to leave

But then I see the pictures of our family by her side
And I know this spark that we all love can never really die
Her eyes may dim, her voice may fade, as she slowly slips away
But a simple shift in focus and her spark is bright as day

For I see it in my sisters' smiles, and in our childrens' eyes
I see it in her friends who have come to say goodbye
And though I've feared the moment when my mother passes on
I know that she's left pieces here, so she won't be really gone.

Acknowledgments

Writing is a solitary activity by nature, but I could never have done this alone.

Thank you to my sisters, my writing muses, for their memories and unwavering support. This would only be half a story without you.

Thank you to my husband, whose steadiness never falters—in the happy times and the sad.

Thank you to my fellow memoirists and instructors at the Westport Writers' Workshop who provided so much invaluable feedback over the years. You kept me going.

Thank you to all my friends who never forgot to ask how my writing was going, no matter how long it was taking.

Thank you to everyone on Minds.com who read, liked and commented on my early reflections. By sharing your own stories of losing your moms, you helped me see that grief can be a bridge to healing, and that this story was not mine alone.

And finally, to my mother—for the life you lived, the love you gave, and the lessons you taught even in your leaving. This book is my thank you—my way of carrying forward what you so bravely placed in my hands.

www.ingramcontent.com/pod-product-compliance
Lightning Source LLC
Chambersburg PA
CBHW031955150726
47990CB00005B/1721